Date Due

BEYOND THE HORIZON

and

'MARCO MILLIONS'

Beyond the Horizon
and
'Marco Millions'

by

Eugene O'Neill

Jonathan Cape Ltd
Thirty Bedford Square London

BEYOND THE HORIZON
and
Gold

FIRST PUBLISHED 1924

★

'*MARCO MILLIONS*'

FIRST PUBLISHED 1927

★

THESE PLAYS FIRST ISSUED IN ONE VOLUME
1960

PRINTED IN GREAT BRITAIN BY BUTLER & TANNER LTD
FROME AND LONDON

Contents

Beyond the Horizon

A Play in Three Acts

TO AGNES

ACT I

ACT II

(Three years later)

ACT III

(Five years later)

Characters

JAMES MAYO, *a farmer*
KATE MAYO, *his wife*
CAPTAIN DICK SCOTT, *of the barque "Sunda," her brother*
ANDREW MAYO ⎫ *sons of James Mayo*
ROBERT MAYO ⎭
RUTH ATKINS,
MRS. ATKINS, *her widowed mother*
MARY,
BEN, *a farm hand*
DOCTOR FAWCETT.

(The "right" and "left" of the stage directions are the audience's.)

Beyond the Horizon

ACT ONE

SCENE ONE

SCENE. *A section of country highway. The road runs diagonally from the left, forward, to the right, rear, and can be seen in the distance winding toward the horizon like a pale ribbon between the low, rolling hills with their freshly ploughed fields clearly divided from each other, checker-board fashion, by the lines of stone walls and rough snake-fences.*

The forward triangle cut off by the road is a section of a field from the dark earth of which myriad bright-green blades of fall-sown rye are sprouting. A straggling line of piled rocks, too low to be called a wall, separates this field from the road.

To the rear of the road is a ditch with a sloping, grassy bank on the far side. From the centre of this an old, gnarled apple tree, just budding into leaf, strains its twisted branches heavenwards, black against the pallor of distance. A snake-fence sidles from left to right along the top of the bank, passing beneath the apple tree.

The hushed twilight of a day in May is just beginning. The horizon hills are still rimmed by a faint line of flame, and the sky above them glows with the crimson flush of the sunset. This fades gradually as the action of the scene progresses.

5

BEYOND THE HORIZON

*At the rise of the curtain, Robert Mayo is dis-
covered sitting on the fence. He is a tall, slender
young man of twenty-three. There is a touch of
the poet about him expressed in his high forehead
and wide, dark eyes. His features are delicate
and refined, leaning to weakness in the mouth
and chin. He is dressed in grey corduroy trousers
pushed into high laced boots, and a blue flannel
shirt with a bright coloured tie. He is reading a
book by the fading sunset light. He shuts this,
keeping a finger in to mark the place, and turns
his head toward the horizon, gazing out over the
fields and hills. His lips move as if he were
reciting something to himself.*

*His brother Andrew comes along the road from
the right, returning from his work in the fields.
He is twenty-seven years old, an opposite type to
Robert — husky, sun-bronzed, handsome in a
large-featured, manly fashion — a son of the soil,
intelligent in a shrewd way, but with nothing of
the intellectual about him. He wears overalls,
leather boots, a grey flannel shirt open at the
neck, and a soft, mud-stained hat pushed back on
his head. He stops to talk to Robert, leaning on
the hoe he carries.*

ANDREW (*seeing Robert has not noticed his presence —
in a loud shout*). Hey there! (*Robert turns with a
start. Seeing who it is, he smiles.*) Gosh, you do
take the prize for day-dreaming! And I see you've

6

carted one of the old books along with you. Want to bust your eyesight reading in this light?

ROBERT (*glancing at the book in his hand with a rather shamefaced air*). I wasn't reading — just then, Andy.

ANDREW. No, but you have been. Shucks, you never will get any sense, Rob. (*He crosses the ditch and sits on the fence near his brother.*) What is it this time — poetry, I'll bet. (*He reaches for the book.*) Let me see.

ROBERT (*handing it to him rather reluctantly*). Yes, it's poetry. Look out you don't get it full of dirt.

ANDREW (*glancing at his hands*). That isn't dirt — it's good clean earth; but I'll be careful of the old thing. I just wanted to take a peep at it. (*He turns over the pages.*)

ROBERT (*slyly*). Better look out for your eyesight, Andy.

ANDREW. Huh! If reading this stuff was the only way to get blind, I'd see for ever. (*His eyes read something and he gives an exclamation of disgust.*) Hump! (*With a provoking grin at his brother he reads aloud in a doleful, sing-song voice.*) "I have loved wind and light, and the bright sea. But holy and most sacred night, not as I love and have loved thee." (*He hands the book back.*) Here! Take it and bury it. Give me a good magazine any time.

ROBERT (*with a trace of irritation*). The Farm Journal?

ANDREW. Sure; anything sensible. I suppose it's that year in college gave you a liking for that kind of stuff. I'm darn glad I stopped with High School, or maybe I'd been crazy too. (*He grins and slaps Robert on the back affectionately.*) Imagine me reading poetry and ploughing at the same time. The team'd run away, I'll bet.

ROBERT (*laughing*). Or picture me ploughing. That'd be worse.

ANDREW (*seriously*). Pa was right never to sick you on to the farm. You surely were never cut out for a farmer, that's a fact — even if you'd never been took sick. (*With concern.*) Say, how'd you feel now, anyway? I've lost track of you. Seems as if I never did get a chance to have a talk alone with you these days, 'count of the work. But you're looking fine as silk.

ROBERT. Why, I feel great — never better.

ANDREW. That's bully. You've surely earned it. You certainly had enough sickness in the old days to last you the rest of your life.

ROBERT. A healthy animal like you, you brute, can hardly understand what I went through — although you saw it. You remember — sick one day and well the next — always weak — never able to last through a whole term at school 'til I was years behind every one my age — not able to get in any games — it was hell! These last few years of comparative health have been heaven to me.

ANDREW. I know; they must have been. (*After a pause.*) You should have gone back to college last fall, like I know you wanted to. You're fitted for that sort of thing — just as I ain't.

ROBERT. You know why I didn't go back, Andy. Pa didn't like the idea, even if he didn't say so, and I know he wanted the money to use improving the farm. And besides, I had pretty much all I cared for in that one year. I'm not keen on being a student, just because you see me reading books all the time. What I want to do now is keep on moving, so that I won't take root in any one place.

ANDREW. Well, the trip you're leaving on to-morrow will keep you moving all right. (*At this mention of the trip they both fall silent. There is a pause. Finally Andrew goes on, awkwardly attempting to speak casually.*) Uncle says you'll be gone three years.

ROBERT. About that, he figures.

ANDREW (*moodily*). That's a long time.

ROBERT. Not so long when you come to consider it. You know the *Sunda* sails around the Horn for Yokohama first, and that's a long voyage on a sailing ship, and if we go to any of the other places Uncle Dick mentions — India, or Australia, or

South Africa, or South America – they'll be long voyages, too.

ANDREW. You can have all those foreign parts for all of me. A trip to the port once in a while, or maybe down to New York a couple of times a year – that's all the travel I'm hankering after. (*He looks down the road to the right.*) Here comes Pa.

> (*The noise of a team of horses coming slowly down the road is heard, and a man's voice urging them on. A moment later James Mayo enters, driving the two weary horses which have been unhitched from the plough. He is his son Andrew over again in body and face – an Andrew sixty-five years old, with a short, square, white beard. He is dressed much the same as Andrew.*)

MAYO (*checking his horses when he sees his sons*). Whoa there! Hello boys! What are you two doin' there roostin' on the fence like a pair of hens?

ROBERT (*laughing*). Oh, just talking things over, Pa.

ANDREW (*with a sly wink*). Rob's trying to get me into reading poetry. He thinks my education's been neglected.

MAYO (*chuckling*). That's good! You kin go out and sing it to the stock at nights to put 'em to sleep. What's that he's got there – 'nother book?

Good Lord, I thought you'd read every book there was in the world, Robert, and here you go and finds 'nother one!

ROBERT (*with a smile*). There's still a few left, Pa.

ANDREW. He's learning a new poem about the "bright sea" so he'll be all prepared to recite when he gets on the boat to-morrow.

MAYO (*a bit rebukingly*). He'll have plenty of time to be thinkin' 'bout the water in the next years. No need to bother 'bout it yet.

ROBERT (*gently*). I wasn't. That's just Andy's fooling.

MAYO (*changing the subject abruptly; turns to Andrew*). How are things lookin' up to the hill lot, Andy?

ANDREW (*enthusiastically*). Fine as silk for this early in the year. Those oats seem to be coming along great.

MAYO. I'm most done ploughin' up the old medder — figger I ought to have it all up by to-morrow noon; then you kin start in with the harrowin'.

ANDREW. Sure. I expect I'll be through up above by then. There ain't but a little left to do.

MAYO (*to the restive team*). Whoa there! You'll get your supper soon enough, you hungry critters. (*Turning again to Andrew.*) It looks like a good year for us, son, with fair luck on the weather —

even if it's hard work gettin' things started.

ANDREW (*with a grin of satisfaction*). I can stand my share of the hard work, I guess — and then some.

MAYO. That's the way to talk, son. Work never done a man harm yet — leastways, not work done out in the open. (*Robert has been trying to pretend an interest in their conversation, but he can't help showing that it bores him. Andrew notices this.*)

ANDREW. But farming ain't poetry, is it, Rob? (*Robert smiles but remains silent.*)

MAYO (*seriously*). There's more satisfaction in the earth than ever was in any book, and Robert'll find it out sooner or later. (*A twinkle comes into his eyes.*) When he's grown up and got some sense.

ROBERT (*whimsically*). I'm never going to grow up — if I can help it.

MAYO. Time'll tell. Well, I'll be movin' along home. Don't you two stay gossipin' too long. (*He winks at Robert.*) 'Specially you, Andy. Ruth and her Maw is comin' to supper, and you'd best be hurryin' to wash up and put on your best Sunday-go-to-meetin' clothes. (*He laughs. Robert's face contracts as if he were wincing at some pain, but he forces a smile. Andrew grows confused and casts a quick side glance at his brother.*)

ANDREW. I'll be along in a minute, Pa.

MAYO. And you, Robert, don't you stay moonin'

at the sky longer'n is needful. You'll get lots o' time for that the next three years you're out on the sea. Remember this is your last night at home, and you've got to make an early start to-morrow (*he hesitates, then finishes earnestly*), 'n' your Ma'll be wantin' to see all she kin o' you the little time left.

ROBERT. I'm not forgetting, Pa. I'll be home right away.

MAYO. That's right. I'll tell your Maw you're acomin'. (*He chucks to the horses.*) Giddap, old bones! Don't you want no supper to-night?

> (*The horses walk off, and he follows them. There is a pause. Andrew and Robert sit silently, without looking at each other.*)

ANDREW (*after a while*). Ma's going to miss you a lot, Rob.

ROBERT. Yes – and I'll miss her.

ANDREW. And Pa ain't feeling none too happy to have you go – though he's been trying not to show it.

ROBERT. I can see how he feels.

ANDREW. And you can bet that I'm not giving any cheers about it. (*He puts one hand on the fence near Robert.*)

ROBERT (*putting one hand on top of Andrew's with a gesture almost of shyness*). I know that too, Andy.

ANDREW. I'll miss you as much as anybody, I guess. I know how lonesome the old place was winter before last when you was away at college – and even then you used to come home once in a while; but this time — (*He stops suddenly.*)

ROBERT. Let's not think about it – 'til afterward. We'll only spoil this last night if we do.

ANDREW. That's good advice. (*But after a pause, he returns to the subject again.*) You see, you and I ain't like most brothers – always fighting and separated a lot of the time, while we've always been together – just the two of us. It's different with us. That's why it hits so hard, I guess.

ROBERT (*with feeling*). It's just as hard for me, Andy – believe that! I hate to leave you and the old folks – but – I feel I've got to. There's something calling me – (*He points to the horizon*) calling to me from over there, beyond – and I feel as if – no matter what happens – Oh, I can't just explain it to you, Andy.

ANDREW. No need to, Rob. (*Angry at himself.*) You needn't try to explain. It's all just as it ought to be. Hell! You want to go. You feel you ought to, and you *got* to! – that's all there is to it; and I wouldn't have you miss this chance for the world.

ROBERT. It's fine of you to feel that way, Andy.

ANDREW. Huh! I'd be a nice son-of-a-gun if I didn't, wouldn't I? When I know how you need

14

this sea trip to make a new man of you — in the body, I mean — and give you your full health back.

ROBERT (*a trifle impatiently*). All of you seem to keep harping on my health. You were so used to seeing me lying around the house in the old days that you never will get over the notion that I'm a chronic invalid, and have to be looked after like a baby all the time, or wheeled round in a chair like Mrs. Atkins. You don't realize how I've bucked up in the past few years. Why, I bet right now I'm just as healthy as you are — I mean just as sound in wind and limb; and if I was staying on at the farm, I'd prove it to you. You're suffering from a fixed idea about my delicateness — and so are Pa and Ma. Every time I've offered to help, Pa has stared at me as if he thought I was contemplating suicide.

ANDREW (*conciliatingly*). Nobody claimed the undertaker was taking your measurements. All I was saying was the sea trip would be bound to do anybody good.

ROBERT. If I had no other excuse for going on Uncle Dick's ship but just my health, I'd stay right here and start in ploughing.

ANDREW. Can't be done. No use in your talking that way, Rob. Farming ain't your nature. There's all the difference shown in just the way us two feel about the farm. I like it, all of it, and you — well, you like the home part of it, I expect; but as a place to work and grow things, you hate it. Ain't that right?

ROBERT. Yes, I suppose it is. I've tried to take an interest but — well, you're the Mayo branch of the family, and I take after Ma and Uncle Dick. It's natural enough when you come to think of it. The Mayos have been farmers from way back, while the Scotts have been mostly seafaring folks, with a school teacher thrown in now and then on the woman's side — just as Ma was before her marriage.

ANDREW. You do favour Ma. I remember she used always to have her nose in a book when I was a kid; but she seems to have given it up of late years.

ROBERT (*with a trace of bitterness*). The farm has claimed her in spite of herself. That's what I'm afraid it might do to me in time, and that's why I feel I ought to get away. (*Fearing he has hurt Andrew's feelings.*) You mustn't misunderstand me, Andy. For you it's a different thing. You're a Mayo through and through. You're wedded to the soil. You're as much a product of it as an ear of corn is, or a tree. Father is the same. This farm is his life-work, and he's happy in knowing that another Mayo, inspired by the same love, will take up the work where he leaves off. I can understand your attitude, and Pa's, and I think it's wonderful and sincere. But I — well, I'm not made that way.

ANDREW. No, you ain't; but when it comes to understanding, I guess I realize that you've got your own angle of looking at things.

ROBERT (*musingly*). I wonder if you do, really.

ANDREW (*confidently*). Sure I do. You've seen a bit of the world, enough to make the farm seem small, and you've got the itch to see it all.

ROBERT. It's more than that, Andy.

ANDREW. Oh, of course. I know you're going to learn navigation, and all about a ship, so's you can be an officer. That's natural, too. There's fair pay in it, I expect, when you consider that you've always got a home and grub thrown in; and if you're set on travelling, you can go anywhere you've a mind to, without paying fare.

ROBERT (*with a smile that is half-sad*). It's more than that, Andy.

ANDREW. Sure it is. There's always a chance of a good thing coming your way in some of those foreign ports or other. I've heard there are great opportunities for a young fellow with his eyes open in some of those new countries that are just being opened up. And with your education you ought to pick up the language quick. (*Jovially.*) I'll bet that's what you've been turning over in your mind under all your quietness! (*He slaps his brother on the back with a laugh.*) Well, if you get to be a millionaire all of a sudden, call 'round once in a while and I'll pass the plate to you. We could use a lot of money right here on the farm without hurting it any.

ROBERT (*forced to laugh*). I've never considered that practical side of it for a minute, Andy. (*As Andrew looks incredulous.*) That's the truth.

ANDREW. Well, you ought to.

ROBERT. No, I oughtn't. You're trying to wish an eye-for-business on me I don't possess. (*Pointing to the horizon — dreamily.*) Supposing I was to tell you that it's just Beauty that's calling me, the beauty of the far off and unknown, the mystery and spell of the East, which lures me in the books I've read, the need of the freedom of great wide spaces, the joy of wandering on and on — in quest of the secret which is hidden just over there, beyond the horizon? Suppose I told you that was the one and only reason for my going?

ANDREW. I should say you were nutty.

ROBERT. Then I must be — because it's so.

ANDREW. I don't believe it. You've got that idea out of your poetry books. A good dose of seasickness will get that out of your system.

ROBERT (*frowning*). Don't, Andy. I'm serious.

ANDREW. Then you might as well stay right here, because we've got all you're looking for right on this farm. There's wide space enough, Lord knows, and you can have all the sea you want by walking a mile down to the beach, and there's plenty of horizon to look at, and beauty enough for anyone, except in the winter. (*He grins.*) As for the mystery and spell, and other things you mentioned, I haven't met 'em yet, but they're probably lying around somewheres. I'll have you understand this is a first-class farm with all the fixings. (*He laughs.*)

ROBERT (*joining in the laughter in spite of himself*). It's no use talking to you, you chump!

ANDREW. Maybe; but you'll see I'm right before you've gone far. You're not as big a nut as you'd like to make out. You'd better not say anything to Uncle Dick about spells and things when you're on the ship. He'll likely chuck you overboard for a Jonah. (*He jumps down from fence.*) I'd better run along. I've got to wash up some as long as Ruth's Ma is coming over for supper.

ROBERT (*pointedly – almost bitterly*). And Ruth.

ANDREW (*confused – looking everywhere except at Robert – trying to appear unconcerned*). Yes, Pa did say she was staying too. Well, I better hustle, I guess, and — (*He steps over the ditch to the road while he is talking.*)

ROBERT (*who appears to be fighting some strong inward emotion – impulsively*). Wait a minute, Andy! (*He jumps down from the fence.*) There is something I want to — (*He stops abruptly, biting his lips, his face colouring.*)

19

ANDREW (*facing him; half-defiantly*). Yes?

ROBERT (*confusedly*). No – never mind – it doesn't matter, it was nothing.

ANDREW (*after a pause, during which he stares fixedly at Robert's averted face*). Maybe I can guess – what you were going to say – but I guess you're right not to talk about it. (*He pulls Robert's hand from his side and grips it tensely; the two brothers stand looking into each other's eyes for a minute.*) We can't help those things, Rob. (*He turns away, suddenly releasing Robert's hand.*) You'll be coming along shortly, won't you?

ROBERT (*dully*). Yes.

ANDREW. See you later, then.

(*He walks off down the road to the left. Robert stares after him for a moment; then climbs to the fence rail again, and looks out over the hills, an expression of deep grief on his face. After a moment or so, Ruth enters hurriedly from the left. She is a healthy, blonde, out-of-door girl of twenty, with a graceful, slender figure. Her face, though inclined to roundness, is undeniably pretty, its large eyes of a deep blue set off strikingly by the sun-bronzed complexion. Her small, regular features are marked by a certain strength – an underlying, stubborn fixity of purpose hidden in the frankly-appeal-*)

20

*ing charm of her fresh youthfulness. She
wears a simple white dress but no hat.*)

RUTH (*seeing him*). Hello, Rob!

ROBERT (*startled*). Hello, Ruth!

RUTH (*jumps the ditch and perches on the fence
beside him*). I was looking for you.

ROBERT (*pointedly*). Andy just left here.

RUTH. I know. I met him on the road a second
ago. He told me you were here. (*Tenderly playful.*)
I wasn't looking for Andy, Smarty, if that's what
you mean. I was looking for *you*.

ROBERT. Because I'm going away to-morrow?

RUTH. Because your mother was anxious to have
you come home and asked me to look for you. I
just wheeled Ma over to your house.

ROBERT (*perfunctorily*). How is your mother?

RUTH (*a shadow coming over her face*). She's
about the same. She never seems to get any better
or any worse. Oh, Rob, I do wish she'd pick up a
little or — or try to make the best of things that
can't be helped.

ROBERT. Has she been nagging at you again?

RUTH (*nods her head, and then breaks forth rebelliously*). She never stops nagging. No matter what
I do for her she finds fault. She's growing more
irritable every day. Oh, Rob, you've no idea how
hard it is living there alone with her in that big

lonely house. It's enough to drive anyone mad. If only Pa was still living — (*She stops as if ashamed of her outburst.*) I suppose I shouldn't complain this way. I wouldn't to anyone but you. (*She sighs.*) Poor Ma, Lord knows it's hard enough for her — having to be wheeled around in a chair ever since I was born. I suppose it's natural to be cross when you're not able ever to walk a step. But why should she be in a temper with me all the time? Oh, I'd like to be going away some place — like you!

ROBERT. It's hard to stay — and equally hard to go, sometimes.

RUTH. There! If I'm not the stupid body! I swore I wasn't going to speak about your trip — until after you'd gone, and there I go, first thing!

ROBERT. Why didn't you want to speak of it?

RUTH. Because I didn't want to spoil this last night you're here. Oh, Rob, I'm going to — we're all going to miss you so awfully. Your mother is going around looking as if she'd burst out crying any minute. You ought to know how I feel. Andy and you and I — why, it seems as if we'd always been together.

ROBERT (*with a wry attempt at a smile*). You and Andy will still have each other. It'll be harder for me without anyone.

RUTH. But you'll have new sights and new people

to take your mind off; while we'll be here with the old, familiar place to remind us every minute of the day. It's a shame you're going — just at this time, in spring, when everything is getting so nice. (*With a sigh.*) I oughtn't to talk that way when I know going's the best thing for you — on account of your health. The sea trip's bound to do you so much good, every one says.

ROBERT (*with a half-resentful grimace*). Don't tell me *you* think I'm a hopeless invalid, too! I've heard enough of that talk from the folks. Honestly, Ruth, I feel better than I ever did in my life. I'm disgustingly healthy. I wouldn't even consider my health an excuse for this trip.

RUTH (*vaguely*). Of course you're bound to find all sorts of opportunities to get on, your father says.

ROBERT (*heatedly*). I don't give a damn about that! I wouldn't take a voyage across the road for the best opportunity in the world of the kind Pa thinks of. I'd run away from it instead. (*He smiles at his own irritation.*) Excuse me, Ruth, for getting worked up over it; but Andy gave me an overdose of the practical considerations.

RUTH (*slowly puzzled*). Well, then, if it isn't any of those reasons — (*With sudden intensity.*) Oh, Rob, why *do* you want to go?

ROBERT (*turning to her quickly, in surprise — slowly*). Why do you ask that, Ruth?

23

RUTH (*dropping her eyes before his searching glance*). Because — (*Lamely.*) It seems such a shame.

ROBERT (*insistently*). Why?

RUTH. Oh, because — everything.

ROBERT. I could hardly back out now, even if I wanted to. And I'll be forgotten before you know it.

RUTH (*indignantly*). You won't! I'll never forget — (*She stops and turns away to hide her confusion.*)

ROBERT (*softly*). Will you promise me that?

RUTH (*evasively*). Of course. It's mean of you to think that any of us would forget so easily.

ROBERT (*disappointedly*). Oh!

RUTH (*with an attempt at lightness*). But you haven't told me your reason for leaving yet? Aren't you going to?

ROBERT (*moodily*). I doubt if you'll understand. It's difficult to explain, even to myself. It's more an instinctive longing that won't stand dissection. Either you feel it, or you don't. The cause of it all is in the blood and the bone, I guess, not in the brain, although imagination plays a large part in it. I can remember being conscious of it first when I was only a kid — you haven't forgotten what a sickly specimen I was then, in those days, have you?

24

RUTH (*with a shudder*). They're past. Let's not think about them.

ROBERT. You'll have to, to understand. Well, in those days, when Ma was fixing meals, she used to get me out of the way by pushing my chair to the west window and telling me to look out and be quiet. That wasn't hard. I guess I was always quiet.

RUTH (*compassionately*). Yes, you always were -- and you suffering so much, too!

ROBERT (*musingly*). So I used to stare out over the fields to the hills, out there – (*He points to the horizon*) and somehow after a time I'd forget any pain I was in, and start dreaming. I knew the sea was over beyond those hills – the folks had told me – and I used to wonder what the sea was like, and try to form a picture of it in my mind. (*With a smile.*) There was all the mystery in the world to me then about that – far-off sea – and there still is! It called to me then just as it does now. (*After a slight pause.*) And other times my eyes would follow this road, winding off into the distance, toward the hills, as if it, too, was searching for the sea. And I'd promise myself that when I grew up and was strong, I'd follow that road, and it and I would find the sea together. (*With a smile.*) You see, my making this trip is only keeping that promise of long ago.

RUTH (*charmed by his low, musical voice telling the dreams of his childhood*). Yes, I see.

B
25

ROBERT. Those were the only happy moments of my life then, dreaming there at the window. I liked to be all alone – those times. I got to know all the different kinds of sunsets by heart – the clear ones and the cloudy ones, and all the colour schemes of their countless variations – although I could hardly name more than three or four colours correctly. And all those sunsets took place over there – (*He points*) beyond the horizon. So gradually I came to believe that all the wonders of the world happened on the other side of those hills. There was the home of the good fairies who performed beautiful miracles. (*He smiles.*) I believed in fairies then, although I suppose I ought to have been ashamed of it from a boy's standpoint. But you know how contemptuous of all religion Pa's always been – even the mention of it in the house makes him angry.

RUTH. Yes. (*Wearily.*) It's just the opposite to our house.

ROBERT. He'd bullied Ma into being ashamed of believing in anything and he'd forbidden her to teach Andy or me. There wasn't much about our home but the life on the farm. I didn't like that, so I *had* to believe in fairies. (*With a smile.*) Perhaps I still do believe in them. Anyway, in those days they were real enough, and sometimes – I suppose the mental science folks would explain it by self-hypnosis – I could actually hear them call-

ing to me in soft whispers to come out and play
with them, dance with them down the road in the
dusk in a game of hide-and-seek to find out where
the sun was hiding himself. They sang their little
songs to me, songs that told of all the wonderful
things they had in their home on the other side of
the hills, and they promised to show me all of
them, if I'd only come, come! But I couldn't come
then, and I used to cry sometimes and Ma would
think I was in pain. (*He breaks off suddenly with a
laugh.*) That's why I'm going now, I suppose.
For I can still hear them calling, although I'm a
man and have seen the other side of many hills.
But the horizon is as far away and as luring as ever.
(*He turns to her – softly.*) Do you understand now,
Ruth?

RUTH (*spellbound, in a whisper*). Yes.

ROBERT. You feel it then?

RUTH. Yes, yes, I do! (*Unconsciously she snuggles
close against his side. His arm steals about her as
if he were not aware of the action.*) Oh, Rob, how
could I help feeling it? You tell things so beautifully!

ROBERT (*suddenly realizing that his arm is around
her, and that her head is resting on his shoulder, gently
takes his arm away. Ruth, brought back to herself, is
overcome with confusion.*) So now you know why
I'm going. It's for that reason – that and one
other.

RUTH. You've another? Then you must tell me that, too.

ROBERT (*looking at her searchingly. She drops her eyes before his gaze*). I wonder if I ought to. I wonder if you'd really care to hear it – if you knew. You'll promise not to be angry – whatever it is?

RUTH (*softly, her face still averted*). Yes, I promise.

ROBERT (*simply*). I love you. That's the other reason.

RUTH (*hiding her face in her hands*). Oh, Rob!

ROBERT. You must let me finish now I've begun. I wasn't going to tell you, but I feel I have to. It can't matter to you now that I'm going so far away, and for so long – perhaps for ever. I've loved you all these years, but the realization of it never came to me 'til I agreed to go away with Uncle Dick. Then I thought of leaving you, and the pain of that thought revealed the truth to me in a flash – that I loved you, *had* loved you as long as I could remember. (*He gently pulls one of Ruth's hands away from her face.*) You mustn't mind my telling you this, Ruth. I realize how impossible it all is – and I understand; for the revelation of my own love seemed to open my eyes to the love of others. I saw Andy's love for you – and I knew that you must love him.

RUTH (*breaking out stormily*). I don't! I don't love Andy! I don't! (*Robert stares at her in stupia*

28

astonishment. Ruth weeps hysterically.) Whatever —
put such a fool notion into — into your head? (*She
suddenly throws her arms about his neck and hides her
head on his shoulder.*) Oh, Rob! Don't go away!
Please! You mustn't, now! You can't! I won't
let you! It'd break my — my heart!

ROBERT (*the expression of stupid bewilderment giving
way to one of overwhelming joy. He presses her close
to him — slowly and tenderly*). Do you mean that —
that you love me?

RUTH (*sobbing*). Yes, yes — of course I do — what
d'you s'pose? (*She lifts up her head and looks into
his eyes with a tremulous smile.*) You stupid thing!
(*He kisses her.*) I've loved you right along.

ROBERT (*mystified*). But you and Andy were
always together!

RUTH. Because you never seemed to want to go
any place with me. You were always reading an
old book, and not paying any attention to me. I
was too proud to let you see I cared because I
thought the year you had away to college had made
you stuck-up, and you thought yourself too edu-
cated to waste any time on me.

ROBERT (*kissing her*). And I was thinking —
(*With a laugh.*) What fools we've both been!

RUTH (*overcome by a sudden fear*). You won't go
away on the trip, will you, Rob? You'll tell them
you can't go on account of me, won't you? You
can't go now! You can't!

ROBERT (*bewildered*). Perhaps — you can come too.

RUTH. Oh, Rob, don't be so foolish. You know I can't. Who'd take care of Ma? She has no one in the world but me. I can't leave her — the way she is. It'd be different if she was well and healthy like other people. Don't you see I couldn't go — on her account?

ROBERT (*vaguely*). I could go — and then send for you both — when I'd settled some place out there.

RUTH. Ma never could. She'd never leave the farm for anything, and she couldn't make a trip anywhere 'til she got better — if she ever does. And oh, Rob, I wouldn't want to live in any of those outlandish places you were going to. I couldn't stand it there, I know I couldn't — not knowing anyone. It makes me afraid just to think of it. I've never been away from here, hardly and — I'm just a home body, I'm afraid. (*She clings to him imploringly.*) Please don't go — not now. Tell them you've decided not to. They won't mind. I know your mother and father'll be glad. They'll all be. They don't want you to go so far away from them. Please, Rob! We'll be so happy here together where it's natural and we know things. Please tell me you won't go!

ROBERT (*face to face with a definite, final decision, betrays the conflict going on within him*). But — Ruth — I — Uncle Dick —

30

RUTH. He won't mind when he knows it's for your happiness to stay. How could he? (*As Robert remains silent she bursts into sobs again.*) Oh, Rob! And you said — you loved me!

ROBERT (*conquered by this appeal — an irrevocable decision in his voice*). I won't go, Ruth. I promise you. There! Don't cry! (*He presses her to him, stroking her hair tenderly. After a pause he speaks with happy hopefulness.*) Perhaps after all Andy was right — righter than he knew — when he said I could find all the things I was seeking for here, at home on the farm. The mystery and the wonder — our love should bring them home to us. I think love must have been the secret — the secret that called to me from over the world's rim — the secret beyond every horizon; and when I did not come, it came to me. (*He clasps Ruth to him fiercely.*) Oh, Ruth, you are right! Our love is sweeter than any distant dream. It is the meaning of all life, the whole world. The kingdom of heaven is within — us!

> (*He kisses her passionately and steps to the ground, lifting Ruth in his arms and carrying her to the road, where he puts her down.*)

RUTH (*with a happy laugh*). My, but you're strong!

ROBERT. Come! We'll go and tell them at once.

RUTH (*dismayed*). Oh no, don't, Rob, not 'til

after I've gone. Then you can tell your folks and I'll tell Ma when I get her home. There'd be bound to be such a scene with them all together.

ROBERT (*kissing her – gaily*). As you like – little Miss Common Sense!

RUTH. Let's go, then.

> (*She takes his hand, and they start to go off left. Robert suddenly stops and turns as though for a last look at the hills and the dying sunset flush.*)

ROBERT (*looking upward and pointing*). See! The first star. (*He bends down and kisses her tenderly.*) *Our* star!

RUTH (*in a soft murmur*). Yes. Our very own star. (*They stand for a moment looking up at it, their arms around each other. Then Ruth takes his hand again and starts to lead him away.*) Come, Rob, let's go. (*His eyes are fixed again on the horizon as he half-turns to follow her. Ruth urges.*) We'll be late for supper, Rob.

ROBERT (*shakes his head impatiently, as though he were throwing off some disturbing thought – with a laugh*). All right. We'll run then. Come on! (*They run off laughing as*

The Curtain Falls)

ACT ONE
SCENE TWO

SCENE. *The sitting-room of the Mayo farm-house about nine o'clock the same night. On the left, two windows looking out on the fields. Against the wall between the windows, an old-fashioned walnut desk. In the left corner, rear, a sideboard with a mirror. In the rear wall to the right of the sideboard, a window looking out on the road. Next to the window a door leading out into the yard. Farther right, a black horse-hair sofa, and another door opening on a bedroom. In the corner, a straight-backed chair. In the right wall, near the middle, an open doorway leading to the kitchen. Farther forward a double-heater stove with coal-scuttle, etc. In the centre of the newly carpeted floor, an oak dining-room table with a red cover. In the centre of the table, a large oil reading-lamp. Four chairs, three rocking with crocheted tidies on their backs, and one straight-backed, are placed about the table. The walls are papered a dark red with a scrolly figured pattern.*

Everything in the room is clean, well-kept, and in its exact place, yet there is no suggestion of primness about the whole. Rather the atmosphere is one of the orderly comfort of a simple, hard-earned prosperity, enjoyed and maintained by the family as a unit.

James Mayo, his wife, her brother, Captain

33

Dick Scott, and Andrew are discovered. Mrs. Mayo is a slight, round-faced, rather prim-looking woman of fifty-five, who had once been a school teacher. The labours of a farmer's wife have bent but not broken her, and she retains a certain refinement of movement and expression foreign to the Mayo part of the family. Whatever of resemblance Robert has to his parents may be traced to her. Her brother, the Captain, is short and stocky, with a weather-beaten, jovial face and a white moustache – a typical old salt, loud of voice and given to gesture. He is fifty-eight years old.

James Mayo sits in front of the table. He wears spectacles, and a farm journal which he has been reading lies in his lap. The Captain leans forward from a chair in the rear, his hands on the table in front of him. Andrew is tilted back on the straight-backed chair to the left, his chin sunk forward on his chest, staring at the carpet, preoccupied and frowning.

As the curtain rises the Captain is just finishing the relation of some sea episode. The others are pretending an interest which is belied by the absent-minded expressions on their faces.

THE CAPTAIN (*chuckling*). And that mission woman, she hails me on the dock as I was acomin' ashore, and she says – with her silly face all screwed up serious as judgment – "Captain," she says, "would you be so kind as to tell me where the sea-gulls sleeps at nights?" Blow me if them warn't her exact words! (*He slaps the table with the palms of his hands and laughs loudly. The others force smiles.*) Ain't that just like a fool woman's question? And I looks at her serious as I could, "Ma'm," says I, "I couldn't rightly answer that question. I ain't never seed a sea-gull in his bunk yet. The next time I hears one snorin'," I says, "I'll make a note of where he's turned in, and write you a letter 'bout it." And then she calls me a fool real spiteful and tacks away from me quick. (*He laughs again uproariously.*) So I got rid of her that way. (*The others smile but immediately relapse into expressions of gloom again.*)

MRS. MAYO (*absent-mindedly — feeling that she has to say something*). But when it comes to that, where *do* sea-gulls sleep, Dick?

SCOTT (*slapping the table*). Ho! Ho! Listen to her, James. 'Nother one! Well, if that don't beat all hell — 'scuse me for cussin', Kate.

MAYO (*with a twinkle in his eyes*). They unhitch their wings, Katey, and spreads 'em out on a wave for a bed.

SCOTT. And then they tells the fish to whistle to 'em when it's time to turn out. Ho! Ho!

MRS. MAYO (*with a forced smile*). You men folks are too smart to live, aren't you? (*She resumes her*

35

knitting. Mayo pretends to read his paper; Andrew stares at the floor.)

SCOTT (*looks from one to the other of them with a puzzled air. Finally he is unable to bear the thick silence a minute longer, and blurts out:*) You folks look as if you was settin' up with a corpse. (*With exaggerated concern.*) God A'mighty, there ain't anyone dead, be there?

MAYO (*sharply*). Don't play the dunce, Dick! You know as well as we do there ain't no great cause to be feelin' chipper.

SCOTT (*argumentatively*). And there ain't no cause to be wearin' mourning, either, I can make out.

MRS. MAYO (*indignantly*). How can you talk that way, Dick Scott, when you're taking our Robbie away from us, in the middle of the night, you might say, just to get on that old boat of yours on time! I think you might wait until morning when he's had his breakfast.

SCOTT (*appealing to the others hopelessly*). Ain't that a woman's way o' seein' things for you? God A'mighty, Kate, I can't give orders to the tide that it's got to be high just when it suits me to have it. I ain't gettin' no fun out o' missin' sleep and leavin' here at six bells myself. (*Protestingly.*) And the *Sunda* ain't an old ship — leastways, not very old — and she's good's she ever was. Your boy Robert'll be as safe on board o' her as he'd be home in bed here.

MRS. MAYO. How can you say that, Dick, when we read in almost every paper about wrecks and storms, and ships being sunk.

SCOTT. You've got to take your chances with such things. They don't happen often – not nigh as often as accidents do ashore.

MRS. MAYO (*her lips trembling*). I wish Robbie weren't going – not so far away and for so long.

MAYO (*looking at her over his glasses – consolingly*). There, Katey!

MRS. MAYO (*rebelliously*). Well, I *do* wish he wasn't! It'd be different if he'd ever been away from home before for any length of time. If he was healthy and strong too, it'd be different. I'm so afraid he'll be taken down ill when you're miles from land, and there's no one to take care of him.

MAYO. That's the very reason you was willin' for him to go, Katey – 'count o' your bein' 'fraid for his health.

MRS. MAYO (*illogically*). But he seems to be all right now without Dick taking him away.

SCOTT (*protestingly*). You'd think to hear you, Kate, that I was kidnappin' Robert agin your will. Now I ain't asayin' I ain't tickled to death to have him along, because I be. It's a'mighty lonesome for a captain on a sailin' vessel at times, and Robert'll be company for me. But what I'm sayin' is, I didn't propose it. I never even suspicioned that he was hankerin' to ship out, or that you'd let him go 'til you and James speaks to me 'bout it. And now you blames me for it.

MAYO. That's so. Dick's speaking the truth, Katey.

SCOTT. You shouldn't be taking it so hard, 's far as I kin see. This vige'll make a man of him. I'll see to it he learns how to navigate, 'n' study for a mate's c'tificate right off — and it'll give him a trade for the rest of his life, if he wants to travel.

MRS. MAYO. But I don't want him to travel all his life. You've got to see he comes home when this trip is over. Then he'll be all well, and he'll want to — to marry — (*Andrew sits forward in his chair with an abrupt movement*) — and settle down right here.

SCOTT. Well, in any case it won't hurt him to learn things when he's travellin'. And then he'll get to see a lot of the world in the ports we put in at, 'n' that'll help him afterwards, no matter what he takes up.

MRS. MAYO (*staring down at the knitting in her lap — as if she hadn't heard him*). I never realized how hard it was going to be for me to have Robbie go — or I wouldn't have considered it a minute. (*On the verge of tears.*) Oh, if only he wouldn't go!

SCOTT. It ain't no good goin' on that way, Kate, now it's all settled.

38

MRS. MAYO (*half-sobbing*). It's all right for *you* to talk. You've never had any children of your own, and you don't know what it means to be parted from them – and Robbie my youngest, too. (*Andrew frowns and fidgets in his chair.*)

MAYO (*a trace of command in his voice*). No use takin' on so, Katey! It's best for the boy. We've got to take that into consideration – no matter how much we hate to lose him. (*Firmly.*) And like Dick says, it's all settled now.

ANDREW (*suddenly turning to them*). There's one thing none of you seem to take into consideration – that Rob wants to go. He's dead set on it. He's been dreaming over this trip ever since it was first talked about. It wouldn't be fair to him not to have him go. (*A sudden thought seems to strike him and he continues doubtfully.*) At least, not if he still feels the same way about it he did when he was talking to me this evening.

MAYO (*with an air of decision*). Andy's right, Katey. Robert wants to go. That ends all argyment, you can see that.

MRS. MAYO (*faintly, but resignedly*). Yes. I suppose it must be, then.

MAYO (*looking at his big silver watch*). It's past nine. Wonder what's happened to Robert. He's been gone long enough to wheel the widder home, certain. He can't be out dreamin' at the stars his last night.

39

MRS. MAYO (*a bit reproachfully*). Why didn't you wheel Mrs. Atkins back to-night, Andy? You usually do when she and Ruth come over.

ANDREW (*avoiding her eyes*). I thought maybe Robert wanted to go to-night. He offered to go right away when they were leaving.

MRS. MAYO. He only wanted to be polite.

ANDREW (*gets to his feet*). Well, he'll be right back, I guess. (*He turns to his father.*) Guess I'll go take a look at the black cow, Pa – see if she's ailing any.

MAYO. Yes – better had, son. (*Andrew goes into the kitchen on the right.*)

SCOTT (*as he goes out – in a low tone*). There's the boy that would make a good, strong seafarin' man – if he'd a mind to.

MAYO (*sharply*). Don't you put no such fool notions in Andy's head, Dick – or you 'n' me's goin' to fall out. (*Then he smiles.*) You couldn't tempt him, no ways. Andy's a Mayo bred in the bone, and he's a born farmer, and a damn good one, too. He'll live and die right here on this farm, like I expect to. (*With proud confidence.*) And he'll make this one of the slickest, best-payin' farms in the state, too, afore he gits through!

SCOTT. Seems to me it's a pretty slick place right now.

MAYO (*shaking his head*). It's too small. We need

more land to make it amount to much, and we ain't got the capital to buy it.

>(*Andrew enters from the kitchen. His hat is on, and he carries a lighted lantern in his hand. He goes to the door in the rear leading out.*)

ANDREW (*opens the door and pauses*). Anything else you can think of to be done, Pa?

MAYO. No, nothin' I know of. (*Andrew goes out, shutting the door.*)

MRS. MAYO (*after a pause*). What's come over Andy to-night, I wonder? He acts so strange.

MAYO. He does seem sort o' glum and out of sorts. It's 'count o' Robert leavin', I s'pose. (*To Scott.*) Dick, you wouldn't believe how them boys o' mine sticks together. They ain't like most brothers. They've been thick as thieves all their lives, with nary a quarrel I kin remember.

SCOTT. No need to tell me that. I can see how they take to each other.

MRS. MAYO (*pursuing her train of thought*). Did you notice, James, how queer every one was at supper? Robert seemed stirred up about something, and Ruth was so flustered and giggly, and Andy sat there dumb, looking as if he'd lost his best friend, and all of them only nibbled at their food.

MAYO. Guess they was all thinkin' about to-morrow, same as us.

41

MRS. MAYO (*shaking her head*). No. I'm afraid somethin's happened – somethin' else.

MAYO. You mean – 'bout Ruth?

MRS. MAYO. Yes.

MAYO (*after a pause – frowning*). I hope her and Andy ain't had a serious fallin'-out. I always sorter hoped they'd hitch up together sooner or later. What d'you say, Dick? Don't you think them two'd pair up well?

SCOTT (*nodding his head approvingly*). A sweet, wholesome couple they'd make.

MAYO. It'd be a good thing for Andy in more ways than one. I ain't what you'd call calculatin' generally, and I b'lieve in lettin' young folks run their affairs to suit themselves; but there's advantages for both o' them in this match you can't overlook in reason. The Atkins' farm is right next to ourn. Jined together they'd make a jim-dandy of a place, with plenty o' room to work in. And bein' a widder with only a daughter, and laid up all the time to boot, Mrs. Atkins can't do nothin' with the place as it ought to be done. Her hired help just goes along as they pleases, in spite o' her everlastin' complainin' at 'em. She needs a man, a first-class farmer, to take hold o' things, and Andy's just the one.

MRS. MAYO (*abruptly*). I don't think Ruth loves Andy.

MAYO. You don't? Well, maybe a woman's eyes is sharper in such things, but — they're always together. And if she don't love him now, she'll likely come around to it in time.

MAYO (*as Mrs. Mayo shakes her head*). You seem mighty fixed in your opinion, Katey. How d'you know?

MRS. MAYO. It's just — what I feel.

MAYO (*a light breaking over him*). You don't mean to say — (*Mrs. Mayo nods. Mayo chuckles scornfully*). Shucks! I'm losin' my respect for your eyesight, Katey. Why, Robert ain't got no time for Ruth, 'cept as a friend!

MRS. MAYO (*warningly*). Sss-h-h!

> (*The door from the yard opens, and Robert enters. He is smiling happily, and humming a song to himself, but as he comes into the room an undercurrent of nervous uneasiness manifests itself in his bearing.*)

MAYO. So here you be at last! (*Robert comes forward and sits on Andy's chair. Mayo smiles slyly at his wife.*) What have you been doin' all this time — countin' the stars to see if they all come out right and proper?

ROBERT. There's only one I'll ever look for any more, Pa.

MAYO (*reproachfully*). You might've even not

43

wasted time lookin' for that one – your last night.

MRS. MAYO (*as if she were speaking to a child*). You ought to have worn your coat a sharp night like this, Robbie.

ROBERT. I wasn't cold, Ma. It's beautiful and warm on the road.

SCOTT (*disgustedly*). God A'mighty, Kate, you treat Robert as if he was one year old!

ROBERT (*with a smile*). I'm used to that, Uncle.

SCOTT (*with joking severity*). You'll learn to forget all that baby coddlin' nights down off the Horn when you're haulin' hell-bent on the braces with a green sea up to your neck, and the old hooker doin' summersaults under you. That's the stuff'll put iron in your blood, eh Kate?

MRS. MAYO (*indignantly*). What are you trying to do, Dick Scott – frighten me out of my senses? If you can't say anything cheerful, you'd better keep still.

SCOTT. Don't take on, Kate. I was only joshin' him and you.

MRS. MAYO. You have strange notions of what's a joke, I must say! (*She notices Robert's nervous uneasiness.*) You look all worked up over something, Robbie. What is it?

ROBERT (*swallowing hard, looks quickly from one to the other of them – then begins determinedly*). Yes, there *is* something – something I must tell you –

all of you. (*As he begins to talk Andrew enters quietly from the rear, closing the door behind him, and setting the lighted lantern on the floor. He remains standing by the door, his arms folded, listening to Robert with a repressed expression of pain on his face. Robert is so much taken up with what he is going to say that he does not notice Andrew's presence.*) Something I discovered only this evening – very beautiful and wonderful – something I did not take into consideration previously because I hadn't dared to hope that such happiness could ever come to me. (*Appealingly.*) You must all remember that fact, won't you?

MAYO (*frowning*). Let's get to the point, son.

ROBERT. You were offended because you thought I'd been wasting my time star-gazing on my last night at home. (*With a trace of defiance.*) Well, the point is this, Pa; it *isn't* my last night at home. I'm not going – I mean – I can't go to-morrow with Uncle Dick – or at any future time, either.

MRS. MAYO (*with a sharp sigh of joyful relief*). Oh, Robbie, I'm so glad!

MAYO (*astounded*). You ain't serious, be you, Robert?

ROBERT. Yes, I mean what I say.

MAYO (*severely*). Seems to me it's a pretty late hour in the day for you to be upsettin' all your plans so sudden!

45

ROBERT. I asked you to remember that until this evening I didn't know myself — the wonder which makes everything else in the world seem sordid and pitifully selfish by comparison. I had never dared to dream —

MAYO (*irritably*). Come to the point. What is this foolishness you're talkin' of?

ROBERT (*flushing*). Ruth told me this evening that — she loved me. It was after I'd confessed I loved her. I told her I hadn't been conscious of my love until after the trip had been arranged, and I realized it would mean — leaving her. That was the truth. I *didn't* know until then. (*As if justifying himself to the others.*) I hadn't intended telling her anything but — suddenly — I felt I must. I didn't think it would matter, because I was going away, and before I came back I was sure she'd have forgotten. And I thought she loved — some one else. (*Slowly — his eyes shining.*) And then she cried and said it was I she'd loved all the time, but I hadn't seen it. (*Simply.*) So we're going to be married — very soon — and I'm happy — and that's all there is to say. (*Appealingly.*) But you see, I couldn't go away now — even if I wanted to.

MRS. MAYO (*getting up from her chair*). Of course not! (*Rushes over and throws her arms about him.*) I knew it! I was just telling your father when you came in — and, oh, Robbie, I'm so happy you're not going!

46

ROBERT (*kissing her*). I knew you'd be glad, Ma.

MAYO (*bewilderedly*). Well, I'll be damned! You do beat all for gettin' folks' minds all tangled up, Robert. And Ruth too! Whatever got into her of a sudden? Why, I was thinkin' —

MRS. MAYO (*hurriedly – in a tone of warning*). Never mind what you were thinking, James. It wouldn't be any use telling us that now. (*Meaningly.*) And what you were hoping for turns out just the same almost, doesn't it?

MAYO (*thoughtfully – beginning to see this side of the argument*). Yes; I suppose you're right, Katey. (*Scratching his head in puzzlement.*) But how it ever come about! It do beat anything ever I heard. (*Finally he gets up with a sheepish grin and walks over to Robert.*) We're glad you ain't goin', your Ma and I, for we'd have missed you terrible, that's certain and sure; and we're glad you've found happiness. Ruth's a fine girl and'll make a good wife to you.

ROBERT (*much moved*). Thank you, Pa. (*He grips his father's hand in his.*)

ANDREW (*his face tense and drawn comes forward and holds out his hand, forcing a smile*). I guess it's my turn to offer congratulations, isn't it?

ROBERT (*with a startled cry when his brother appears before him so suddenly*). Andy! (*Confused.*) Why – I – I didn't see you. Were you here when—·

ANDREW. I heard everything you said; and here's wishing you every happiness, you and Ruth. You both deserve the best there is.

ROBERT (*taking his hand*). Thanks, Andy, it's fine of you to — (*His voice dies away as he sees the pain in Andrew's eyes.*)

ANDREW (*giving his brother's hand a final grip*). Good luck to you both!

> (*He turns away and goes back to the rear, when he bends over the lantern, fumbling with it to hide his emotion from the others.*)

MRS. MAYO (*to the Captain, who has been too flabbergasted by Robert's decision to say a word*). What's the matter, Dick? Aren't you going to congratulate Robbie?

SCOTT (*embarrassed*). Of course I be! (*He gets to his feet and shakes Robert's hand, muttering a vague*) Luck to you, boy.

> (*He stands beside Robert as if he wanted to say something more but doesn't know how to go about it.*)

ROBERT. Thanks, Uncle Dick.

SCOTT. So you're not acomin' on the *Sunda* with me? (*His voice indicates disbelief.*)

ROBERT. I can't, Uncle — not now. I'm very grateful to you for having wanted to take me. I wouldn't miss it for anything else in the world under any other circumstances. (*He sighs uncon-sciously.*) But you see I've found – a bigger dream.

SCOTT (*gruffly*). Bring the girl along with you. I'll fix it so there's room.

MRS. MAYO (*sharply*). How can you propose such a crazy idea, Dick – to take a young girl on a sail-boat all over the world and not a woman on the boat but herself. Have you lost your senses?

ROBERT (*regretfully*). It would be wonderful if we could both go with you, Uncle – but it's impossible. Ruth couldn't go on account of her mother, and besides, I'm afraid she doesn't like the idea of the sea.

SCOTT (*putting all his disapproval into an exclamation*). Humph!

(*He goes back and sits down at the table.*)

ROBERT (*in joyous high spirits*). I want you all to understand one thing – I'm not going to be a loafer on your hands any longer. This means the beginning of a new life for me in every way. I'm sick and disgusted at myself for sitting around and seeing every one else hard at work, while all I've been doing is keep the accounts – a couple of hours' work a week! I'm going to settle right down and take a real interest in the farm, and do my share. I'll prove to you, Pa, that I'm as good a Mayo as you are – or Andy, when I want to be.

MAYO (*kindly but sceptically*). That's the right

spirit, Robert, but it ain't needful for you to —

MRS. MAYO (*interrupting him*). No one said you weren't doing your part, Robbie. You've got to look out for —

ROBERT. I know what you're going to say, and that's another false idea you've got to get out of your heads. It's ridiculous for you to persist in looking on me as an invalid. I'm as well as anyone, and I'll prove it to you if you'll give me half a chance. Once I get the hang of it, I'll be able to do as hard a day's work as anyone. You wait and see.

MAYO. Ain't none of us doubts your willin'ness, but you ain't never learned —

ROBERT. Then I'm going to start learning right away, and you'll teach me, won't you?

MAYO (*mollifyingly*). Of course I will, boy, and be glad to, only you'd best go easy at first.

ROBERT. With the two farms to look after, you'll need me; and when I marry Ruth I'll have to know how to take care of things for her and her mother.

MAYO. That's so, son.

SCOTT (*who has listened to this conversation in mingled consternation and amazement*). You don't mean to tell me you're goin' to let him stay, do you, James?

MAYO. Why, things bein' as they be, Robert's free to do as he's a mind to.

MRS. MAYO. *Let him!* The very idea!

SCOTT (*more and more ruffled*). Then all I got to say is, you're a soft, weak-willed critter to be permittin' a boy — and women, too — to be layin' your course for you wherever they damn pleases.

MAYO (*slyly amused*). It's just the same with me as 'twas with you, Dick. You can't order the tides on the seas to suit you, and I ain't pretendin' I can reg'late love for young folks.

SCOTT (*scornfully*). Love! They ain't old enough to know love when they sight it! Love! I'm ashamed of you, Robert, to go lettin' a little huggin' and kissin' in the dark spile your chances to make a man out o' yourself. It ain't common sense — no sirree, it ain't — not by a hell of a sight!

(*He pounds the table with his fists in exasperation.*)

ROBERT (*smiling*). I'm afraid I can't help it, Uncle.

SCOTT. Humph! You ain't got any sand, that's what! And you, James Mayo, lettin' boys and women run things to the devil and back — you've got less sense than he has!

MAYO (*with a grin*). If Robert can't help it, I'm sure I ain't able, Dick.

MRS. MAYO (*laughing provokingly at her brother*). A fine one you are to be talking about love, Dick — an old cranky bachelor like you. Goodness sakes!

SCOTT (*exasperated by their joking*). I've never been a damn fool like most, if that's what you're steerin' at.

MRS. MAYO (*tauntingly*). Sour grapes, aren't they, Dick? (*She laughs. Robert and his father chuckle. Scott sputters with annoyance.*) Good gracious, Dick, you do act silly, flying into a temper over nothing.

SCOTT (*indignantly*). Nothin'! Is that what you call it — nothin'? You talk as if I wasn't concerned nohow in this here business. Seems to me I've got a right to have my say. Ain't I gone to all sorts o' trouble gettin' the sta'b'd cabin all cleaned out and painted and fixed up so's that Robert o' yours'd be comfortable? Ain't I made all arrangements with the owners and stocked up with some special grub all on Robert's account?

ROBERT. You've been fine, Uncle Dick; and I appreciate it. Truly.

MAYO. 'Course; we all does, Dick.

MRS. MAYO. And don't spoil it now by getting angry at us.

SCOTT (*unplacated*). It's all right for you to say don't this and don't that; but you ain't seen things from my side of it. I've been countin' sure on havin' Robert for company on this vige — to sorta talk to and show things to, and teach, kinda, and I got my mind so set on havin' him I'm goin' to be

52

double lonesome this vige. (*He pounds on the table, attempting to cover up this confession of weakness.*) Darn all this silly lovin' business, anyway.

MRS. MAYO (*touched*). It's too bad you have to be so lonesome, Dick. Why don't you give up the old boat? You've been on the sea long enough, heaven knows. Why don't you make up your mind and settle down here with us?

SCOTT (*emphatically*). And go diggin' up the dirt and plantin' things? Not by a hell of a sight! You can have all the darned dirt in the earth for all o' me. I ain't sayin' it ain't all right – if you're made that way – but *I ain't*. No settlin' down for me. No sirree! (*Irritably.*) But all this talk ain't tellin' me what I'm to do with that sta'b'd cabin I fixed up. It's all painted white, an' a bran new mattress on the bunk, 'n' new sheets 'n' blankets 'n' things. And Chips built in a book-case so's Robert could take his books along – with a slidin' bar fixed across't it, mind, so's they couldn't fall out no matter how she rolled. (*With excited consternation.*) What d'you suppose my officers is goin' to think when there's no one comes aboard to occupy that sta'b'd cabin? And the men what did the work on it – what'll *they* think? (*He shakes his finger indignantly.*) They're liable as not to suspicion it was a *woman* I'd planned to ship along, and that she gave me the go-by at the last moment! (*He wipes his perspiring brow in anguish at this thought.*) Gawd A'mighty! They're only lookin' to have the laugh on me for something like that. They're liable to b'lieve anything, those fellers is!

MAYO (*with a wink*). Then there's nothing to it but for you to get right out and hunt up a wife somewheres for that spic 'n' span cabin. She'll have to be a pretty one, too, to match it. (*He looks at his watch with exaggerated concern.*) You ain't got much time to find her, Dick.

SCOTT (*as the others smile — sulkily*). You kin go to thunder, Jim Mayo!

ANDREW (*comes forward from where he has been standing by the door, rear, brooding. His face is set in a look of grim determination*). You needn't worry about that spare cabin, Uncle Dick, if you've a mind to take me in Robert's place.

ROBERT (*turning to him quickly*). Andy! (*He sees at once the fixed resolve in his brother's eyes, and realizes immediately the reason for it — in consternation.*) Andy, you mustn't!

ANDREW. You've made your decision, Rob, and now I've made mine. You're out of this, remember.

ROBERT (*hurt by his brother's tone*). But Andy—

ANDREW. Don't interfere, Rob — that's all I ask. (*Turning to his uncle.*) You haven't answered my question, Uncle Dick.

SCOTT (*clearing his throat, with an uneasy side*

glance at James Mayo, who is staring at his elder son as if he thought he had suddenly gone mad. O' course, I'd be glad to have you, Andy.

ANDREW. It's settled then. I can pack the little I want to take in a few minutes.

MRS. MAYO. Don't be a fool, Dick. Andy's only joking you. He wouldn't go for anything.

SCOTT (*disgruntledly*). It's hard to tell who's jokin' and who's not in this house.

ANDREW (*firmly*). I'm not joking, Uncle Dick – and since I've got your permission, I'm going with you. (*As Scott looks at him uncertainly.*) You needn't be afraid I'll go back on my word. When I say I'll go, I'll go.

ROBERT (*hurt by the insinuation he feels in Andrew's tone*). Andy! That isn't fair!

MRS. MAYO (*beginning to be disturbed*). But I know he must be fooling us. Aren't you, Andy?

ANDREW. No, Ma, I'm not.

MAYO (*frowning*). Seems to me this ain't no subject to joke over – not for Andy.

ANDREW (*facing his father*). I agree with you, Pa, and I tell you again, once and for all, that I've made up my mind to go.

MAYO (*dumbfounded – unable to doubt the determination in Andrew's voice – helplessly*). But why, son? Why?

ANDREW (*evasively*). I've always wanted to go, even if I ain't said anything about it

ROBERT. Andy!

ANDREW (*half-angrily*). You shut up, Rob! I told you to keep out of this. (*Turning to his father again.*) I didn't ever mention it because as long as Rob was going I knew it was no use; but now Rob's staying on here, and Uncle Dick wants some one along with him, there isn't any reason for me not to go.

MAYO (*breathing hard*). No reason? Can you stand there and say that to me, Andrew?

MRS. MAYO (*hastily — seeing the gathering storm*). He doesn't mean a word of it, James.

MAYO (*making a gesture to her to keep silence*). Let me talk, Katey. (*In a more kindly tone.*) What's come over you so sudden, Andy? You know's well as I do that it wouldn't be fair o' you to run off at a moment's notice right now when we're up to our necks in hard work.

ANDREW (*avoiding his eyes*). Rob'll hold his end up as soon as he learns.

MAYO. You know that ain't so. Robert was never cut out for a farmer, and you was.

ANDREW. You can easily get a man to do my work.

MAYO (*restraining his anger with an effort*). It sounds strange to hear you, Andy, that I always

56

thought had good sense, talkin' crazy like that. And you don't believe yourself one bit of what you've been sayin' — not 'less you've suddenly gone out of your mind. (*Scornfully.*) Get a man to take your place? Where'd I get him, tell me, with the shortage of farm labour hereabouts? And if I could get one, what int'rest d'you suppose he'd take beyond doin' as little work as he could for the money I paid him? You ain't been workin' here for no hire, Andy, that you kin give me your notice to quit like you've done. The farm is your'n as well as mine. You've always worked on it with that understanding; and what you're sayin' you intend doin' is just skulkin' out o' your rightful responsibility.

ANDREW (*looking at the floor — simply*). I'm sorry, Pa. (*After a slight pause.*) It's no use talking any more about it.

MRS. MAYO (*in relief*). There! I knew Andy'd come to his senses!

ANDREW. Don't get the wrong idea, Ma. I'm not backing out.

MAYO. You mean you're goin' in spite of — everythin'?

ANDREW. Yes. I'm going. I want to — and — I've got to. (*He looks at his father defiantly.*) I feel I oughtn't to miss this chance to go out into the world and see things, and — I want to go.

MAYO (*with bitter scorn*). So — you want to go out

C   57

into the world and see thin's! (*His voice raised and quivering with anger.*) I never thought I'd live to see the day when a son o' mine'd look me in the face and tell a barefaced lie! (*Bursting out.*) You're a liar, Andy Mayo, and a mean one to boot!

MRS. MAYO. James!

ROBERT. Pa!

SCOTT. Steady there, Jim!

MAYO (*waving their protests aside*). He is and he knows it.

ANDREW (*his face flushed*). I won't argue with you, Pa. You can think as badly of me as you like. I can't help that. Let's not talk about it any more. I've made up my mind, and nothing you can say will change it.

MAYO (*shaking his finger at Andy, in a cold rage*). You know I'm speakin' truth — that's why you're afraid to argy! You lie when you say you want to go 'way — and see things! You ain't got no likin' in the world to go. Your place is right here on this farm — the place you was born to by nature — and you can't tell me no different. I've watched you grow up, and I know your ways, and they're my ways. You're runnin' against your own nature, and you're goin' to be a'mighty sorry for it if you do. You're tryin' to pretend to me something that don't fit in with your make-up, and it's damn fool pretendin' if you think you're foolin' me. 'S if I didn't know your real reason for runnin' away! And runnin' away's the only words to fit it. You're runnin' away 'cause you're put out and riled 'cause your own brother's got Ruth 'stead o' you, and——

ANDREW (*his face crimson – tensely*). Stop, Pa! I won't stand hearing that – not even from you!

MRS. MAYO (*rushing to Andy and putting her arms about him protectingly*). Don't mind him, Andy dear. He don't mean a word he's saying!

> (*Robert stands rigidly, his hands clenched, his face contracted by pain. Scott sits dumbfounded and open-mouthed. Andrew soothes his mother, who is on the verge of tears.*)

MAYO (*in angry triumph*). It's the truth, Andy Mayo! And you ought to be bowed in shame to think of it!

ROBERT (*protestingly*). Pa! You've gone far enough. It's a shame for you to talk that way!

MRS. MAYO (*coming from Andrew to his father; puts her hands on his shoulders as though to try and push him back in the chair from which he has risen*). Won't you be still, James? Please won't you?

MAYO (*looking at Andrew over his wife's shoulder – stubbornly*). The truth – God's truth!

MRS. MAYO. Sh-h-h! (*She tries to put a finger across his lips, but he twists his head away.*)

ANDREW (*who has regained control over himself*). You're wrong, Pa, it isn't truth. (*With defiant assertiveness.*) I don't love Ruth. I never loved her, and the thought of such a thing never entered my head.

MAYO (*with an angry snort of disbelief*). Hump! You're pilin' lie on lie!

ANDREW (*losing his temper — bitterly*). I suppose it'd be hard for you to explain anyone's wanting to leave this blessed farm except for some outside reason like that. You think these few measly acres are heaven, and that none'd want to ever do nothing in all their lives but stay right here and work like a dog all the time. But I'm sick and tired of it — whether you want to believe me or not — and that's why I'm glad to get a chance to move on. I've been sick and tired of farm life for a long time, and if I hadn't said anything about it, it was only to save your feelings. Just because you love it here, you've got your mind set that I like it, too. You want me to stay on so's you can know that I'll be taking care of the rotten farm after you're gone. Well, Rob'll be here, and he's a Mayo, too. You can leave it in his hands.

ROBERT. Andy! Don't! You're only making it worse.

ANDREW (*sulkily*). I don't care. I've done my share of work here. I've earned my right to quit when I want to. (*Suddenly overcome with anger and*

60

grief; with rising intensity.) I'm sick and tired of the whole damn business. I hate the farm and every inch of ground in it. I'm sick of digging in the dirt and sweating in the sun like a slave without getting a word of thanks for it. (*Tears of rage starting to his eyes – hoarsely.*) I'm through, through for good and all; and if Uncle Dick won't take me on his ship, I'll find another. I'll get away somewhere, somehow.

MRS. MAYO (*in a frightened voice*). Don't you answer him, James. He doesn't know what he's saying to you. Don't say a word to him 'til he's in his right senses again. Please James, don't—

MAYO (*pushes her away from him; his face is drawn and pale with the violence of his passion. He glares at Andrew as if he hated him*). You dare to – you dare to speak like that to me? You talk like that 'bout this farm – the Mayo farm – where you was born – you – you— (*He clenches his fist above his head and advances threateningly on Andrew.*) You damned whelp!

MRS. MAYO (*with a shriek*). James!

(*She covers her face with her hands and sinks weakly into Mayo's chair. Andrew remains standing motionless, his face pale and set.*)

SCOTT (*starting to his feet and stretching his arms across the table toward Mayo*). Easy there, Jim!

61

ROBERT (*throwing himself between father and brother*). Stop! Are you mad?

MAYO (*grabs Robert's arm and pushes him aside — then stands for a moment gasping for breath before Andrew. He points to the door with a shaking finger*). Yes — go! — go! — You're no son o' mine — no son o' mine! You can go to hell if you want to! Don't let me find you here — in the mornin' — or — or — I'll *throw* you out!

ROBERT. Pa! For God's sake!

(*Mrs. Mayo bursts into noisy sobbing.*)

SCOTT (*placatingly*). Ain't you goin' too far, Jim?

MAYO (*turning on him furiously*). Shut up, you — you Dick! It's your fault — a lot o' this — you and your cussed ship! Don't you take him — if you do — don't you dare darken this door again. Let him go by himself and learn to starve — *starve!* (*He gulps convulsively and turns again to Andrew.*) And you go — to-morrow mornin' — and by God — don't come back — don't dare come back — by God, not while I'm livin' — or I'll — I'll—

(*He shakes over his muttered threat and strides toward the door rear, right.*)

MRS. MAYO (*rising and throwing her arms around him — hysterically*). James! James! Where are you going?

MAYO (*incoherently*). I'm goin' — to bed, Katey. It's late, Katey — it's late. (*He goes out.*)

62

MRS. MAYO (*following him, pleading hysterically*). James! Take back what you've said to Andy. James!

> (*She follows him out. Robert and the Captain stare after them with horrified eyes. Andrew stands rigidly looking straight in front of him, his fists clenched at his sides.*)

SCOTT (*the first to find his voice — with an explosive sigh*). Well, if he ain't the devil himself when he's roused! You oughtn't to have talked to him that way, Andy, 'bout the damn farm, knowin' how touchy he is about it. (*With another sigh.*) Well, you won't mind what he's said in anger. He'll be sorry for it when he's calmed down a bit.

ANDREW (*in a dead voice*). No, he won't. You don't know him. (*Defiantly.*) What's said is said and can't be unsaid; and I've chosen.

SCOTT (*uncertainly*). You don't mean — you're still a mind to go — go with me, do you?

ANDREW (*stubbornly*). I haven't said I've changed my mind, have I? There's all the reason in the world for me to go — now. And I'm going if you're not afraid to take me after what he said.

ROBERT (*with violent protest*). Andy! You can't! Don't be a fool! This is all so stupid — and terrible.

ANDREW (*coldly*). I'll talk to you in a minute,

63

BEYOND THE HORIZON

Rob, when we're alone. This is between Uncle and me. (*Crushed by his brother's cold indifference, Robert sinks down into a chair, holding his head in his hands. Andrew turns again to Scott.*) If you don't want to take me, it's all right — there's no hard feelings. I can understand you don't like to fall out with Pa.

SCOTT (*indignantly*). Gawd A'mighty, Andy, I ain't scared o' your Pa, nor no man livin', I want t'have you come along! Only I was thinkin' o' Kate. We don't want her to have to suffer from his contrariness. Let's see. (*He screws up his brows in thought.*) S'posing we both lie a little, eh? I'll tell 'em you're not comin' with me, and you tell 'em you're goin' to the port to get another ship. We can leave here in the team together. That's natural enough. They can't suspect nothin' from that. And then you can write home the first port we touch and explain things. (*He winks at Andrew cunningly.*) Are you on to the course?

ANDREW (*frowning*). Yes — if you think it's best.

SCOTT. For your Ma's sake. I wouldn't ask it, else.

ANDREW (*shrugging his shoulders*). All right then.

SCOTT (*with a great sigh of relief — comes and slaps Andrew on the back — beaming*). I'm damned glad you're shippin' on, Andy. I like your spirit, and the way you spoke up to him. (*Lowering his voice to a cautious whisper.*) You was right not to want

64

to waste your life ploughin' dirt and pattin' it down again. The sea's the place for a young feller like you that isn't half dead 'n' alive. (*He gives Andy a final approving slap.*) You 'n' me'll get along like twins, see if we don't. I'm durned glad you're comin', boy.

ANDREW (*wearily*). Let's not talk about it any more, Uncle. I'm tired of talking.

SCOTT. Right! I'm goin' aloft to turn in, and leave you two alone. Don't forget to pack your dunnage. And git some sleep, if you kin. We'll want to sneak out extra early b'fore they're up. It'll do away with more argyments. Robert can drive us down to the town, and bring back the team. (*He goes to the door in the rear, left.*) Well, good night.

ANDREW. Good night. (*Scott goes out. The two brothers remain silent for a moment. Then Andrew comes over to his brother and puts a hand on his back. He speaks in a low voice, full of feeling.*) Buck up, Rob. It ain't any use crying over spilt milk; and it'll all turn out for the best — let's hope. It couldn't be helped — what's happened.

ROBERT (*wildly*). But it's a lie, Andy, a lie!

ANDREW. Of course it's a lie. You know it and I know it — but that's all ought to know it.

ROBERT. Pa'll never forgive you. Oh, why did you want to anger him like that? You know how he feels about the farm. Oh, the whole affair is so senseless – and tragic. Why did you think you must go away?

ANDREW. You know better than to ask that. You know why. (*Fiercely*.) I can wish you and Ruth all the good luck in the world, and I do, and I mean it; but you can't expect me to stay around here and watch you two together, day after day – and me alone. You couldn't expect that! I couldn't stand it – not after all the plans I'd made to happen on this place thinking— (*His voice breaks*.) Thinking she cared for me.

ROBERT (*putting a hand on his brother's arm*). God! It's horrible! I feel so guilty – to think that I should be the cause of your suffering, after we've been such pals all our lives. If I could have foreseen what'd happen, I swear to you I'd have never said a word to Ruth. I swear I wouldn't have, Andy.

ANDREW. I know you wouldn't; and that would've been worse, for Ruth would've suffered then. (*He pats his brother's shoulder*.) It's best as it is. It had to be, and I've got to stand the gaff, that's all. Pa'll see how I felt – after a time (*as Robert shakes his head*) – and if he don't – well, it can't be helped.

ROBERT. But think of Ma! God, Andy, you can't go! You can't!

66

ANDREW (*fiercely*). I've got to go – to get away! I've got to, I tell you. I'd die here. I'd kill myself! Can't you understand what it'd mean to me, how I'd suffer? You don't know how I'd planned – for Ruth and me – the hopes I'd had about what the future'd be like. You can't blame me to go. You'd do the same yourself. I'd go crazy here, bein' reminded every second of the day how my life's been smashed, and what a fool I'd made of myself. I'd have nothing to hope or live for. I've got to get away and try and forget, if I can. I never could stay here – seeing her. And I'd hate the farm if I stayed, hate it for bringin' things back. I couldn't take interest in the work any more, work with no purpose in sight. Can't you see what a hell it'd be? You love her too, Rob. Put yourself in my place, and remember I haven't stopped loving her, and couldn't if I was to stay. Would that be fair to you or to her? Put yourself in my place. (*He shakes his brother fiercely by the shoulder.*) What'd you do then? Tell me the truth! You love her. What'd you do? In spite of all hell, what'd you do?

ROBERT (*chokingly*). I'd – I'd go, Andy! (*He buries his face in his hands with a shuddering sob.*) God!

ANDREW (*seeming to relax suddenly all over his body – in a low, steady voice.*) Then you know why I got to go; and there's nothing more to be said.

67

ROBERT (*in a frenzy of rebellion*). Why did this have to happen to us? It's damnable!

> (*He looks about him wildly, as if his vengeance were seeking the responsible Fate.*)

ANDREW (*soothingly — again putting his hands on his brother's shoulder*). It's no use fussing any more, Rob. It's done. (*Affectionately.*) You'll forget anything I said to hurt when I was mad, won't you? I wanted to keep you out of it.

ROBERT. Oh, Andy, it's me who ought to be asking your forgiveness for the suffering I've brought on you.

ANDREW (*forcing a smile*). I guess Ruth's got a right to have who she likes; you ain't to blame for that. She made a good choice — and God bless her for it!

ROBERT. Andy! Oh, I wish I could tell you half I feel of how fine you are!

ANDREW (*interrupting him quickly*). Shut up! Let's go to bed. We've talked long enough, and I've got to be up long before sun-up. You, too, if you're going to drive us down.

ROBERT. Yes. Yes.

ANDREW (*turning down the lamp*). And I've got to pack yet. (*He yawns with utter weariness.*) I'm as tired as if I'd been ploughing twenty-four hours at a stretch. (*Dully.*) I feel — dead. (*Robert covers his*

68

face again with his hands. Andrew shakes his head as if to get rid of his thoughts, and continues with a poor attempt at cheery briskness.) I'm going to douse the light. Come on. (*He slaps his brother on the back. Robert does not move. Andrew bends over and blows out the lamp. His voice comes from the darkness.*) Don't sit there mourning, Rob. It'll all come out in the wash. Come on and get some sleep. Everything'll turn out all right in the end.

> (*Robert can be heard stumbling to his feet, and the dark figures of the two brothers can be seen groping their way toward the doorway in the rear as*
>
> *The Curtain Falls*)

ACT TWO

SCENE ONE

SCENE. *Same as Act One, Scene Two. Sitting-room of the farm-house about half-past twelve in the afternoon of a hot, sun-baked day in midsummer, three years later. All the windows are open, but no breeze stirs the soiled white curtains. A patched screen door is in the rear. Through it the yard can be seen, its small stretch of lawn divided by the dirt path leading to the door from the gate in the white picket fence which borders the road.*

The room has changed, not so much in its outward appearance as in its general atmosphere. Little significant details give evidence of carelessness, of inefficiency, of an industry gone to seed. The chairs appear shabby from lack of paint; the table cover is spotted and askew; holes show in the curtains; a child's doll, with one arm gone, lies under the table; a hoe stands in a corner; a man's coat is flung on the couch in the rear; the desk is cluttered up with odds and ends; a number of books are piled carelessly on the sideboard. The noon enervation of the sultry, scorching day seems to have penetrated indoors, causing even inanimate objects to wear an aspect of despondent exhaustion.

A place is set at the end of the table, left, for some one's dinner. Through the open door to the kitchen comes the clatter of dishes being washed,

71

*interrupted at intervals by a woman's irritated
voice and the peevish whining of a child.*

*At the rise of the curtain Mrs. Mayo and Mrs.
Atkins are discovered sitting facing each other,
Mrs. Mayo to the rear, Mrs. Atkins to the right
of the table. Mrs. Mayo's face has lost all character, disintegrated, become a weak mask wearing a helpless, doleful expression of being constantly on the verge of comfortless tears. She
speaks in an uncertain voice, without assertiveness, as if all power of willing had deserted her.
Mrs. Atkins is in her wheel chair. She is a
thin, pale-faced, unintelligent-looking woman of
about forty-eight, with hard, bright eyes. A
victim of partial paralysis for many years, con-
demned to be pushed from day to day of her life
in a wheel chair, she has developed the selfish
irritable nature of the chronic invalid. Both
women are dressed in black. Mrs. Atkins knits
nervously as she talks. A ball of unused yarn,
with needles stuck through it, lies on the table
before Mrs. Mayo.*

MRS. ATKINS (*with a disapproving glance at the
place set on the table*). Robert's late for his dinner
again, as usual. I don't see why Ruth puts up
with it, and I've told her so. Many's the time I've
said to her "It's about time you put a stop to his
nonsense. Does he suppose you're runnin' an
hotel — with no one to help with things?" But she

don't pay no attention. She's as bad as he is, a'most — thinks she knows better than an old, sick body like me.

MRS. MAYO (*dully*). Robbie's always late for things. He can't help it, Sarah.

MRS. ATKINS (*with a snort*). Can't help it! How you do go on, Kate, findin' excuses for him! Anybody can help anything they've a mind to — as long as they've got health, and ain't rendered helpless like me (*she adds as a pious afterthought*) — through the will of God.

MRS. MAYO. Robbie can't.

MRS. ATKINS. Can't! It do make me mad, Kate Mayo, to see folks that God gave all the use of their limbs to potterin' round and wastin' time doin' everything the wrong way — and me powerless to help and at their mercy, you might say. And it ain't that I haven't pointed the right way to 'em. I've talked to Robert thousands of times and told him how things ought to be done. You know that, Kate Mayo. But d'you s'pose he takes any notice of what I say? Or Ruth, either — my own daughter? No, they think I'm a crazy, cranky old woman, half-dead a'ready, and the sooner I'm in the grave and out o' their way the better it'd suit them.

MRS. MAYO. You mustn't talk that way, Sarah. They're not as wicked as that. And you've got years and years before you.

MRS. ATKINS. You're like the rest, Kate. You don't know how near the end I am. Well, at least I can go to my eternal rest with a clear conscience. I've done all a body could do to avert ruin from this house. On their heads be it!

MRS. MAYO (*with hopeless indifference*). Things might be worse. Robert never had any experience in farming. You can't expect him to learn in a day.

MRS. ATKINS (*snappily*). He's had three years to learn, and he's gettin' worse 'stead of better. He hasn't got it in him, that's what; and I do say it to you, Kate Mayo, even if he is your son. He doesn't want to learn. Everything I've told him he's that pig-headed he's gone and done the exact opposite. And now look where things are! They couldn't be worse, spite o' what you say. Not on'y your place but mine too is driftin' to rack and ruin, and I can't do nothin' to prevent, 'cause Ruth backs him up in his folly and shiftlessness.

MRS. MAYO (*with a spark of assertiveness*). You can't say but Robbie works hard, Sarah.

MRS. ATKINS. What good's workin' hard if it don't accomplish anythin', I'd like to know?

MRS. MAYO. Robbie's had bad luck against him.

MRS. ATKINS. Say what you've a mind to, Kate, the proof of the puddin's in the eatin'; and you can't deny that things have been goin' from bad to worse ever since your husband died two years back.

MRS. MAYO (*wiping tears from her eyes with her handkerchief*). It was God's will that he should be taken.

MRS. ATKINS (*triumphantly*). It was God's punishment on James Mayo for the blasphemin' and denyin' of God he done all his sinful life! (*Mrs. Mayo begins to weep softly.*) There, Kate, I shouldn't be remindin' you, I know. He's at peace, poor man, and forgiven, let's pray.

MRS. MAYO (*wiping her eyes – simply*). James was a good man.

MRS. ATKINS (*ignoring this remark*). What I was sayin' was that since Robert's been in charge things've been goin' downhill steady. You don't know *how* bad they are. Robert don't let on to you what's happinin'; and you'd never see it yourself if 'twas under your nose. But, thank God, Ruth still comes to me once in a while for advice when she's worried near out of her senses by his goin's-on. Do you know what she told me last night? But I forgot, she said not to tell you – still I think you've got a right to know, and it's my duty not to let such things go on behind your back.

MRS. MAYO (*wearily*). You can tell me if you want to.

MRS. ATKINS (*bending over toward her – in a low*

voice). Ruth was almost crazy about it. Robert told her he'd have to mortgage the farm — said he didn't know how he'd pull through 'til harvest without it, and he can't get money any other way. (*She straightens up — indignantly.*) Now what do you think of your Robert?

MRS. MAYO (*resignedly*). If it has to be—

MRS. ATKINS. You don't mean to say you're goin' to sign away your farm, Kate Mayo — after me warnin' you?

MRS. MAYO. I'll do what Robbie says is needful.

MRS. ATKINS (*holding up her hands*). Well, of all the foolishness! — well, it's your farm, not mine, and I've nothin' more to say.

MRS. MAYO. Maybe Robbie'll manage till Andy gets back and sees to things. It can't be long now.

MRS. ATKINS (*with keen interest*). Ruth says Andy ought to turn up any day. When does Robert figger he'll get here?

MRS. MAYO. He says he can't calculate exactly on account o' the *Sunda* being a sail-boat. Last letter he got was from England, the day they were sailing for home. That was over a month ago, and Robbie thinks they're overdue now.

MRS. ATKINS. We can give praise to God then that he'll be back in the nick o' time. I've got confidence in Andy and always did have, when it comes to farmin'; and he ought to be tired of

76

travellin' and anxious to get home and settle down to work again.

MRS. MAYO. Andy *has* been working. He's head officer on Dick's boat, he wrote Robbie. You know that.

MRS. ATKINS. That foolin' on ships is all right for a spell, but he must be right sick of it by this. Andy's got to the age where it's time he took hold of things serious and got this farm workin' as it ought to be again.

MRS. MAYO (*musingly*). I wonder if he's changed much. He used to be so fine-looking and strong. (*With a sigh.*) Three years! It seems more like three hundred. (*Her eyes filling – piteously.*) Oh, if James could only have lived 'til he came back – and forgiven him!

MRS. ATKINS. He never would have – not James Mayo! Didn't he keep his heart hardened against him till the last in spite of all you and Robert did to soften him?

MRS. MAYO (*with a feeble flash of anger*). Don't you dare say that! (*Brokenly.*) Oh, I know deep down in his heart he forgave Andy, though he was too stubborn ever to own up to it. It was that brought on his death – breaking his heart just on account of his stubborn pride.

(*She wipes her eyes with her handkerchief and sobs.*)

MRS. ATKINS (*piously*). It was the will of God. (*The whining crying of the child sounds from the kitchen. Mrs. Atkins frowns irritably.*) Drat that young one! Seems as if she cries all the time on purpose to set a body's nerves on edge.

MRS. MAYO (*wiping her eyes*). It's the heat upsets her. Mary doesn't feel any too well these days, poor little child!

MRS. ATKINS. She gets it right from her Pa — bein' sickly all the time. You can't deny Robert was always ailin' as a child. (*She sighs heavily.*) It was a crazy mistake for them two to get married. I argyed against it at the time, but Ruth was so spelled with Robert's wild poetry notions she wouldn't listen to sense. Andy was the one would have been the match for her. I always thought so in those days, same as your James did; and I know she liked Andy. Then 'long comes Robert with his book-learnin' and high-fangled talk — and off she goes and marries him.

MRS. MAYO. I've often thought since it might have been better the other way. But Ruth and Robbie seem happy enough together.

MRS. ATKINS. At any rate it was God's work — and His will be done.

> (*The two women sit in silence for a moment. Ruth enters from the kitchen, carrying in her arms her two-year-old daughter, Mary, a pretty but sickly and anæmic-*

78

> *looking child with a tear-stained face.*
> *Ruth has aged appreciably. Her face*
> *has lost its youth and freshness. There*
> *is a trace in her expression of something*
> *hard and spiteful. She sits in the rocker*
> *in front of the table and sighs wearily.*
> *She wears a gingham dress with a*
> *soiled apron tied around her waist.*)

RUTH. Land sakes, if this isn't a scorcher! That kitchen's like a furnace. Phew!

> (*She pushes the damp hair back from her forehead.*)

MRS. MAYO. Why didn't you call me to help with the dishes?

RUTH (*shortly*). No. The heat in there'd kill you.

MARY (*sees the doll under the table and struggles on her mother's lap*). Mary wants Dolly, Mamma! Give Mary Dolly!

RUTH (*pulling her back*). It's time for your nap. You can't play with Dolly now.

MARY (*commencing to cry whiningly*). Mary wants Dolly!

MRS. ATKINS (*irritably*). Can't you keep that child still? Her racket's enough to split a body's ears. Put her down and let her play with the doll if it'll quiet her.

RUTH (*lifting Mary to the floor*). There! I hope

79

you'll be satisfied and keep still. You're only to play for a minute, remember. Then you've got to take your nap. (*Mary sits down on the floor before the table and plays with the doll in silence. Ruth glances at the place set on the table.*) It's a wonder Rob wouldn't try to get to meals on time once in a while. Does he think I've nothing to do on a hot day like this but stand in that kitchen washing dishes?

MRS. MAYO (*dully*). Something must have gone wrong again.

RUTH (*wearily*). I s'pose so. Something's always going wrong these days, it looks like.

MRS. ATKINS (*snappily*). It wouldn't if you possessed a bit of spunk. The idea of you permittin' him to come in to meals at all hours — and you doin' the work! You ought to force him to have more consideration. I never heard of such a thin'. You mind my words and let him go to the kitchen and get his own once in a while, and see if he don't toe the mark. You're too easy goin', that's the trouble.

RUTH. Do stop your nagging at me, Ma! I'm sick of hearing you. I'll do as I please about it; and thank you for not interfering. (*She wipes her moist forehead — wearily.*) Phew! It's too hot to argue. Let's talk of something pleasant. (*Curiously.*) Didn't I hear you speaking about Andy a while ago?

MRS. MAYO. We were wondering when he'd get home.

RUTH (*brightening*). Rob says any day now he's liable to drop in and surprise us — him and the Captain. I wonder if he's changed much — what he'll be like. It'll certainly look natural to see him around the farm again.

MRS. ATKINS. Let's hope the farm'll look more natural, too, when he's had a hand at it. The way thin's are now!

RUTH (*irritably*). Will you stop harping on that, Ma? We all know things aren't as they might be. What's the good of your complaining all the time?

MRS. ATKINS. There, Kate Mayo! Ain't that just what I told you? I can't say a word of advice to my own daughter even, she's that stubborn and self-willed.

RUTH (*putting her hands over her ears — in exasperation*). For goodness sakes, Ma!

MRS. MAYO (*dully*). Never mind. Andy'll fix everything when he comes.

RUTH (*hopefully*). Oh yes, I know he will. He always did know just the right thing ought to be done. (*With weary vexation.*) It's a shame for him to come home and have to start in with things in such a topsy-turvy.

MRS. MAYO. Andy'll manage.

RUTH (*sighing*). I s'pose it isn't Rob's fault things go wrong with him.

MRS. ATKINS (*scornfully*). Hump! (*She fans herself nervously.*) Land o' Goshen, but it's bakin' in here! Let's go out in under the trees in back where there's a breath of fresh air. Come, Kate. (*Mrs. Mayo gets up obediently and starts to wheel the invalid's chair toward the screen door.*) You better come too, Ruth. It'll do you good. Learn him a lesson and let him get his own dinner. Don't be such a fool.

RUTH (*going and holding the screen door open for them — listlessly*). He wouldn't mind. He tells me never to wait — but he wouldn't know where to find anything.

MRS. ATKINS. Let him go hungry then — and serve him right.

RUTH. He wouldn't mind that, either. He doesn't eat much. But I can't go anyway. I've got to put baby to bed.

MRS. ATKINS. Let's go, Kate. I'm boilin' in here.

(*Mrs. Mayo wheels her out and off left. Ruth comes back and sits down in her chair.*)

RUTH (*mechanically*). Come and let me take off your shoes and stockings, Mary, that's a good girl. You've got to take your nap now.

(*The child continues to play as if she hadn't heard, absorbed in her doll. An eager*

82

*expression comes over Ruth's tired face.
She glances toward the door furtively —
then gets up and goes to the desk. Her
movements indicate a guilty fear of dis-
covery. She takes a letter from a pigeon-
hole and retreats swiftly to her chair
with it. She opens the envelope and
reads the letter with great interest, a
flush of excitement coming to her cheeks.
Robert walks up the path and opens the
screen door quietly and comes into the
room. He, too, has aged. His shoulders
are stooped as if under too great a bur-
den. His eyes are dull and lifeless, his
face burned by the sun and unshaven for
days. Streaks of sweat have smudged
the layer of dust on his cheeks. His lips,
drawn down at the corners, give him a
hopeless, resigned expression. The three
years have accentuated the weakness of
his mouth and chin. He is dressed in
overalls, laced boots, and a flannel shirt
open at the neck.)*

ROBERT (*throwing his hat over on the sofa — with a
great sigh of exhaustion*). Phew! The sun's hot to-
day!

*(Ruth is startled. At first she makes an in-
stinctive motion as if to hide the letter in
her bosom. She immediately thinks better
of this and sits with the letter in her*

hands looking at him with defiant eyes.
He bends down and kisses her.)

RUTH (*feeling her cheek — irritably*). Why don't you shave? You look awful.

ROBERT (*indifferently*). I forgot — and it's too much trouble this weather.

MARY (*throwing aside her doll, runs to him with a happy cry*). Dadda! Dadda!

ROBERT (*swinging her up above his head — lovingly*). And how's this little girl of mine this hot day, eh?

MARY (*screeching happily*). Dadda! Dadda!

RUTH (*in annoyance*). Don't do that to her! You know it's time for her nap and you'll get her all waked up; then I'll be the one that'll have to sit beside her till she falls asleep.

ROBERT (*sitting down in the chair on the left of table and cuddling Mary on his lap*). You needn't bother. I'll put her to bed.

RUTH (*shortly*). You've got to get back to your work, I s'pose.

ROBERT (*with a sigh*). Yes, I was forgetting. (*He glances at the open letter on Ruth's lap.*) Reading Andy's letter again? I should think you'd know it by heart by this time.

RUTH (*colouring as if she'd been accused of something — defiantly*). I've got a right to read it, haven't I? He says it's meant for all of us.

84

ROBERT (*with a trace of irritation*). Right? Don't be so silly. There's no question of right. I was only saying that you must know all that's in it after so many readings.

RUTH. Well, I don't. (*She puts the letter on the table and gets wearily to her feet.*) I s'pose you'll be wanting your dinner now.

ROBERT (*listlessly*). I don't care. I'm not hungry. It's almost too hot to eat.

RUTH. And here I been keeping it hot for you!

ROBERT (*irritably*). Oh, all right then. Bring it in and I'll try to eat.

RUTH. I've got to get her to bed first. (*She goes to lift Mary off his lap.*) Come, dear. It's after time and you can hardly keep your eyes open now.

MARY (*crying*). No, no, I don't wanter sleep! (*Appealing to her father.*) Dadda! No!

RUTH (*accusingly to Robert*). There! Now see what you've done! I told you not to —

ROBERT (*shortly*). Let her alone, then. She's all right where she is. She'll fall asleep on my lap in a minute if you'll stop bothering her.

RUTH (*hotly*). She'll not do any such thing! She's got to learn to mind me, that she has! (*Shaking her finger at Mary.*) You naughty child! Will you come with Mamma when she tells you for your own good?

MARY (*clinging to her father*). No, Dadda!

RUTH (*losing her temper*). A good spanking's what you need, my young lady — and you'll get one from me if you don't mind better, d'you hear? (*Mary starts to whimper frightenedly.*)

ROBERT (*with sudden anger*). Leave her alone! How often have I told you not to threaten her with whipping? It's barbarous, and I won't have it. That's got to be understood. (*Soothing the wailing Mary.*) There! There, little girl! Baby mustn't cry. Dadda won't like you if you do. Dadda'll hold you and you must promise to go to sleep like a good little girl. Will you when Dadda asks you?

MARY (*cuddling up to him*). Yes, Dadda.

RUTH (*looking at them, her pale face set and drawn*). I won't be ordered by you! She's my child as much as yours. A fine one you are to be telling folks how to do things, you — (*She bites her lips. Husband and wife look into each other's eyes with something akin to hatred in their expressions; then Ruth turns away with a shrug of affected indifference.*) All right, take care of her then, if you think it's so easy. You'll be whipping her yourself inside of a week. (*She walks away into the kitchen.*)

ROBERT (*smoothing Mary's hair — tenderly*). We'll show Mamma you're a good little girl, won't we?

MARY (*crooning drowsily*). Dadda, Dadda.

ROBERT. Let's see: Does your mother take off your shoes and stockings before your nap?

MARY (*nodding with half-shut eyes*). Yes, Dadda.

ROBERT (*taking off her shoes and stockings*). We'll show Mamma we know how to do those things, won't we? There's one old shoe off — and there's the other old shoe — and here's one old stocking — and there's the other old stocking. There we are, all nice and cool and comfy. (*He bends down and kisses her.*) And now will you promise to go right to sleep if Dadda takes you to bed? (*Mary nods sleepily.*) That's the good little girl.

> (*He gathers her up in his arms carefully and carries her into the bedroom. His voice can be heard faintly as he lulls the child to sleep. Ruth comes out of the kitchen and gets the plate from the table. She hears the voice from the room and tiptoes to the door to look in. Then she starts for the kitchen but stands for a moment thinking, a look of ill-concealed jealousy on her face. At a noise from inside she hurriedly disappears into the kitchen. A moment later Robert re-enters. He comes forward and picks up the shoes and stockings which he shoves carelessly under the table. Then, seeing no one about, he goes to the sideboard and selects a book. Coming back to his chair,*

87

he sits down and immediately becomes absorbed in reading. Ruth returns from the kitchen bringing his plate heaped with food, and a cup of tea. She sets those before him and sits down in her former place. Robert continues to read, oblivious to the food on the table.)

RUTH (*after watching him irritably for a moment*). For heaven's sakes, put down that old book! Don't you see your dinner's getting cold?

ROBERT (*closing his book*). Excuse me, Ruth. I didn't notice.

(*He picks up his knife and fork and begins to eat gingerly, without appetite.*)

RUTH. I should think you might have some feeling for me, Rob, and not always be late for meals. If you think it's fun sweltering in that oven of a kitchen to keep things warm for you, you're mistaken.

ROBERT. I'm sorry, Ruth, really I am.

RUTH. That's what you always say; but you keep coming late just the same.

ROBERT. I know; and I can't seem to help it. Something crops up every day to delay me. I mean to be here on time.

RUTH (*with a sigh*). Mean-tos don't count.

ROBERT (*with a conciliating smile*). Then punish me, Ruth. Let the food get cold and don't bother about me. Just set it to one side. I won't mind.

RUTH. I'd have to wait just the same to wash up after you.

ROBERT. But I can wash up.

RUTH. A nice mess there'd be then!

ROBERT (*with an attempt at lightness*). The food is lucky to be able to get cold this weather.

> (*As Ruth doesn't answer or smile he opens his book and resumes his reading, forcing himself to take a mouthful of food every now and then. Ruth stares at him in annoyance.*)

RUTH. And besides, you've got your own work that's got to be done.

ROBERT (*absent-mindedly, without taking his eyes from the book*). Yes, of course.

RUTH (*spitefully*). Work you'll never get done by reading books all the time.

ROBERT (*shutting the book with a snap*). Why do you persist in nagging at me for getting pleasure out of reading? Is it because — (*He checks himself abruptly.*)

RUTH (*colouring*). Because I'm too stupid to understand them, I s'pose you were going to say.

ROBERT (*shamefacedly*). No – no. (*In exasperation.*) Oh, Ruth, why do you want to pick quarrels like this? Why do you goad me into saying things

I don't mean? Haven't I got my share of troubles trying to work this cursed farm without your adding to them? You know how hard I've tried to keep things going in spite of bad luck —

RUTH (*scornfully*). Bad luck!

ROBERT. And my own very apparent unfitness for the job, I was going to add; but you can't deny there's been bad luck in it, too. You know how unsuited I am to the work and how I hate it; and I've managed to fight along somehow. Why don't you take things into consideration? Why can't we pull together? We used to. I know it's hard on you also. Then why can't we help each other instead of hindering? That's the only way we can make life bearable for each other.

RUTH (*sullenly*). I do the best I know how.

ROBERT (*gets up and puts his hand on her shoulder*). I know you do. But let's both of us try to do better. We can both improve. Say a word of encouragement once in a while when things go wrong, even if it is my fault. You know the odds I've been up against since Pa died. I'm not a farmer. I've never claimed to be one. But there's nothing else I can do under the circumstances, and I've got to pull things through somehow. With your help, I can do it. With you against me — (*He shrugs his shoulders. There is a pause. Then he bends down and kisses her hair — with an attempt at cheerfulness.*) So you promise that; and I'll promise to be here when the clock strikes – and anything else you tell me to. Is it a bargain?

RUTH (*dully*). I s'pose so.

ROBERT. The reason I was late to-day – it's more bad news, so be prepared.

RUTH (*as if this was only what she expected*). Oh! (*They are interrupted by the sound of a loud knock at the kitchen door.*) There's some one at the kitchen door. (*She hurries out. A moment later she reappears.*) It's Ben. He says he wants to see you.

ROBERT (*frowning*). What's the trouble now, I wonder? (*In a loud voice.*) Come on in here, Ben. (*Ben slouches in from the kitchen. He is a hulking, awkward young fellow with a heavy, stupid face and shifty, cunning eyes. He is dressed in overalls, boots, etc., and wears a broad-brimmed hat of coarse straw pushed back on his head.*) Well, Ben, what's the matter?

BEN (*drawlingly*). The mowin' machine's bust.

ROBERT. Why, that can't be. The man fixed it only last week.

BEN. It's bust just the same.

ROBERT. And can't you fix it?

BEN. No. Don't know what's the matter with the goll-darned thing. 'Twon't work, anyhow.

ROBERT (*getting up and going for his hat*). Wait a minute and I'll go look it over. There can't be much the matter with it.

BEN (*impudently*). Don't make no diff'rence t'me whether there be or not. I'm quittin'.

ROBERT (*anxiously*). You're quitting? You don't mean you're throwing up your job here?

BEN. That's what! My month's up to-day and I want what's owin' t'me.

ROBERT. But why are you quitting now, Ben, when you know I've so much work on hand? I'll have a hard time getting another man at such short notice.

BEN. That's for you to figger. I'm quittin'.

ROBERT. But what's your reason? You haven't any complaint to make about the way you've been treated, have you?

BEN. No. 'Tain't that. (*Shaking his finger.*) Look-a-here. I'm sick o' bein' made fun at, that's what; an' I got a job up to Timms' place; an' I'm quittin' here.

ROBERT. Being made fun of? I don't understand you. Who's making fun of you?

BEN. They all do. When I drive down with the milk in the mornin' they all laughs and jokes at me — that boy up at Harris' and the new feller up at Slocum's, and Bill Evans down at Meade's, and all the rest of 'em.

ROBERT. That's a queer reason for leaving me flat. Won't they laugh at you just the same when you're working for Timms?

BEN. They wouldn't dare to. Timms is the best farm hereabouts. They was laughin' at me for workin' for *you*, that's what! "How're things up at the Mayo place?" they hollers every mornin'. "What's Robert doin' now — pasturin' the cattle in the corn-lot? Is he seasonin' his hay with rain this year, same as last?" they shouts. "Or is he inventin' some 'lectrical milkin' engine to fool them dry cows o' his into givin' hard cider?" (*Very much ruffled.*) That's like they talks; and I ain't goin' to put up with it no longer. Every one's always knowd me as a first-class hand hereabouts, and I ain't wantin' 'em to get no different notion. So I'm quittin' you. And I wants what's comin' to me.

ROBERT (*coldly*). Oh, if that's the case, you can go to the devil.

BEN. This farm'd take me there quick 'nuff if I was fool 'nuff to stay.

ROBERT (*angrily*). None of your damned cheek! You'll get your money to-morrow when I get back from town — not before!

BEN (*turning to doorway to kitchen*). That suits me. (*As he goes out he speaks back over his shoulder.*) And see that I do get it, or there'll be trouble.

> (*He disappears and the slamming of the kitchen door is heard.*)

ROBERT (*as Ruth comes from where she has been*

standing by the doorway and sits down dejectedly in her old place). The stupid damn fool! And now what about the haying? That's an example of what I'm up against. No one can say I'm responsible for that.

RUTH. Yes you are! He wouldn't dare act that way with anyone else. They do like they please with you, because you don't know how to treat 'em. They think you're easy — and you are!

ROBERT (*indignantly*). I suppose I ought to be a slave driver like the rest of the farmers — stand right beside them all day watching every move they make, and work them to their last ounce of strength? Well, I can't do it, and I won't do it!

RUTH. It's better to do that than have to ask your Ma to sign a mortgage on the place.

ROBERT (*distractedly*). Oh, damn the place! (*He walks to the window on left and stands looking out.*)

RUTH (*after a pause, with a glance at Andrew's letter on the table*). It's lucky Andy's coming back.

ROBERT (*coming back and sitting down*). Yes, Andy 'll see the right thing to do in a jiffy. He has the knack of it; and he ought to be home any time now. The *Sunda's* overdue. Must have met with head winds all the way across.

RUTH (*anxiously*). You don't think — anything's happened to the boat?

ROBERT. Trust Uncle Dick to bring her through

all right! He's too good a sailor to be caught napping. Besides, we'll never know the ship's here till Andy steps in the door. He'll want to surprise us. (*With an affectionate smile.*) I wonder if the old chump's changed much? He doesn't seem to from his letters, does he? Still the same practical hardhead. (*Shaking his head.*) But just the same, I doubt if he'll want to settle down to a humdrum farm life, after all he's been through.

RUTH (*resentfully*). Andy's not like you. He likes the farm.

ROBERT (*immersed in his own thoughts — enthusiastically*). Gad, the things he's seen and experienced! Think of the places he's been! Hong-Kong, Yokohama, Batavia, Singapore, Bangkok, Rangoon, Bombay — all the marvellous East! And Honolulu, Sydney, Buenos Aires! All the wonderful far places I used to dream about! God, how I envy him! What a trip!

> (*He springs to his feet and instinctively goes to the window and stares out at the horizon.*)

RUTH (*bitterly*). I s'pose you're sorry now you didn't go?

ROBERT (*too occupied with his own thoughts to hear her — vindictively*). Oh, those cursed hills out there that I used to think promised me so much! How I've grown to hate the sight of them! They're like the walls of a narrow prison yard shutting me in from all the freedom and wonder of life! (*He turns back to the room with a gesture of loathing.*) Sometimes I think if it wasn't for you, Ruth, and — (*his voice softening*) — little Mary, I'd chuck everything up and walk down the road with just one desire in my heart — to put the whole rim of the world between me and those hills, and be able to breathe freely once more! (*He sinks down into his chair and smiles with bitter self-scorn.*) There I go dreaming again — my old fool dreams.

RUTH (*in a low, repressed voice — her eyes smouldering*). You're not the only one!

ROBERT (*buried in his own thoughts — bitterly*). And Andy, who's had the chance — what has he got out of it? His letters read like the diary of a — of a farmer! "We're in Singapore now. It's a dirty hole of a place and hotter than hell. Two of the crew are down with fever, and we're short-handed on the work. I'll be damn glad when we sail again, although tacking back and forth in these blistering seas is a rotten job too!" (*Scornfully.*) That's about the way he summed up his impressions of the East. Every port they touched at he found the same silly fault with. God! The only place he appeared to like was Buenos Aires — and that only because he saw the business opportunities in a booming country like Argentine.

RUTH (*her repressed voice trembling*). You needn't make fun of Andy.

ROBERT. Perhaps I am too hard on him; but when I think — but what's the use? You know I wasn't making fun of Andy personally. No one loves him better than I do, the old chump! But his attitude toward things is — is rank, in my estimation.

RUTH (*her eyes flashing — bursting into uncontrollable rage*). You was too making fun of him! And I ain't going to stand for it! You ought to be ashamed of yourself! A fine one you be! (*Robert stares at her in amazement. She continues furiously.*) A fine one to talk about anyone else — after the way you've ruined everything with your lazy loafing! — and the stupid way you do things!

ROBERT (*angrily*). Stop that kind of talk, do you hear?

RUTH. You findin' fault — with your own brother who's ten times the man you ever was or ever will be — a thing like you to be talking. You're jealous, that's what! Jealous because he's made a man of himself, while you're nothing but a — but a — (*She stutters incoherently, overcome by rage.*)

ROBERT. Ruth! Ruth! Don't you dare —! You'll be sorry for talking like that.

RUTH. I won't! I won't never be sorry! I'm only saying what I've been thinking for years.

ROBERT (*aghast*). Ruth! You can't mean that!

RUTH. What do you think — living with a man

97

like you – having to suffer all the time because you've never been man enough to work and do things like other people. But no! You never own up to that. You think you're so much better than other folks, with your college education, where you never learned a thing, and always reading your stupid books instead of working. I s'pose you think I ought to be *proud* to be your wife – a poor, ignorant thing like me! (*Fiercely.*) But I'm not. I hate it! I hate the sight of you! Oh, if I'd only known! If I hadn't been such a fool to listen to your cheap, silly, poetry talk that you learned out of books! If I could have seen how you were in your true self – like you are now – I'd have killed myself before I'd have married you! I was sorry for it before we'd been together a month. I knew what you were really like – when it was too late.

ROBERT (*his voice raised loudly*). And now – I'm finding out what you're really like – what a – a creature I've been living with. (*With a harsh laugh.*) God! It wasn't that I haven't guessed how mean and small you are – but I've kept on telling myself that I must be wrong – like a fool! – like a damned fool!

RUTH. You were saying you'd go out on the road if it wasn't for me. Well, you can go, and the sooner the better! I don't care! I'll be glad to get rid of you! The farm 'll be better off too. There's been a curse on it ever since you took hold. So go!

Go and be a tramp, like you've always wanted. It's all you're good for. I can get along without you, don't you worry. I'll get some peace. (*Exulting fiercely.*) And Andy's coming back, don't forget that! He'll attend to things like they should be. He'll show what a man can do! I don't need you. Andy's coming!

ROBERT (*they are both standing. Robert grabs her by the shoulders and glares into her eyes*). What do you mean? (*He shakes her violently.*) What are you thinking of? What's in your evil mind, you – you —? (*His voice is a harsh shout.*)

RUTH (*in a defiant scream*). Yes, I do mean it! I'd say it if you was to kill me! I do love Andy. I do! I do! I always loved him. (*Exultantly.*) And he loves me! He loves me! I know he does. He always did! And you know he did, too! So go! Go if you want to!

ROBERT (*throwing her away from him. She staggers back against the table – thickly*). You – you slut!

(*He stands glaring at her as she leans back, supporting herself by the table, gasping for breath. A loud frightened whimper sounds from the awakened child in the bedroom. It continues. The man and woman stand looking at one another in horror, the extent of their terrible quarrel suddenly brought home to them. A pause. The noise of a horse and carriage*

99

comes from the road before the house.
The two, suddenly struck by the same
premonition, listen to it breathlessly, as
to a sound heard in a dream. It stops.
They hear Andy's voice from the road
shouting a long hail — "*Ahoy there!*")

RUTH (*with a strangled cry of joy*). Andy! Andy!

(*She rushes and grabs the knob of the screen*
door, about to fling it open.)

ROBERT (*in a voice of command that forces obedience*).
Stop! (*He goes to the door and gently pushes the*
trembling Ruth away from it. The child's crying rises
to a louder pitch.) I'll meet Andy. You better go
in to Mary, Ruth.

(*She looks at him defiantly for a moment, but*
there is something in his eyes that makes
her turn and walk slowly into the bed-
room.)

ANDY'S VOICE (*in a louder shout*). Ahoy there, Rob!

ROBERT (*in an answering shout of forced cheeriness*).
Hallo, Andy!

(*He opens the door and walks out as*

The Curtain Falls)

ACT TWO
SCENE TWO

SCENE. *The top of a hill on the farm. It is about eleven o'clock the next morning. The day is hot and cloudless. In the distance the sea can be seen.*

The top of the hill slopes downward slightly toward the left. A big boulder stands in the centre toward the rear. Farther right, a large oak tree. The faint trace of a path leading upward to it from the left foreground can be detected through the bleached, sun-scorched grass.

Robert is discovered sitting on the boulder, his chin resting on his hands, staring out toward the horizon seaward. His face is pale and haggard, his expression one of utter despondency. Mary is sitting on the grass near him in the shade, playing with her doll, singing happily to herself. Presently she casts a curious glance at her father, and, propping her doll up against the tree, comes over and clambers to his side.

MARY (*pulling at his hand – solicitously*). Is Dadda sick?

ROBERT (*looking at her with a forced smile*). No, dear. Why?

MARY. Then why don't he play with Mary?

ROBERT (*gently*). No, dear, not to-day. Dadda doesn't feel like playing to-day.

MARY (*protestingly*). Yes, please, Dadda!

101

ROBERT. No, dear. Dadda does feel sick – a little. He's got a bad headache.

MARY. Let Mary see. (*He bends his head. She pats his hair.*) Bad head.

ROBERT (*kissing her – with a smile*). There! It's better now, dear, thank you.

(*She cuddles up close against him. There is a pause during which each of them looks out seaward.*)

MARY (*pointing toward the sea*). Is that all wa-wa, Dadda?

ROBERT. Yes, dear.

MARY (*amazed by the magnitude of this conception*). Oh-oh! (*She points to the horizon.*) And it all stops there, over farver?

ROBERT. No, it doesn't stop. That line you see is called the horizon. It's where the sea and sky meet. Just beyond that is where the good fairies live. (*Checking himself – with a harsh laugh.*) But you mustn't ever believe in fairies. It's bad luck. And besides, there aren't any good fairies.

(*Mary looks up into his face with a puzzled expression.*)

MARY. Then if fairies don't live there, what lives there?

ROBERT (*bitterly*). God knows! Mocking devils, I've found them. (*Mary frowns in puzzlement,*) *turning this over in her mind. There is a pause. Finally Robert turns to her tenderly.*) Would you miss Dadda very much if he went away?

MARY. Far — far away?

ROBERT. Yes. Far, far away.

MARY. And Mary wouldn't see him, never?

ROBERT. No; but Mary'd forget him very soon, I'm sure.

MARY (*tearfully*). No! No! Dadda mustn't go 'way. No, Dadda, no!

ROBERT. Don't you like Uncle Andy — the man that came yesterday — not the old man with the white moustache — the other?

MARY. But Dadda mustn't go 'way. Mary loves Dadda.

ROBERT (*with fierce determination*). He won't go away, baby. He was only joking. He couldn't leave his little Mary. (*He presses the child in his arms.*)

MARY (*with an exclamation of pain*). Oh! Dadda hurts!

ROBERT. I'm sorry, little girl. (*He lifts her down to the grass.*) Go play with Dolly, that's a good girl; and be careful to keep in the shade.

> (*She reluctantly leaves him and takes up her doll again. A moment later she points down the hill to the left.*)

MARY. Here comes mans, Dadda.

ROBERT (*looking that way*). It's your Uncle Andy.

MARY. Will he play wiv me, Dadda?

ROBERT. Not now, dear. You mustn't bother him. After awhile he will, maybe.

> (*A moment later Andrew comes up from the left, whistling cheerfully. He has changed but little in appearance, except for the fact that his face has been deeply bronzed by his years in the tropics; but there is a decided change in his manner. The old easy-going good-nature seems to have been partly lost in a breezy, business-like briskness of voice and gesture. There is an authoritative note in his speech as though he were accustomed to give orders and have them obeyed as a matter of course. He is dressed in the simple blue uniform and cap of a merchant ship's officer.*)

ANDREW. Here you are, eh?

ROBERT. Hallo, Andy.

ANDREW (*going over to Mary*). And who's this young lady I find you all alone with, eh? Who's this pretty young lady? (*He tickles the laughing, squirming Mary, then lifts her up at arm's length over his head.*) Upsy – daisy! (*He sets her down on the ground again.*) And there you are! (*He walks over*

104

*and sits down on the boulder beside Robert who moves
to one side to make room for him.*) Ruth told me I'd
probably find you up top-side here; but I'd have
guessed it, anyway. (*He digs his brother in the ribs
affectionately.*) Still up to your old tricks, you old
beggar! I can remember how you used to come
up here to mope and dream in the old days.

ROBERT (*with a smile*). I come up here now because it's the coolest place on the farm. I've given
up dreaming.

ANDREW (*grinning*). I don't believe it. You can't
have changed that much.

ROBERT (*wearily*). One gets tired of dreaming —
when they never come true.

ANDREW (*scrutinizing his brother's face*). You've
changed in looks all right. You look all done up,
as if you'd been working too hard. Better let up
on yourself for awhile.

ROBERT. Oh, I'm all right!

ANDREW. Take a fool's advice and go it easy. You
remember — your old trouble. You wouldn't want
that coming back on you, eh? It pays to keep top-
notch in your case.

ROBERT (*betraying annoyance*). Oh, that's all a
thing of the past, Andy. Forget it!

ANDREW. Well — a word to the wise does no
harm? Don't be touchy about it. (*Slapping his*

brother on the back.) You know I mean well, old man, even if I do put my foot in it.

ROBERT. Of course, Andy. I'm not touchy about it. I don't want you to worry about dead things, that's all. I've a headache to-day, and I expect I do look done up.

ANDREW. Mum's the word, then! (*After a pause – with boyish enthusiasm.*) Say, it sure brings back old times to be up here with you having a chin all by our lonesomes again. I feel great being back home.

ROBERT. It's great for us to have you back.

ANDREW (*after a pause – meaningly*). I've been looking over the old place with Ruth. Things don't seem to be —

ROBERT (*his face flushing – interrupts his brother shortly*). Never mind the damn farm! There's nothing about it we don't both know by heart. Let's talk about something interesting. This is the first chance I've had to have a word with you alone. To the devil with the farm for the present. They think of nothing else at home. Tell me about your trip. That's what I've been anxious to hear about.

ANDREW (*with a quick glance of concern at Robert*). I suppose you do get an overdose of the farm at home. (*Indignantly.*) Say, I never realized that Ruth's mother was such an old rip till she talked to me this morning. (*With a grin.*) Phew! I pity you, Rob, when she gets on her ear!

ROBERT. She is – difficult sometimes; but one must make allowances. (*Again changing the subject abruptly.*) But this isn't telling me about the trip.

ANDREW. Why, I thought I told you everything in my letters.

ROBERT (*smiling*). Your letters were – sketchy, to say the least.

ANDREW. Oh, I know I'm no author. You needn't be afraid of hurting my feelings. I'd rather go through a typhoon again than write a letter.

ROBERT (*with eager interest*). Then you were through a typhoon?

ANDREW. Yes – in the China Sea. Had to run before it under bare poles for two days. I thought we were bound down for Davy Jones, sure. Never dreamed waves could get so big or the wind blow so hard. If it hadn't been for Uncle Dick being such a good skipper we'd have gone to the sharks, all of us. As it was we came out minus a main top-mast, and had to beat back to Hong-Kong for repairs. But I must have written you all this.

ROBERT. You never mentioned it.

ANDREW. Well, there was so much dirty work getting things ship-shape again I must have forgotten about it.

ROBERT (*looking at Andrew – marvelling*). Forget a typhoon? (*With a trace of scorn.*) You're a

107

strange combination, Andy. And is what you've told me all you remember about it?

ANDREW. Oh, I could give you your bellyful of details if I wanted to turn loose on you; but they're not the kind of things to fit in with your pretty notions of life on the ocean wave, I'll give you that straight.

ROBERT (*earnestly*). Tell me. I'd like to hear them — honestly!

ANDREW. What's the use? They'd make a man want to live in the middle of America without even a river in a hundred miles of him so he'd feel safe. It was rotten, that's what it was! Talk about work! I was wishin' the ship 'd sink and give me a rest, I was so dog tired toward the finish. We didn't get a warm thing to eat for nearly two weeks. There was enough China Sea in the galley to float the stove, and the fo'c'sle was flooded, too. And you couldn't sleep a wink. No place on the darned old tub stayed still long enough for you to lie on it. And every one was soaked to the skin all the time, with green seas boiling over the deck keeping you busy jumping for the rat-lines to keep from being washed over. Oh, it was all-wool-and-a-yard-wide-Hell, I'll tell you. You ought to have been there. I remember thinking about you at the worst of it when you couldn't force a breath out against the wind, and saying to myself: "This'd cure Rob of them ideas of his about the beautiful sea, if he could see it." And it would have too, you bet! (*He nods emphatically.*)

ROBERT. And you don't see any romance in that?

ANDREW. Romance be blowed! It was hell! (*As an afterthought.*) Oh, I was forgetting! One of the men *was* washed overboard — a Norwegian — Ollie we called him. (*With a grin of sarcasm.*) I suppose that's romance, eh? Well, it might be for a fish, but not for me, old man!

ROBERT (*dryly*). The sea doesn't seem to have impressed you very favourably.

ANDREW. I should say it didn't! It's a dog's life. You work like the devil and put up with all kinds of hardships — for what? For a rotten wage you'd be ashamed to take on shore.

ROBERT. Then you're not going to — follow it up?

ANDREW. Not me! I'm through! I'll never set foot on a ship again if I can help it — except to carry me some place I can't get to by train. No. I've had enough. Dry land is the only place for me.

ROBERT. But you studied to become an officer!

ANDREW. Had to do something or I'd gone mad. The days were like years. Nothing to look at but sea and sky. No place to go. A regular prison. (*He laughs.*) And as for the East you used to rave about — well, you ought to see it, and *smell* it! And the Chinks and Japs and Hindus and the rest of them — you can have them! One walk down one of their filthy narrow streets with the tropic sun beating on it would sicken you for life with the "wonder and mystery" you used to dream of. I can say one thing for it though — it certainly has the stink market cornered.

ROBERT (*shrinking from his brother with a glance of aversion*). So all you found in the East was a stench?

ANDREW. *A* stench! Ten thousand of them! That and the damned fever! You can have the tropics, old man. I never want to see them again. At that, there's lots of money to be made down there — for a white man. The natives are too lazy to work, that's the only trouble.

ROBERT. But you did like some of the places, judging from your letters — Sydney, Buenos Aires —

ANDREW. Yes, Sydney's a good town. (*Enthusiastically.*) But Buenos Aires — there's the place for you. Argentine's a country where a fellow has a chance to make good. You're right I liked it. And I'll tell you, Rob, that's right where I'm going just as soon as I've seen you folks awhile and can get a ship. I don't intend to pay for my passage now I can get a berth as second officer, and I'll jump the ship when I get there. I'll need every cent of the wages Uncle's paid me to get a start at something in B.A.

BEYOND THE HORIZON

ROBERT (*staring at his brother – slowly*). So you're not going to stay on the farm.

ANDREW. Why sure not! Did you think I was? There wouldn't be any sense. One of us is enough to run this little place.

ROBERT. I suppose it does seem small to you now.

ANDREW (*not noticing the sarcasm in Robert's tone*). You've no idea, Rob, what a splendid place Argentine is. I went around Buenos Aires quite a lot and got to know people – English-speaking people, of course. The town is full of them. It's foreign capital that's developed the country, you know. I had a letter from a marine insurance chap that I'd made friends with in Hong-Kong to his brother, who's in the grain business in Buenos Aires. He took quite a fancy to me, and what's more important, he offered me a job if I'd come back there. I'd have taken it on the spot, only I couldn't leave Uncle Dick in the lurch, and I'd promised you folks to come home. But I'm going back there very soon, you bet, and then you watch me get on! (*He slaps Robert on the back.*) But don't you think it's a big chance, Rob?

ROBERT. It's fine – for you, Andy.

ANDREW. We call this a farm – but you ought to hear about the farms down there – ten square miles where we've got an acre. It's a new country where big things are opening up – and I want to get in on something big before I die. That job

111

I'm offered 'll furnish the wedge. I'm no fool when it comes to farming, and I know something about grain. I've been reading up a lot on it, too, lately. (*He notices Robert's absent-minded expression and laughs.*) Wake up, you old poetry book-worm, you! I know my talking about business makes you want to choke me, doesn't it?

ROBERT (*with an embarrassed smile*). No, Andy, I — I just happened to think of something else. (*Frowning.*) There've been lots of times lately that I've wished I had some of your faculty for business.

ANDREW (*soberly*). There's something I want to talk about, Rob — the farm. You don't mind, do you?

ROBERT. No.

ANDREW. I walked over it this morning with Ruth — and she told me about things — (*evasively*) — the hard luck you'd had and how things stood at present — and about your thinking of raising a mortgage.

ROBERT (*bitterly*). It's all true, I guess, and probably worse than she told you.

ANDREW. I could see the place had run down; but you mustn't blame yourself. When luck's against anyone —

ROBERT. Don't, Andy! It *is* my fault — my inability. You know it as well as I do. The best I've ever done was to make ends meet, and this year I can't do that without the mortgage.

ANDREW (*after a pause*). You mustn't raise the mortgage, Rob. I've got over a thousand saved, and you can have that.

ROBERT (*firmly*). No. You need that for your start in Buenos Aires.

ANDREW. I don't. I can —

ROBERT (*determinedly*). No, Andy! Once and for all, no! I won't hear of it!

ANDREW (*protestingly*). You obstinate old son of a gun! (*There is a pause.*) Well, I'll do the best I can while I'm here. I'll get a real man to superintend things for you – if he can be got. That'll relieve you some. If he gets results, you can afford to pay him.

ROBERT. Oh, everything 'll be on a sound footing after harvest. Don't worry about it.

ANDREW (*doubtfully*). Maybe. The prospects don't look so bad.

ROBERT. And then I can pay the mortgage off again. It's just to tide over.

ANDREW (*after a pause*). I wish you'd let me help, Rob.

ROBERT (*with a tone of finality*). No. Please don't suggest it any more. My mind's made up on that point.

ANDREW (*slapping his brother on the back – with forced joviality*). Well, anyway, you've got to promise to let me step in when I've made my pile, and I'll make it down there, I'm certain, and it won't take me long, either.

ROBERT. I've no doubt you will with your determination.

ANDREW. I'll be able to pay off all the mortgages you can raise! Still, a mortgage isn't such a bad thing at that — it makes a place heaps easier to sell — and you may want to cut loose from this farm some day — come down and join me in Buenos Aires, that's the ticket.

ROBERT. If I had only myself to consider —

ANDREW. Yes, I suppose they wouldn't want to come. (*After a pause.*) It's too bad Pa couldn't have lived to see things through. (*With feeling.*) It cut me up a lot — hearing he was dead. Tell me about it. You didn't say much in your letter.

ROBERT (*evasively*). He's at peace, Andy. It'll only make you feel bad to talk of it.

ANDREW. He never — softened up, did he — about me, I mean?

ROBERT. He never understood, that's a kinder way of putting it. He does now.

ANDREW (*after a pause*). You've forgotten all about what — caused me to go, haven't you, Rob? (*Robert nods but keeps his face averted.*) I was a slushier damn fool in those days than you were. But it was an act of Providence I did go. It opened my eyes to how I'd been fooling myself. Why, I'd forgotten all about — that — before I'd been at sea six months.

ROBERT (*turns and looks into Andrew's eyes searchingly*). You're speaking of — Ruth?

ANDREW (*confused*). Yes. I didn't want you to get false notions in your head, or I wouldn't say anything. (*Looking Robert squarely in the eyes.*) I'm telling you the truth when I say I'd forgotten long ago. It don't sound well for me, getting over things so easy, but I guess it never really amounted to more than a kid idea I was letting rule me. I'm certain now I never was in love — I was getting fun out of thinking I was — and being a hero to myself. (*He heaves a great sigh of relief.*) There! Gosh, I'm glad that's off my chest. I've been feeling sort of awkward ever since I've been home, thinking of what you two might think. (*A trace of appeal in his voice.*) You've got it all straight now, haven't you, Rob?

ROBERT (*in a low voice*). Yes, Andy.

ANDREW. And I'll tell Ruth, too, if I can get up the nerve. She must feel kind of funny having me round — after what used to be — and not knowing how I feel about it.

ROBERT (*slowly*). Perhaps — for her sake — you'd better not tell her.

ANDREW. For her sake? Oh, you mean she

wouldn't want to be reminded of my foolishness? Still, I think it'd be worse if —

ROBERT (*breaking out — in an agonized voice*). Do as you please, Andy; but for God's sake, let's not talk about it! (*There is a pause. Andrew stares at Robert in hurt stupefaction. Robert continues after a moment in a voice which he vainly attempts to keep calm.*) Excuse me, Andy. This rotten headache has my nerves shot to pieces.

ANDREW (*mumbling*). It's all right, Rob — long as you're not sore at me.

ROBERT. Where did Uncle Dick disappear to this morning?

ANDREW. He went down to the port to see to things on the *Sunda*. He said he didn't know exactly when he'd be back. I'll have to go down and tend to the ship when he comes. That's why I dressed up in these togs.

MARY (*pointing down the hill to the left*). See Dadda! Mamma! Mamma!

(*She jumps to her feet and starts to run down the path.*)

ANDREW (*standing and looking down*). Yes, here comes Ruth. Must be looking for you, I guess. (*Jumping forward and stopping Mary.*) Hey up! You mustn't run downhill like that, little girl. You'll take a bad fall, don't you know it?

ROBERT. Stay here and wait for your mother. Mary.

MARY (*struggling to her feet*). No! No! Mamma! Dadda!

ANDREW. Here she is!

(*Ruth appears at left. She is dressed in white, shows she has been fixing up. She looks pretty, flushed and full of life.*)

MARY (*running to her mother*). Mamma!

RUTH (*kissing her*). Hello, dear! (*She walks toward the rock and addresses Robert coldly.*) Jake wants to see you about something. He finished working where he was. He's waiting for you at the road.

ROBERT (*getting up – wearily*). I'll go down right away.

(*As he looks at Ruth, noting her changed appearance, his face darkens with pain.*)

RUTH. And take Mary with you, please. (*To Mary.*) Go with Dadda, that's a good girl. Grandma has your dinner most ready for you.

ROBERT (*shortly*). Come, Mary!

MARY (*taking his hand and dancing happily beside him*). Dadda! Dadda! (*They go down the hill to the left. Ruth looks after them for a moment, frowning – then turns to Andy with a smile.*) I'm going to sit down. Come on, Andy. It'll be like old times. (*She jumps lightly to the top of the rock and sits down.*) It's so fine and cool up here after the house.

117

ANDREW (*half-sitting on the side of the boulder*). Yes. It's great.

RUTH. I've taken a holiday in honour of your arrival — from work in the kitchen. (*Laughing excitedly.*) I feel so free I'd like to have wings and fly over the sea. You're a man. You can't know how awful and stupid it is — cooking and washing dishes all the time.

ANDREW (*making a wry face*). I can guess.

RUTH. Besides, your mother just insisted on getting your first dinner at home, she's that happy at having you back. You'd think I was planning to poison you the flurried way she shooed me out of the kitchen.

ANDREW. That's just like Ma, bless her!

RUTH. She's missed you terrible. We all have. And you can't deny the farm has, after what I showed you and told you when we was looking over the place this morning.

ANDREW (*with a frown*). Things are run down, that's a fact! It's too darn hard on poor old Rob.

RUTH (*scornfully*). It's his own fault. He never takes any interest in things.

ANDREW (*reprovingly*). You can't blame him. He wasn't born for it; but I know he's done his best for your sake and the old folks and the little girl.

RUTH (*indifferently*). Yes, I suppose he has.

(*Gaily.*) But thank the Lord, all those days are over now. The "hard luck" Rob's always blaming won't last long when you take hold, Andy. All the farm's ever needed was some one with the knack of looking ahead and preparing for what's going to happen.

ANDREW. Yes, Rob hasn't got that. He's frank to own up to that himself. I'm going to try and hire a good man for him — an experienced farmer — to work the place on a salary and percentage. That'll take it off of Rob's hands, and he needn't be worrying himself to death any more. He looks all worn out, Ruth. He ought to be careful.

RUTH (*absent-mindedly*). Yes, I s'pose. (*Her mind is filled with premonitions by the first part of his statement.*)

ANDREW. It would be a good idea if Rob could pull out of here — get a job in town on a newspaper, or something connected with writing — and this plan of mine'd give him a chance.

RUTH (*vaguely*). He's always wanted to get away. (*Suspiciously.*) Why do you want to hire a man to oversee things? Seems as if now that you're back it wouldn't be needful.

ANDREW. Oh, of course I'll attend to everything while I'm here. I mean after I'm gone.

RUTH (*as if she couldn't believe her ears*). Gone!

ANDREW. Yes. When I leave for the Argentine again.

RUTH (*aghast*). You're going away to sea again!

ANDREW. Not to sea, no; I'm through with the sea for good as a job. I'm going down to Buenos Aires to get in the grain business.

RUTH. But — that's way far off — isn't it?

ANDREW (*easily*). Six thousand miles more or less. It's quite a trip. (*With enthusiasm.*) I've got a peach of a chance down there, Ruth. Ask Rob if I haven't. I've just been telling him all about it. I won't bother you by repeating. Rob can tell you.

RUTH (*a flush of anger coming over her face*). And didn't he try to stop you from going?

ANDREW (*in surprise*). No, of course not. Why?

RUTH (*slowly and vindictively*). That's just like him — not to.

ANDREW (*resentfully*). Rob's too good a chum to try and stop me when he knows I'm set on a thing. And he could see just as soon's I told him what a good chance it was. You ask him about it.

RUTH (*dazedly*). And you're bound on going?

ANDREW. Sure thing. Oh, I don't mean right off. I'll have to wait for a ship sailing there for quite a while, likely. Anyway, I want to stay at home and visit with you folks a spell before I go.

RUTH (*dumbly*). I s'pose. (*With sudden anguish.*) Oh, Andy, you can't go! You can't. Why we've all thought — we've all been hoping and praying you was coming home to stay, to settle down on the farm and see to things. You mustn't go! Think of how your Ma'll take on if you go – and how the farm'll be ruined if you leave it to Rob to look after. You can see that.

ANDREW (*frowning*). Rob hasn't done so bad. When I get a man to direct things the farm'll be safe enough.

RUTH (*insistently*). But your Ma – think of her.

ANDREW. She's used to me being away. She won't object when she knows it's best for her and all of us for me to go. You ask Rob. In a couple of years down there I'll make my pile, see if I don't, and then I'll come back and settle down and turn this farm to the crackiest place in the whole state. In the meantime, I can help you both from down there. (*Earnestly.*) I tell you, Ruth, I'm going to make good right from the minute I land, if working hard and a determination to get on can do it, and I *know* they can! I'll have money and lots of it before long, and none of you'll have to worry about this pesky little farm any more. (*Excitedly – in a rather boastful tone.*) I tell you, I feel ripe for bigger things than settling down here. The trip did that for me, anyway. It showed me the world in a larger proposition than ever I thought it was in the old days. I couldn't be content any more stuck here like a fly in molasses. There ain't enough to do. It all seems trifling, somehow. You ought to be able to understand what I feel.

RUTH (*dully*). Yes – I s'pose I ought.

ANDREW. I felt sure you'd see, and wait till Rob tells you about —

RUTH (*a dim suspicion forming in her mind – interrupting him*). What did he tell you – about me?

ANDREW. Tell? About you? Why, nothing.

RUTH (*staring at him intensely*). Are you telling me the truth, Andy Mayo? Didn't he say – I — (*She stops confusedly.*)

ANDREW (*surprised*). No, he didn't mention you, I can remember. Why? What made you think he did?

RUTH (*wringing her hands*). Oh, I wish I could tell if you're lying or not!

ANDREW (*indignantly*). What're you talking about? I didn't used to lie to you, did I? And what in the name of God is there to lie for?

RUTH (*still unconvinced*). Are you sure – will you swear – it isn't the reason — (*She lowers her eyes and half-turns away from him.*) The same reason that made you go last time that's driving you away again? 'Cause if it is – I was going to say – you mustn't go – on that account. (*Her voice sinks to a tremulous, tender whisper as she finishes.*)

ANDREW (*confused – forces a laugh*). Oh, is *that*

what you're driving at? Well, you needn't worry about that no more — (*Soberly.*) I don't blame you, Ruth, feeling embarrassed having me around again, after the way I played the dumb fool about going away last time. You'll have to put it down to me just being young and foolish and not responsible for my actions — and forgive me and forget it. Will you?

RUTH (*in anguish buries her face in her hands*). Oh, Andy!

ANDREW (*misunderstanding*). I know I oughtn't to talk about such foolishness to you. Still I figure it's better to get it out of my system so's we three can be together same's years ago, and not be worried thinking one of us might have the wrong notion. No, don't you fret about me having any such reason for going this time. I'm not a calf any more. Why honest, Ruth, before the ship got to Hong Kong I'd near forgat all that part of it. All I remembered was the awful scrap I'd had with Pa — and I was darned cut up about that.

RUTH. Andy! Please! Don't!

ANDREW. Let me finish now that I've started. It'll help clear things up. I don't want you to think once a fool always a fool, and be upset all the time I'm here on my fool account. I want you to believe I put all that silly nonsense back of me a long time ago — and now — it seems — well — as if you'd always been my sister, that's what, Ruth.

RUTH (*at the end of her endurance — laughing hysterically*). For God's sake, Andy — won't you please stop talking!

> (*She again hides her face in her hands, her bowed shoulders trembling.*)

ANDREW (*ruefully*). Seem's if I put my foot in it whenever I open my mouth to-day. Rob shut me up with almost them same words when I tried speaking to him about it.

RUTH (*fiercely*). You told him — what you've told me?

ANDREW (*astounded*). Why sure! Why not?

RUTH (*shuddering*). Oh, my God!

ANDREW (*alarmed*). Why? Shouldn't I have?

RUTH (*hysterically*). Oh, I don't care what you do! I don't care! Leave me alone!

> (*Andrew gets up and walks down the hill to the left, embarrassed, hurt, and greatly puzzled by her behaviour.*)

ANDREW (*after a pause — pointing down the hill*). Hello! Here they come back — and the Captain's with them. How'd he come to get back so soon, I wonder? That means I've got to hustle down to the port and get on board. Rob's got the baby with him. (*He comes back to the boulder. Ruth keeps her face averted from him.*) Gosh, I never saw a father so tied up in a kid as Rob is! He just watches every move she makes. And I don't blame him. You both got a right to feel proud of her. She's surely a little winner. (*He glances at Ruth to see if this very obvious attempt to get back in her good graces is having any effect.*) I can see the likeness to Rob standing out all over her, can't you? But there's no denying she's your young one, either. There's something about her eyes —

RUTH (*piteously*). Oh, Andy, I've a headache! I don't want to talk! Leave me alone, won't you, please?

ANDREW (*stands staring at her for a moment — then walks away, saying in a hurt tone*). Everybody hereabouts seems to be on edge to-day. I begin to feel as if I'm not wanted around.

> (*He stands near the path, left, kicking at the grass with the toe of his shoe. A moment later Captain Dick Scott enters, followed by Robert carrying Mary. The Captain seems scarcely to have changed at all from the jovial, booming person he was three years before. He wears a uniform similar to Andrew's. He is puffing and breathless from his climb and mops wildly at his perspiring countenance. Robert casts a quick glance at Andrew, noticing the latter's discomfited look, and then turns his eyes on Ruth who, at their approach, has moved so*

125

> *her back is toward them, her chin rest-*
> *ing on her hands as she stares out sea-*
> *ward.*)

MARY. Mamma! Mamma!

> (*Robert puts her down and she runs to her*
> *mother. Ruth turns and grabs her up*
> *in her arms with a sudden fierce tender-*
> *ness, quickly turning away again from*
> *the others. During the following scene*
> *she keeps Mary in her arms.*)

SCOTT (*wheezily*). Phew! I got great news for you, Andy. Let me get my wind first. Phew! God A'mighty, mountin' this damned hill is worser'n goin' aloft to the skys'l yard in a blow. I got to lay to a while.

(*He sits down on the grass, mopping his face.*)

ANDREW. I didn't look for you this soon, Uncle.

SCOTT. I didn't figger it, neither; but I run across a bit o' news down to the Seamen's Home made me 'bout ship and set all sail back here to find you.

ANDREW (*eagerly*). What is it, Uncle?

SCOTT. Passin' by the Home I thought I'd drop in an' let 'em know I'd be lackin' a mate next trip count o' your leavin'. Their man in charge o' the shippin' asked after you 'special curious. 'Do you think he'd consider a berth as Second on a steamer, Captain?' he asks. I was goin' to say no when I thinks o' you wantin' to get back down south to

126

the Plate agen; so I asks him: 'What is she and where's she bound?' 'She's the *El Paso*, a brand-new tramp,' he says, 'and she's bound for Buenos Aires.'

ANDREW (*his eyes lighting up – excitedly*). Gosh, that is luck! When does she sail?

SCOTT. To-morrow mornin'. I didn't know if you'd want to ship away agen so quick an' I told him so. 'Tell him I'll hold the berth open for him until late this afternoon,' he says. So I said I'd tell you, an' I catches the first car back to town. So there you be, an' you can make your own choice.

ANDREW. I'd like to take it. There may not be another ship for Buenos Aires with a vacancy in months. (*His eyes roving from Robert to Ruth and back again – uncertainly.*) Still – damn it all – to-morrow morning *is* soon. I wish she wasn't leaving for a week or so. That'd give me a chance – it seems hard to go right away again when I've just got home. And yet it's a chance in a thousand — (*Appealing to Robert.*) What do you think, Rob? What would you do?

ROBERT (*forcing a smile*). He who hesitates, you know. (*Frowning.*) It's a piece of good luck thrown in your way – and – from what you've told me of your plans – I think you owe it to yourself to jump at it. But don't ask me to decide for you.

RUTH (*turning to look at Andrew – in a tone of fierce resentment*). Yes, go, Andy!

(*She turns quickly away again. There is a
moment of embarrassed silence.*)

ANDREW (*thoughtfully*). Yes, I guess I will. It'll
be the best thing for all of us in the end, don't
you think so, Rob? (*Robert nods but remains
silent.*)

SCOTT (*getting to his feet*). Then, that's settled.

ANDREW (*now that he has definitely made a decision
his voice rings with hopeful strength and energy*).
Yes, I'll take the berth. The sooner I go the
sooner I'll be back, that's a certainty, and I won't
come back with empty hands next time. You bet
I won't!

SCOTT. You ain't got so much time, Andy. To
make sure you'd best leave here soon's you kin.
You can't put too much trust in them fellers. I got
to get right back aboard. You'd best come with
me.

ANDREW. I'll go to the house and repack my bag
right away.

ROBERT (*quietly*). You'll both be here for dinner,
won't you?

ANDREW (*worriedly*). I don't know. Will there
be time? What time is it now, I wonder?

ROBERT (*reproachfully*). Ma's been getting dinner
especially for you, Andy.

ANDREW (*flushing – shamefacedly*). Hell! And I
was forgetting! I'm a damn fool. Of course I'll

128

stay for dinner if I missed every damned ship in the world. (*He turns to the Captain — briskly.*) Come on, Uncle. Walk down with me to the house and you can tell me more about this berth on the way. I've got to pack before dinner. (*He and the Captain start down to the left. Andrew calls back over his shoulder.*) You're coming soon, aren't you, Rob?

ROBERT. Yes. I'll be right down.

> (*Andrew and the Captain leave. Ruth puts Mary on the ground and hides her face in her hands. Her shoulders shake as if she were sobbing. Robert stares at her with a grim, sombre expression. Mary walks backward toward Robert, her wondering eyes fixed on her mother.*)

MARY (*her voice vaguely frightened, taking her father's hand*). Dadda, Mamma's cryin', Dadda.

ROBERT (*bending down and stroking her hair — in a voice he endeavours to keep from being harsh*). No, she isn't, little girl. The sun hurts her eyes, that's all. Aren't you beginning to feel hungry, Mary?

MARY (*decidedly*). Yes, Dadda.

ROBERT (*meaningly*). It must be your dinner time now.

RUTH (*in a muffled voice*). I'm coming, Mary. (*She wipes her eyes quickly and, without looking at*

Robert, comes and takes Mary's hand — in a dead voice. Come on and I'll get your dinner for you.

(*She walks out left, her eyes fixed on the ground, the skipping Mary tugging at her hand. Robert waits a moment for them to get ahead and then slowly follows as*

The Curtain Falls)

ACT THREE

SCENE ONE

SCENE. *Same as Act Two, Scene One. The sitting-room of the farm house about six o'clock in the morning of a day toward the end of October five years later. It is not yet dawn, but as the action progresses the darkness outside the windows gradually fades to grey.*

The room, seen by the light of the shadeless oil lamp with a smoky chimney which stands on the table, presents an appearance of decay, of dis-solution. The curtains at the windows are torn and dirty and one of them is missing. The closed desk is grey with accumulated dust as if it had not been used in years. Blotches of dampness disfigure the wall-paper. Threadbare trails, leading to the kitchen and outer doors, show in the faded carpet. The top of the coverless table is stained with the imprints of hot dishes and spilt food. The rung of one rocker has been clumsily mended with a piece of plain board. A brown coating of rust covers the unblacked stove. A pile of wood is stacked up carelessly against the wall by the stove.

The whole atmosphere of the room, contrasted with that of former years, is one of an habitual poverty too hopelessly resigned to be any longer ashamed or even conscious of itself.

At the rise of the curtain Ruth is discovered sitting by the stove, with hands outstretched to

131

the warmth as if the air in the room were damp and cold. A heavy shawl is wrapped about her shoulders, half-concealing her dress of deep mourning. She has aged horribly. Her pale, deeply lined face has the stony lack of expression of one to whom nothing more can ever happen, whose capacity for emotion has been exhausted. When she speaks her voice is without timbre, low and monotonous. The negligent disorder of her dress, the slovenly arrangement of her hair, now streaked with grey, her muddied shoes run down at the heel, give full evidence of the apathy in which she lives.

Her mother is asleep in her wheel chair beside the stove toward the rear, wrapped up in a blanket.

There is a sound from the open bedroom door in the rear as if some one were getting out of bed. Ruth turns in that direction with a look of dull annoyance. A moment later Robert appears in the doorway, leaning weakly against it for support. His hair is long and unkempt, his face and body emaciated. There are bright patches of crimson over his cheek-bones and his eyes are burning with fever. He is dressed in corduroy pants, a flannel shirt, and wears worn carpet slippers on his bare feet.

RUTH (*dully*). S-s-s-h-h! Ma's asleep.

ROBERT (*speaking with an effort*). I won't wake her.

132

(*He walks weakly to a rocker by the side of
the table and sinks down in it exhausted.*)

RUTH (*staring at the stove*). You better come near
the fire where it's warm.

ROBERT. No. I'm burning up now.

RUTH. That's the fever. You know the doctor
told you not to get up and move round.

ROBERT (*irritably*). That old fossil! He doesn't
know anything. Go to bed and stay there – that's
his only prescription.

RUTH (*indifferently*). How are you feeling now?

ROBERT (*buoyantly*). Better! Much better than
I've felt in ages. Really I'm quite healthy now –
only very weak. It's the turning-point, I guess.
From now on I'll pick up so quick I'll surprise you
– and no thanks to that old fool of a country quack,
either.

RUTH. He's always tended to us.

ROBERT. Always helped us to die, you mean! He
"tended" to Pa and Ma and – (*his voice breaks*) –
and to – Mary.

RUTH (*dully*). He did the best he knew, I s'pose.
(*After a pause.*) Well, Andy's bringing a specialist
with him when he comes. That ought to suit you.

ROBERT (*bitterly*). Is that why you're waiting up
all night?

RUTH. Yes.

133

ROBERT. For Andy?

RUTH (*without a trace of feeling*). Somebody had got to, when he's bringing that doctor with him. You can't tell when he might get here if he's coming from the port in an auto like he telegraphed us. And besides, it's only right for some one to meet him after he's been gone five years.

ROBERT (*with bitter mockery*). Five years! It's a long time.

RUTH. Yes.

ROBERT (*meaningly*). To *wait*!

RUTH (*indifferently*). It's past now.

ROBERT. Yes, it's past. (*After a pause.*) Have you got his two telegrams with you? (*Ruth nods.*) Let me see them, will you? My head was so full of fever when they came I couldn't make head or tail of them. (*Hastily.*) But I'm feeling fine now. Let me read them again.

> (*Ruth takes them from the bosom of her dress and hands them to him.*)

RUTH. Here. The first one's on top.

ROBERT (*opening it*). New York. "Just landed from steamer. Have important business to wind up here. Will be home as soon as deal is completed." (*He smiles bitterly.*) Business first was always Andy's motto. (*He reads.*) "Hope you are all well. Andy." (*He repeats ironically.*) "Hope you are all well!"

134

RUTH (*dully*). He couldn't know you'd been took sick till I answered that and told him.

ROBERT (*contritely*). Of course he couldn't. You're right. I'm a fool. I'm touchy about nothing lately. Just what did you say in your reply? I forget.

RUTH (*inconsequentially*). I had to send it collect. (*Robert frowns.*) I wrote you were pretty low and for him to hurry up here.

ROBERT (*irritably*). He'll think I'm dying or some such foolishness. What an idiotic exaggeration! What did you say was the matter with me? Did you mention that?

RUTH. I wrote you had lung trouble – just those two words. (*Dully.*) The boy said it wouldn't cost any more for two words.

ROBERT (*flying into a petty temper*)- You *are* a fool! How often have I explained to you that it's *pleurisy* is the matter with me. You can't seem to get it in your head that the pleura is outside the lungs, not in them!

RUTH (*callously*). I only wrote what Doctor Smith told me.

ROBERT (*angrily*). He's a damned ignoramus!

RUTH (*dully*). Makes no difference. I had to tell Andy something, didn't I?

ROBERT (*after a pause, opening the other telegram*). He sent this last evening. Let's see. (*He reads.*)

"Leave for home on midnight train. Just received your wire. Am bringing specialist to see Rob. Will motor to farm from Port." (*He calculates.*) The midnight gets in the Port about four-thirty, I think, or five. It should take a car an hour or more to get here. What time is it now?

RUTH. Round six, must be.

ROBERT. He ought to be here soon. I'm glad he's bringing a doctor who knows something. I'm tired of being at the mercy of that cheap old quack. A specialist will tell you in a second that there's nothing the matter with my lungs.

RUTH (*stolidly*). You've been coughing an awful lot lately.

ROBERT (*irritably*). What nonsense! For God's sake, haven't you ever had a bad cold yourself? (*Ruth stares at the stove in silence. Robert fidgets in his chair. There is a pause. Finally Robert's eyes are fixed on the sleeping Mrs. Atkins.*) Your mother is lucky to be able to sleep so soundly.

RUTH. Ma's tired. She's been sitting up with me most of the night.

ROBERT (*mockingly*). Is she waiting for Andy, too? (*There is a pause. Robert sighs.*) I couldn't get to sleep to save my soul. I counted ten million sheep if I counted one. No use! My brain kept pounding out thoughts as if its life depended on it. I gave up trying finally and just laid there in the dark thinking. (*He pauses, then continues in a tone*

136

of tender sympathy.) I was thinking about you, Ruth — of how hard these last years must have been for you. (*Appealingly.*) I'm sorry, Ruth.

RUTH (*in a dead voice*). I don't know. They're past now. They were hard on all of us.

ROBERT. Yes; on all of us but Andy. (*With a flash of sick jealousy.*) Andy's made a big success of himself — the kind he wanted. He's got lots of money and, I suppose, a reputation for being a sharp business man. (*Mockingly.*) What else is there in life to wish for, eh, Ruth? And now he's coming home to let us admire his greatness. (*Frowning — irritably.*) What does it matter? What am I talking about? My brain must be sick, too. (*After a pause.*) Yes, these years have been terrible for both of us. (*His voice is lowered to a trembling whisper.*) Especially the last eight months since Mary — died. (*He forces back a sob with a convulsive shudder — then breaks out in a passionate agony.*) Our last hope of happiness! I could curse God from the bottom of my soul — if there was a God!

> (*He is racked by a violent fit of coughing and hurriedly puts his handkerchief to his lips.*)

RUTH (*without looking at him*). Mary's better off — being dead.

ROBERT (*gloomily*). We'd all be better off for that matter. (*With sudden exasperation.*) You tell that mother of yours she's got to stop saying that

Mary's death was due to a weak constitution inherited from me. (*On the verge of tears of weakness.*) It's got to stop, I tell you!

RUTH (*sullenly*). She's only saying what Doctor Smith said.

ROBERT (*fiercely*). He's an old ass, and I'll tell him if —

RUTH (*sharply*). S-h-h! You'll wake her, and then she'll nag at me — not you.

ROBERT (*coughs and lies back in his chair weakly — a pause*). It's all because your mother's down on me for not begging Andy for help when things got worse here.

RUTH (*resentfully*). You might have. He's got plenty, if what he says is true.

ROBERT. How can *you* of all people think of taking money from *him*?

RUTH (*dully*). I don't see the harm. He's your own brother.

ROBERT (*shrugging his shoulders*). What's the use of talking to you? Well, *I* couldn't. (*Proudly.*) And I've managed to keep things going, thank God. You can't deny that without help I've succeeded in — (*He breaks off with a bitter laugh.*) My God, what am I boasting of? Debts to this one and that, taxes, interest unpaid! I'm a fool! (*He lies back in his chair closing his eyes for a moment, then speaks in a low voice.*) I'll be frank, Ruth. I've been an utter failure, and I've dragged you with me. I couldn't blame you in all justice – for hating me.

RUTH (*without feeling*). I don't hate you. It's been my fault too, I s'pose.

ROBERT. No. You couldn't help loving – Andy.

RUTH (*dully*). I don't love anyone.

ROBERT (*waving her remark aside*). You needn't deny it. It doesn't matter. (*After a pause – with a tender smile.*) Do you know, Ruth, what I've been dreaming back there in the dark? (*With a short laugh.*) It may sound silly of me but – I was planning our future when I get well. (*He looks at her with appealing eyes as if afraid she will sneer at him. Her expression does not change. She stares at the stove. His voice takes on a note of eagerness.*) After all, why shouldn't we have a future? We're young yet. If we can only shake off the curse of this farm! It's the farm that's ruined our lives, damn it! And now that Andy's coming back – I'm going to sink my foolish pride, Ruth! I'll borrow the money from him to give us a good start in the city. We'll go where people live instead of stagnating, and start all over again. (*Confidently.*) I won't be the failure there that I've been here, Ruth. You won't need to be ashamed of me there. I'll prove to you the reading I've done can be put to some use. (*Vaguely.*) I'll write, or something of that sort.

I've always wanted to write. (*Pleadingly.*) You'll want to do that, won't you, Ruth?

RUTH (*dully*). There's Ma.

ROBERT. She can come with us.

RUTH. She wouldn't.

ROBERT (*angrily*). So that's your answer! (*He trembles with violent passion. His voice is so strange that Ruth turns to look at him in alarm.*) You're lying, Ruth! Your mother's just an excuse. You want to stay here. You think that because Andy's coming back that — (*He chokes and has an attack of coughing.*)

RUTH (*getting up – in a frightened voice*). What's the matter? (*She goes to him.*) I'll go with you, Rob. I don't care for Andy like you think. Stop that coughing for goodness' sake! It's awful bad for you. (*She soothes him in dull tones.*) I'll go with you to the city – soon's you're well again. Honest I will, Rob, I promise! (*Rob lies back and closes his eyes. She stands looking down at him anxiously*). Do you feel better now?

ROBERT. Yes. (*Ruth goes back to her chair. After a pause he opens his eyes and sits up in his chair. His face is flushed and happy.*) Then you *will* go, Ruth?

RUTH. Yes.

ROBERT (*excitedly*). We'll make a new start, Ruth – just you and I. Life owes us some happiness after what we've been through. (*Vehemently.*) It must! Otherwise our suffering would be meaningless — and that is unthinkable.

RUTH (*worried by his excitement*). Yes, yes, of course, Rob, but you mustn't —

ROBERT. Oh, don't be afraid. I feel completely well, really I do — now that I can hope again. Oh, if you knew how glorious it feels to have something to look forward to — not just a dream, but something tangible, something already within our grasp! Can't you feel the thrill of it, too — the vision of a new life opening up after all the horrible years?

RUTH. Yes, yes, but do be —

ROBERT. Nonsense! I won't be careful. I'm getting back all my strength. (*He gets lightly to his feet.*) See! I feel light as a feather. (*He walks to her chair and bends down to kiss her smilingly.*) One kiss — the first in years, isn't it? — to greet the dawn of a new life together.

RUTH (*submitting to his kiss — worriedly*). Sit down, Rob, for goodness' sake!

ROBERT (*with tender obstinacy — stroking her hair*). I won't sit down. You're silly to worry. (*He rests one hand on the back of her chair.*) Listen. All our suffering has been a test through which we had to pass to prove ourselves worthy of a finer realization. (*Exultingly.*) And we did pass through it! It hasn't broken us! And now the dream is to come true! Don't you see?

RUTH (*looking at him with frightened eyes as if she thought he had gone mad*). Yes, Rob, I see; but won't you go back to bed now and rest?

ROBERT. No. I'm going to see the sun rise. It's an augury of good fortune. (*He goes quickly to the window in the rear, left, and pushing the curtains aside, stands looking out. Ruth springs to her feet and comes quickly to the table, left, where she remains watching Robert in a tense, expectant attitude. As he peers out his body seems gradually to sag, to grow limp and tired. His voice is mournful as he speaks.*) No sun yet. It isn't time. All I can see is the black rim of the damned hills outlined against a creeping greyness. (*He turns around, letting the curtains fall back, stretching a hand out to the wall to support himself. His false strength of a moment has evaporated, leaving his face drawn and hollow eyed. He makes a pitiful attempt to smile.*) That's not a very happy augury, is it? But the sun'll come – soon. (*He sways weakly.*)

RUTH (*hurrying to his side and supporting him*). Please go to bed, won't you, Rob? You don't want to be all wore out when the specialist comes, do you?

ROBERT (*quickly*). No. That's right. He mustn't think I'm sicker than I am. And I feel as if I could sleep now – (*cheerfully.*) – a good, sound, restful sleep.

RUTH (*helping him to the bedroom door*). That's

what you need most. (*They go inside. A moment later she reappears, calling back*). I'll shut this door so's you'll be quiet. (*She closes the door and goes quickly to her mother and shakes her by the shoulder.*) Ma! Ma! Wake up!

MRS. ATKINS (*coming out of her sleep with a start*). Glory be! What's the matter with you?

RUTH. It was Rob. He's just been talking to me out here. I put him back to bed. (*Now that she is sure her mother is awake her fear passes and she relapses into dull indifference. She sits down in her chair and stares at the stove – dully.*) He acted – funny; and his eyes looked so – so wild like.

MRS. ATKINS (*with asperity*). And is that all you woke me out of a sound sleep for, and scared me near out of my wits?

RUTH. I was afraid. He talked so crazy – staring out of the window as if he saw – something – and speaking about the hills, and wanting to see the sun rise – and all such notions. I couldn't quiet him. It was like he used to talk – only mad, kind of. I didn't want to be alone with him that way. Lord knows what he might do.

MRS. ATKINS (*scornfully*). Humph! A poor help I'd be to you and me not able to move a step! Why didn't you run and get Jake?

RUTH (*dully*). Jake isn't here. I thought I'd told you. He quit last night. He hasn't been paid in three months. You can't blame him.

143

MRS. ATKINS (*indignantly*). No, I can't blame him when I come to think of it. What decent person'd want to work on a place like this? (*With sudden exasperation.*) Oh, I wish you'd never married that man!

RUTH (*wearily*). You oughtn't to talk about him now when he's sick in his bed.

MRS. ATKINS (*working herself into a fit of rage*). It's lucky for me and you, too, I took my part of the place out of his hands years ago. You know very well, Ruth Mayo, if it wasn't for me helpin' you on the sly out of my savin's, you'd both been in the poor house — and all 'count of his pig-headed pride in not lettin' Andy know the state thin's were in. A nice thing for me to have to support him out of what I'd saved for my last days — and me an invalid with no one to look to!

RUTH. Andy'll pay you back, Ma. I can tell him so's Rob'll never know.

MRS. ATKINS (*with a snort*). What'd Rob think you and him was livin' on, I'd like to know?

RUTH (*dully*). He didn't think about it, I s'pose. (*After a slight pause.*) He said he'd made up his mind to ask Andy for help when he comes. (*As a clock in the kitchen strikes six.*) Six o'clock. Andy ought to get here directly.

MRS. ATKINS. D'you think this special doctor'll do Rob any good?

RUTH (*hopelessly*). I don't know. (*The two women remain silent for a time staring dejectedly at the stove.*)

MRS. ATKINS (*shivering irritably*). For goodness' sake put some wood on that fire. I'm most freezin'!

RUTH (*pointing to the door in the rear*). Don't talk so loud. Let him sleep if he can.

> (*She gets wearily from the chair and puts a few pieces of wood in the stove. Then she tiptoes to the bedroom door and listens.*)

MRS. ATKINS (*in a sharp whisper*). Is he sleepin'?

RUTH (*coming back*). I couldn't hear him move. I s'pose he is. (*She puts another stick in the stove.*) This is the last of the wood in the pile. I don't know who'll cut more now that Jake's left. (*She sighs and walks to the window in the rear, left, pulls the curtains aside, and looks out.*) It's getting grey out. It'll be light soon and we can put out that lamp. (*She comes back to the stove.*) Looks like it'd be a nice day. (*She stretches out her hands to warm them.*) Must've been a heavy frost last night. We're paying for the spell of warm weather we've been having. (*The throbbing whine of a motor sounds from the distance outside.*)

MRS. ATKINS (*sharply*). S-h-h! Listen! Ain't that an auto I hear?

RUTH (*without interest*). Yes. It's Andy, I s'pose.

MRS. ATKINS (*with nervous irritation*). Don't sit there like a silly goose. Look at the state of this room! What'll this strange doctor think of us? Look at that lamp chimney all smoke! Gracious sakes, Ruth—

RUTH (*indifferently*). I've got a lamp all cleaned up in the kitchen.

MRS. ATKINS (*peremptorily*). Wheel me in there this minute. I don't want him to see me looking a sight. I'll lay down in the room the other side. You don't need me now and I'm dead for sleep. I'll have plenty of time to see Andy.

> (*Ruth wheels her mother off right. The noise of the motor grows louder and finally ceases as the car stops on the road before the farm-house. Ruth returns from the kitchen with a lighted lamp in her hand which she sets on the table beside the other. The sound of footsteps on the path is heard — then a sharp rap on the door. Ruth goes and opens it. Andrew enters, followed by Doctor Fawcett carrying a small black bag. Andrew has changed greatly. His face seems to have grown high-strung, hardened by the look of decisiveness which comes from being constantly under a strain where judgments on the spur of the moment are compelled to be accurate.*)

146

BEYOND THE HORIZON

*His eyes are keener and more alert.
There is even a suggestion of ruthless
cunning about them. At present, however, his expression is one of tense
anxiety. Doctor Fawcett is a short, dark,
middle-aged man with a Vandyke
beard. He wears glasses.)*

RUTH. Hello, Andy! I've been waiting—

ANDREW (*kissing her hastily*). I know. I got here
as soon as I could. (*He throws off his cap and heavy
overcoat on the table, introducing Ruth and the Doctor as he does so. He is dressed in an expensive business suit and appears stouter.*) My sister-in-law,
Mrs. Mayo — Doctor Fawcett. (*They bow to each
other silently. Andrew casts a quick glance about the
room.*) Where's Rob?

RUTH (*pointing*). In there.

ANDREW. I'll take your coat and hat, Doctor.
(*As he helps the Doctor with his things.*) Is he very
bad, Ruth?

RUTH (*dully*). He's been getting weaker.

ANDREW. Damn! This way, Doctor. Bring the
lamp, Ruth.

(*He goes into the bedroom, followed by the
Doctor and Ruth carrying the clean
lamp. Ruth reappears almost immediately closing the door behind her, and
goes slowly to the outside door, which she*

147

*opens, and stands in the doorway look-
ing out. The sound of Andrew's and
Robert's voices comes from the bedroom.
A moment later Andrew re-enters,
closing the door softly. He comes forward and sinks down on the rocker on
the right of table, leaning his head on his
hand. His face is drawn in a shocked
expression of great grief. He sighs
heavily, staring mournfully in front of
him. Ruth turns and stands watching
him. Then she shuts the door and returns to her chair by the stove, turning
it so she can face him.*)

ANDREW (*glancing up quickly — in a harsh voice*).
How long has this been going on?

RUTH. You mean — how long has he been sick?

ANDREW (*shortly*). Of course! What else?

RUTH. It was last summer he had a bad spell
first, but he's been ailin' ever since Mary died —
eight months ago.

ANDREW (*harshly*). Why didn't you let me know
— cable me? Do you want him to die, all of you?
I'm damned if it doesn't look that way! (*His voice
breaking.*) Poor old chap! To be sick in this out-
of-the-way hole without anyone to attend to him
but a country quack! It's a damned shame!

RUTH (*dully*). I wanted to send you word once,

148

but he only got mad when I told him. He was too proud to ask anything, he said.

ANDREW. Proud? To ask *me*? (*He jumps to his feet and paces nervously back and forth.*) I can't understand the way you've acted. Didn't you see how sick he was getting? Couldn't you realize — why, I nearly dropped in my tracks when I saw him! He looks (*he shudders.*) — terrible! (*With fierce scorn.*) I suppose you're so used to the idea of his being delicate that you took his sickness as a matter of course. God, if I'd only known!

RUTH (*without emotion*). A letter takes so long to get where you were — and we couldn't afford to telegraph. We owed every one already, and I couldn't ask Ma. She'd been giving me money out of her savings for the last two years till she hadn't much left. Don't say anything to Rob about it. I never told him. He'd only be mad at me if he knew. But I had to, because — God knows how we'd have got on if I hadn't.

ANDREW. You mean to say — (*His eyes seem to take in the poverty-stricken appearance of the room for the first time.*) You sent that telegram to me collect. Was it because — (*Ruth nods silently. Andrew pounds on the table with his fist.*) Good God! And all this time I've been — why I've had everything! (*He sits down in his chair and pulls it close to Ruth's — impulsively.*) But — I can't get it through my head. Why? Why? What has happened? How did it ever come about? Tell me!

RUTH (*dully*). There's nothing much to tell. Things kept getting worse, that's all — and Rob didn't seem to care.

ANDREW. But hasn't he been working the farm?

RUTH. He never took any interest since way back when your Ma died. After that he got men to take charge, and they nearly all cheated him — he couldn't tell — and left one after another. And then there'd be times when there was no one to see to it, when he'd be looking to hire some one new. And the hands wouldn't stay. It was hard to get them. They didn't want to work here, and as soon as they'd get a chance to work some other place they'd leave. Then after Mary died he didn't pay no heed to anything any more — just stayed indoors and took to reading books again. So I had to ask Ma if she wouldn't help us some.

ANDREW (*surprised and horrified*). Why, damn it, this is frightful! Rob must be mad not to have let me know. Too proud to ask help of *me*! It's an insane idea! It's crazy! And for Rob, of all people, to feel that way! What's the matter with him in God's name? He didn't appear to have changed when I was talking to him a second ago. He seemed the same old Rob — only very sick physically. (*A sudden, horrible suspicion entering his mind.*) Ruth! Tell me the truth. His mind hasn't gone back on him, has it?

150

RUTH (*dully*). I don't know. Mary's dying broke him up terrible — but he's used to her being gone by this, I s'pose.

ANDREW (*looking at her queerly*). Do you mean to say *you're* used to it?

RUTH (*in a dead tone*). There's a time comes — when you don't mind any more — anything.

ANDREW (*looks at her fixedly for a moment — with great pity*). I'm sorry I talked the way I did just now, Ruth — if I seemed to blame you. I didn't realize —— The sight of Rob lying in bed there, so gone to pieces — it made me furious at every one. Forgive me, Ruth.

RUTH. There's nothing to forgive. It doesn't matter.

ANDREW (*springing to his feet again and pacing up and down*). Thank God I came back before it was too late. This doctor will know exactly what to do to bring him back to health. That's the first thing to think of. When Rob's on his feet again we can get the farm working on a sound basis once more. I'll see to it so that you'll never have any more trouble — before I leave.

RUTH. You're going away again?

ANDREW. Yes. Back to Argentine. I've got to.

RUTH. You wrote Rob you was coming back to stay this time.

ANDREW. I expected to – until I got to New York. Then I learned certain facts that make it necessary. (*With a short laugh.*) To be candid, Ruth, I'm not the rich man you've probably been led to believe by my letters – not now. I was when I wrote them. I made money hand over fist as long as I stuck to legitimate trading; but I wasn't content with that. I wanted it to come easier, so like all the rest of the idiots, I tried speculation. It was funny, too. I'd always been dead set against that form of gambling before. I guess there's still enough of the farmer in me to make me feel squeamish about Wheat Pits. But I got into it just the same, and it seemed as if I never had a chance to get out. Oh, I won all right! Several times I've been almost a millionaire – on paper – and then come down to earth again with a bump. Finally the strain was too much. I got disgusted with myself and made up my mind to get out and come home and forget it and really live again. I got out – with just a quarter of a million dollars more than I'd had when I landed there five years before. (*He gives a harsh laugh.*) And now comes the funny part. The day before the steamer sailed I saw what I thought was a chance to become a millionaire again. (*He snaps his fingers.*) That easy! I plunged. Then, before things broke, I left – I was so confident I couldn't be wrong – and I left explicit orders to *friends*. (*Bitterly.*) Friends! Well, maybe it wasn't their fault. A fool deserves what he gets. Anyway, when I landed in New York – I wired you I had business to wind up, didn't I? Well, it was the business that wound me up! (*He smiles grimly, pacing up and down, his hands in his pockets.*)

RUTH (*dully*). You found – you'd lost everything?

ANDREW (*sitting down again*). Practically. (*He takes a cigar from his pocket, bites the end off, and lights it.*) Oh, I don't mean I'm dead broke. I've saved ten thousand from the wreckage, maybe twenty. But that's a poor showing for five years' hard work. That's why I'll have to go back. (*Confidently.*) I can make it up in a year or so down there – and I don't need but a shoestring to start with. (*A weary expression comes over his face and he sighs heavily.*) I wish I didn't have to. I'm sick of it all. And I'd made so many plans about converting this place into a real home for all of us, and a working proposition that'd pay big at the same time. (*With another sigh.*) It'll have to wait.

RUTH. It's too bad – things seem to go wrong so.

ANDREW (*shaking off his depression – briskly*). They might be much worse. There's enough left to fix the farm O.K. before I go. I won't leave 'til Rob's on his feet again. In the meantime I'll make things fly around here. (*With satisfaction.*) I need a rest, and the kind of rest I need is hard work in the open – just like I used to do in the

F   153

old days. I'll organize things on a working basis and get a real man to carry out my plans while I'm away — what I intended to do the last time. (*Stopping abruptly and lowering his voice cautiously.*) Not a word to Rob about my losing money! Remember that, Ruth! You can see why. If he's grown so touchy he'd never accept a cent if he thought I was hard up; see?

RUTH. Yes, Andy.

> (*After a pause, during which Andrew puffs at his cigar abstractedly, his mind evidently busy with plans for the future, the bedroom door is opened and Doctor Fawcett enters, carrying a bag. He closes the door quietly behind him and comes forward, a grave expression on his face. Andrew springs out of his chair.*)

ANDREW. Ah, Doctor! (*He pushes a chair between his own and Ruth's.*) Won't you have a chair?

FAWCETT (*glancing at his watch*). I must catch the nine o'clock back to the city. It's imperative. I have only a moment. (*Sitting down and clearing his throat — in a perfunctory, impersonal voice.*) The case of your brother, Mr. Mayo, is — (*He stops and glances at Ruth and says meaningly to Andrew.*) Perhaps it would be better if you and I —

RUTH (*with dogged resentment*). I know what you

mean, Doctor; but I'm not going. I'm his wife, and I've got a right to hear what you're going to say. (*Dully.*) Don't be afraid I can't stand it. I'm used to bearing trouble by this; and I can guess what you've found out. Don't you s'pose I could see it staring out of his eyes at me these last days? (*She hesitates for a moment — then continues in a monotonous voice.*) Rob's going to die.

ANDREW (*angrily*). Ruth!

FAWCETT (*raising his hand as if to command silence*). In view of what you have said, Mrs. Mayo, I see no reason to withhold the facts from you. (*He turns to Andrew.*) I am afraid my diagnosis of your brother's condition forces me to the same conclusion as Mrs. Mayo's.

ANDREW (*groaning*). But Doctor, surely —

FAWCETT (*calmly*). I am concerned only with facts, my dear sir, and this is one of them. Your brother has not long to live — perhaps a few days, perhaps only a few hours. I would not dare to venture a prediction on that score. It is a marvel that he is alive at this moment. My examination revealed that both of his lungs are terribly affected. A hæmorrhage, resulting from any exertion or merely through the unaided progress of the disease itself, will undoubtedly prove fatal.

ANDREW (*brokenly*). Good God! (*Ruth keeps her eyes fixed on her lap in a trance-like stare.*)

FAWCETT. I am sorry I have to tell you this, sorry my trip should prove to be of such little avail. If there was anything that could be done —

ANDREW. There isn't anything?

FAWCETT (*shaking his head*). I am afraid not. It is too late. Six months ago there might have —

ANDREW (*in anguish*). But if we were to take him to the mountains – or to Arizona – or —

FAWCETT. That might have prolonged his life six months ago. (*Andrew groans.*) But now — (*He shrugs his shoulders significantly.*) I would only be raising a hope in you foredoomed to disappointment if I encouraged any belief that a change of air could accomplish the impossible. He could not make a journey. The excitement, the effort required, would inevitably bring on the end.

ANDREW (*appalled by a sudden thought*). Good heavens, you haven't told him this, have you, Doctor?

FAWCETT. No. I lied to him. I said a change of climate to the mountains, the desert would bring about a cure. (*Perplexedly.*) He laughed at that. He seemed to find it amusing for some reason or other. I am sure he knew I was lying. A clear foresight seems to come to people as near death as he is. (*He sighs.*) One feels foolish lying to them; and yet one feels one ought to do it, I don't know why. (*He looks at his watch again nervously.*)

I must take my leave of you. It is really imperative that I take no risk of missing — (*He gets up.*)

ANDREW (*getting to his feet — insistently*). But there must still be a chance for him, isn't there, Doctor?

FAWCETT (*as if he were reassuring a child*). There is always that last chance — the miracle. We doctors see it happen too often to disbelieve in it. (*He puts on his hat and coat — bowing to Ruth.*) Good-bye, Mrs. Mayo.

RUTH (*without raising her eyes — dully*). Good-bye.

ANDREW (*mechanically*). I'll walk to the car with you, Doctor. (*They go out the door. Ruth sits motionlessly. The motor is heard starting and the noise gradually recedes into the distance. Andrew re-enters and sits down in his chair, holding his head in his hands.*) Ruth! (*She lifts her eyes to his.*) Hadn't we better go in and see him? God! I'm afraid to! I know he'll read it in my face. (*The bedroom door is noiselessly opened and Robert appears in the doorway. His cheeks are flushed with fever, and his eyes appear unusually large and brilliant. Andrew continues with a groan.*) It can't be, Ruth. It can't be as hopeless as he said. There's always a fighting chance. We'll take Rob to Arizona. He's *got* to get well. There *must* be a chance!

ROBERT (*in a gentle tone*). Why must there, Andy? (*Ruth turns and stares at him with terrified eyes.*)

ANDREW (*whirling around*). Rob! (*Scoldingly.*)

157

What are you doing out of bed? (*He gets up and goes to him.*) Get right back now and obey the Doc, or you're going to get a licking from me!

ROBERT (*ignoring these remarks*). Help me over to the chair, please, Andy.

ANDREW. Like hell I will! You're going right back to bed, that's where you're going, and stay there! (*He takes hold of Robert's arm.*)

ROBERT (*mockingly*). Stay there 'til I die, eh, Andy? (*Coldly.*) Don't behave like a child. I'm sick of lying down. I'll be more rested sitting up. (*As Andrew hesitates — violently.*) I swear I'll get out of bed every time you put me there. You'll have to sit on my chest, and that wouldn't help my health any. Come on, Andy. Don't play the fool. I want to talk to you, and I'm going to. (*With a grim smile.*) A dying man has some rights, hasn't he?

ANDREW (*with a shudder*). Don't talk that way, for God's sake! I'll only let you sit down if you'll promise that. Remember. (*He helps Rob to the chair between his own and Ruth's.*) Easy now! There you are! Wait, and I'll get a pillow for you. (*He goes into the bedroom. Robert looks at Ruth who shrinks away from him in terror. Robert smiles bitterly. Andrew comes back with the pillow which he places behind Robert's back.*) How's that?

ROBERT (*with an affectionate smile*). Fine! Thank you! (*As Andrew sits down.*) Listen, Andy.

You've asked me not to talk — and I won't after I've made my position clear. (*Slowly*.) In the first place I know I'm dying.

> (*Ruth bows her head and covers her face with her hands. She remains like this all during the scene between the two brothers.*)

ANDREW. Rob! That isn't so!

ROBERT (*wearily*). It *is* so! Don't lie to me. It's useless and it irritates me. After Ruth put me to bed before you came, I saw it clearly for the first time. (*Bitterly*.) I'd been making plans for our future — Ruth's and mine — so it came hard at first — the realization. Then when the Doctor examined me, I knew — although he tried to lie about it. And then to make sure I listened at the door to what he told you. So, for my sake, don't mock me with fairy tales about Arizona, or any such rot as that. Because I'm dying is no reason you should treat me as an imbecile or a coward. Now that I'm sure what's happening I can say Kismet to it with all my heart. It was only the silly uncertainty that hurt. (*There is a pause. Andrew looks around in impotent anguish, not knowing what to say. Robert regards him with an affectionate smile.*)

ANDREW (*finally blurts out*). It isn't foolish. You *have* got a chance. If you heard all the Doctor said that ought to prove it to you.

ROBERT. Oh, you mean when he spoke of the possibility of a miracle? (*Dryly.*) The Doctor and I disagree on that point. I don't believe in miracles — in my case. Beside, I know more than any doctor in earth *could* know — because I *feel* what's coming. (*Dismissing the subject.*) But we've agreed not to talk of it. Tell me about yourself, Andy, and what you've done all these years. That's what I'm interested in. Your letters were too brief and far apart to be illuminating.

ANDREW. I meant to write oftener.

ROBERT (*with a faint trace of irony*). I judge from them you've accomplished all you set out to do five years ago?

ANDREW. That isn't much to boast of.

ROBERT (*surprised*). Have you really, honestly reached that conclusion?

ANDREW. Well, it doesn't seem to amount to much now.

ROBERT. But you're rich, aren't you?

ANDREW (*with a quick glance at Ruth*). Yes, I s'pose so.

ROBERT. I'm glad. You can do to the farm all I've undone. (*With a smile.*) Do you know I was too proud to ask you for money when things went bad here? You'll have to forgive me for that, Andy.

ANDREW. I knew it wasn't like you to feel that way.

ROBERT. But what did you do down there? Tell me. You went in the grain business with that friend of yours?

ANDREW. Yes. After two years I had a share in it. I sold out last year. (*He is answering Rob's questions with great reluctance.*)

ROBERT. And then?

ANDREW. I went in on my own.

ROBERT. Your own business?

ANDREW. I s'pose you'd call it that.

ROBERT. Still in grain?

ANDREW. Yes.

ROBERT. What's the matter? What's there to be ashamed of? You look as if I was accusing you of crimes.

ANDREW. I'm proud enough of the first four years. It's after that I'm not boasting of. You see, I couldn't make money easy enough that way, so I took to speculating.

ROBERT. In wheat?

ANDREW. Yes.

ROBERT. And you made money — gambling?

ANDREW. Yes.

ROBERT. I can't imagine you as the easy-come-easy-go kind.

ANDREW. I'm not. I'm sick of it.

ROBERT (*thoughtfully*). I've been wondering what the great change was in you. I can see now. It's your eyes. There's an expression about them as if you were constantly waiting to hear a cannon go off, and wincing at the bang beforehand.

ANDREW (*grimly*). I've felt just that way all the past year.

ROBERT (*after a pause during which his eyes search Andrew's face*). Why haven't you ever married?

ANDREW. Never wanted to. Didn't have time to think of it, I guess.

ROBERT (*after a pause*). You — a farmer — to gamble in a wheat pit with scraps of paper. There's a spiritual significance in that picture, Andy. (*He smiles bitterly.*) I'm a failure, and Ruth's another — but we can both justly lay some of the blame for our stumbling on God. But you're the deepest-dyed failure of the three, Andy. You've spent eight years running away from yourself. Do you see what I mean? You used to be a creator when you loved the farm. You and life were in harmonious partnership. And now — (*He stops as if seeking vainly for words.*) My brain is muddled. But part of what I mean is that your gambling with the thing you used to love to create proves how far astray you've gotten from the truth. So you'll be punished. You'll have to suffer to win back — (*His voice grows weaker and he sighs wearily.*) It's no use. I can't say it.

(*He lies back and closes his eyes, breathing pantingly.*)

ANDREW (*slowly*). I think I know what you're driving at, Rob — and it's true, I guess.

(*Robert smiles gratefully and stretches out his hand, which Andrew takes in his.*)

ROBERT. I want you to promise me to do one thing, Andy, after —

ANDREW. I'll promise anything, as God is my Judge!

ROBERT. Remember, Andy, Ruth has suffered double her share, and you haven't suffered at all. (*His voice faltering with weakness.*) Only through contact with suffering, Andy, will you — awaken. Listen. You must marry Ruth — afterwards.

RUTH (*with a cry*). Rob! (*Robert lies back, his eyes closed, gasping heavily for breath.*)

ANDREW (*making signs to her to humour him — gently*). You're tired out, Rob. You shouldn't have talked so much. You better lie down and rest a while, don't you think? We can talk later on.

ROBERT (*with a mocking smile*). Later on! You always were an optimist, Andy! (*He sighs with exhaustion.*) Yes, I'll go and rest a while. (*As An-*

drew comes to help him.) It must be near sunrise, isn't it? It's getting grey out.

ANDREW. Yes – pretty near. It's after six.

ROBERT (*as Andrew helps him to the bedroom*). Pull the bed around so it'll face the window, will you, Andy? I can't sleep, but I'll rest and forget if I can watch the rim of the hills and dream of what is waiting beyond. (*They go into the bedroom.*) And the shut door, Andy. I want to be alone.

> (*Andrew reappears and shuts the door softly. He comes and sits down on his chair again, supporting his head on his hands. His face is drawn with the intensity of his dry-eyed anguish.*)

RUTH (*glancing at him – fearfully*). He's out of his mind now, isn't he?

ANDREW. He may be a little delirious. The fever would do that. (*With impotent rage.*) God, what a shame! And there's nothing we can do but sit and – wait! (*He springs from his chair and walks to the stove.*)

RUTH (*dully*). He was talking – wild – like he used to – only this time it sounded – unnatural, don't you think?

ANDREW. I don't know. The things he said to me had truth in them – even if he did talk them way up in the air, like he always sees things. Still — (*He glances down at Ruth keenly.*) Why do you

164

suppose he wanted us to promise we'd — (*Confusedly*.) You know what he said.

RUTH (*dully*). His mind was wandering, I s'pose.

ANDREW (*with conviction*). No — there was something back of it.

RUTH. He wanted to make sure I'd be all right — after he'd gone, I expect.

ANDREW. No, it wasn't that. He knows very well I'd naturally look after you without — anything like that.

RUTH. He might be thinking of — something happened five years back, the time you came home from the trip.

ANDREW. What happened? What do you mean?

RUTH (*dully*). It was the day you came. We had a fight.

ANDREW. A fight? What has that to do with me?

RUTH. It was about you — in a way.

ANDREW (*amazed*). About *me*?

RUTH. Yes, mostly. You see I'd found out I'd made a mistake about Rob soon after we were married — when it was too late.

ANDREW. Mistake? (*Slowly*.) You mean — you found out you didn't love Rob?

RUTH. Yes.

ANDREW. Good God!

RUTH. And then I thought that when Mary came it'd be different, and I'd love him; but it didn't happen that way. And I couldn't bear with his blundering and book-reading – and I grew to hate him, almost.

ANDREW. Ruth!

RUTH. I couldn't help it. No woman could. It had to be because I loved some one else, I'd found out. (*She sighs wearily.*) It can't do no harm to tell you now – when it's all past and gone – and dead. *You* were the one I really loved – only I didn't come to the knowledge of it 'til too late.

ANDREW (*stunned*). Ruth! Do you know what you're saying?

RUTH. It was true – then. (*With sudden fierceness.*) How could I help it? No woman could.

ANDREW. Then – you loved me – that time I came home?

RUTH. Yes.

ANDREW. But – couldn't you see – I didn't love you – that way?

RUTH (*doggedly*). Yes – I saw then; but I'd known your real reason for leaving home the first time – everybody knew it – and for three years I'd been thinking —

ANDREW. That I loved you?

166

RUTH. Yes. Then that day on the hill you laughed about what a fool you'd been for loving me once — and I knew it was all over.

ANDREW. Good God, but I never thought — (*He stops, shuddering at his remembrance.*) And did Rob —

RUTH. That was what I'd started to tell. We'd had a fight just before you came and I got crazy mad — and I told him all I've told you.

ANDREW (*gaping at her speechlessly for a moment*). You told Rob — you loved me?

RUTH. Yes.

ANDREW (*shrinking away from her in horror*). You — you — you mad fool, you! How could you do such a thing?

RUTH. I couldn't help it. I'd got to the end of bearing things — without talking.

ANDREW. And the thought of the child — his child and yours — couldn't keep your mouth shut?

RUTH. I was crazy mad at him — when I told.

ANDREW. Then Rob must have known every moment I stayed here! And yet he never said or showed — God, how he must have suffered! Didn't you know how much he loved you?

RUTH (*dully*). Yes. I knew he liked me.

ANDREW. Liked you! How can you talk in that cold tone — now — when he's dying! What kind of a woman are you? I'd never believe it was in you to be so — Couldn't you have kept silent — no matter what you felt or thought? Did you have to torture him? No wonder he's dying. I don't see how he's lived through it as long as he has. I couldn't. No. I'd have killed myself — or killed you.

RUTH (*dully*). I wish he had — killed me.

ANDREW. And you've lived together for five years with this horrible secret between you?

RUTH. We've lived in the same house — not as man and wife.

ANDREW. But what does he feel about it now? Tell me! Does he still think —

RUTH. I don't know. We've never spoke a word about it since that day. Maybe, from the way he went on, he s'poses I care for you yet. Maybe that's one reason he said what he did.

ANDREW. But you don't. You can't. It's outrageous. It's stupid! You don't love me!

RUTH (*slowly*). I wouldn't know how to feel love, even if I tried, any more.

ANDREW (*brutally*). And I don't love you, that's sure! (*He sinks into his chair, his head between his hands.*) It's damnable such a thing should be between Rob and me — we that have been pals ever since we were born, almost. Why, I love Rob better'n anybody in the world and always did.

There isn't a thing on God's green earth I wouldn't have done to keep trouble away from him. And now I have to be the very one — it's admnable! How am I going to face him again? What can I say to him now? (*He groans with anguished rage. After a pause.*) He asked me to promise — what am I going to do?

RUTH. You can promise — so's it'll ease his mind — and not mean anything.

ANDREW. What? Lie to him now — when he's dying? Can you believe I'd descend as low as that? And there's no sense in my lying. He knows I don't love you. (*Determinedly.*) No! It's *you* who'll have to do the lying, since it must be done. You're the cause of all this. You've got to! You've got a chance now to undo some of all the suffering you've brought on Rob. Go in to him! Tell him you never loved me — it was all a mistake. Tell him you only said so because you were mad and didn't know what you were saying, and you've been ashamed to own up to the truth before this. Tell him something, anything, that'll bring him peace and make him believe you've loved him all the time.

RUTH (*dully*). It's no good. He wouldn't believe me.

ANDREW (*furiously*). You've got to make him believe you, do you hear? You've got to — now — hurry — you never know when it may be too late.

(*As she hesitates — imploringly.*) For God's sake, Ruth! Don't you see you owe it to him? You'll never forgive yourself if you don't.

RUTH (*dully*). I'll go. (*She gets wearily to her feet and walks slowly toward the bedroom.*) But it won't do any good. (*Andrew's eyes are fixed on her anxiously. She opens the door and steps inside the room. She remains standing there for a minute. Then she calls in a frightened voice.*) Rob! Where are you? (*Then she hurries back, trembling with fright.*) Andy! Andy! He's gone!

ANDREW (*misunderstanding her — his face pale with dread*). He's not —

RUTH (*interrupting him — hysterically*). He's gone! He isn't in there. The bed's empty. The window's wide open. He must have crawled out into the yard!

ANDREW (*springing to his feet. He rushes into the bedroom and returns immediately with an expression of alarmed amazement on his face*). Come! He can't have gone far! We've got to find him! (*Grabbing his hat he takes Ruth's arm and shoves her toward the door.*) Come on! (*Opening the door.*) Let's hope to God — (*The door closes behind them, cutting off his words as*

The Curtain Falls)

ACT THREE

SCENE. *Same as Act One, Scene One. A section of country highway. The sky to the east is already alight with bright colour and a thin, quivering line of flame is spreading slowly along the horizon rim of the dark hills. The roadside, however, is still steeped in the greyness of the dawn, shadowy and vague. The field in the foreground has a wild uncultivated appearance as if it had been allowed to remain fallow the preceding summer. Parts of the snake-fence in the rear have been broken down. The apple tree is leafless and seems dead.*

Robert staggers weakly in from the left. He stumbles into the ditch and lies there for a moment; then crawls with a great effort to the top of the bank where he can see the sun rise, and collapses weakly. Ruth and Andrew come hurriedly along the road from the left.

ANDREW (*stopping and looking about him*). There he is! I knew it! I knew we'd find him here.

ROBERT (*trying to raise himself to a sitting position as they hasten to his side — with a wan smile.*) I thought I'd given you the slip.

ANDREW (*with kindly bullying*). Well, you didn't, you old scoundrel, and we're going to take you right back where you belong — in bed. (*He makes*

171

a motion to lift Robert.) What d'you mean by running away like this, eh?

ROBERT. Don't, Andy. Don't, I tell you! I can't bear it!

ANDREW. You're in pain?

ROBERT (*simply*). No. I'm dying. (*He falls back weakly. Ruth sinks down beside him with a sob and pillows his head on her lap.*) Don't try to move me, Andy. It would mean — I had a bad hæmorrhage — trying to get here. I knew then — it was only — a few minutes more. (*Andrew stands looking down at him helplessly. Robert moves his head restlessly on Ruth's lap.*) There! Just so I can see — the sun. I couldn't stand it back there in the room. It seemed as if all my life — I'd been cooped in a room. So I thought I'd try to end as I might have — if I'd had the courage to live my dream. Alone — in a ditch by the open road — watching the sun rise.

ANDREW. Rob! Don't talk. You're wasting your strength. Rest a while and then we'll carry you —

ROBERT. Still hoping, Andy? Don't. I know. (*There is a pause during which he breathes heavily, straining his eyes toward the horizon.*) The sun comes so slowly. I haven't long — to wait. (*With an ironical smile.*) The Doctor told me to go to the far-off places — and I'd be cured. He was right. That was always the cure for me. It's too late — for this world — but in the next I'll not miss — the secret. (*He has a fit of coughing which racks his body.*)

ANDREW (*with a hoarse sob*). Rob! (*He clenches his fists in an impotent rage against Fate.*) God! God!

    (*Ruth sobs brokenly and wipes Robert's lips with her handkerchief.*)

ROBERT (*in a voice which is suddenly ringing with the happiness of hope*). You mustn't feel sorry for me. It's ridiculous! Don't you see I'm happy at last – because I'm making a start to the far-off places – free – free! – freed from the farm – free to wander on and on – eternally! Even the hills are powerless to shut me in now. (*He raises himself on his elbow, his face radiant, and points to the horizon.*) Look! Isn't it beautiful beyond the hills? I can hear the old voices calling me to come — (*Exultantly.*) And this time I'm going – I'm free! It isn't the end. It's a free beginning – the start of my voyage! Don't you see? I've won to my trip – the right of release – beyond the horizon! Oh, you ought to be glad – glad – for my sake! (*He collapses weakly.*) Andy! (*Andrew bends down to him.*) Remember RUTH —

ANDREW. I'll take care of her, I swear to you, Rob!

ROBERT. Ruth has suffered – and for your own sake and hers – remember, Andy – only through sacrifice – the secret beyond there — (*He suddenly raises himself with his last remaining strength and points to the horizon where the edge of the sun's disc is rising from the rim of the hills.)* The sun! *(He remains with his eyes fixed on it for a moment. A rattling noise throbs from his throat. He mumbles:)* Remember!

> *(And falls back and is still. Ruth gives a cry of horror and springs to her feet, shuddering, her hands over her eyes. Andrew bends on one knee beside the body, placing a hand over Robert's heart, then he kisses his brother reverentially on the forehead and stands up.)*

ANDREW *(facing Ruth, the body between them — in a dead voice).* He's dead. *(With a sudden burst of fury.)* God damn you, you never told him!

RUTH *(piteously).* He was so happy without my lying to him.

ANDREW *(pointing to the body — trembling with the violence of his rage).* This is your doing, you damn woman, you coward, you murderess! He's dead because you've killed him, do you hear?

RUTH *(sobbing).* Don't, Andy! Stop! I couldn't help it — and he knew how I'd suffered, too. He told you — to remember.

ANDREW *(stares at her for a moment, his rage ebbing away, an expression of deep pity gradually coming over his face. Then he glances down at his brother*

and speaks brokenly in a compassionate voice). Forgive me, Ruth – for his sake. I know he was right
– and I'll remember what he said. (*Ruth lets her
hands fall from her face and looks at him uncompre-
hendingly. He lifts his eyes to hers and forces out
falteringly:*) I – you – we've both made such a
mess of things! We must try to help each other –
and – in time – we'll come to know what's right to
do — (*Desperately.*) And perhaps we —

> (*But Ruth, if she is aware of his words, gives
> no sign. She remains silent, gazing at
> him dully with the sad humility of ex-
> haustion, her mind already sinking back
> into that spent calm beyond the further
> troubling of any hope.*)

(*The Curtain Falls*)

Gold

A Play in Four Acts

Gold

A Play in Four Acts

SCENES OF ACTS

ACT ONE. A barren coral island on the fringe of the Malay Archipelago – Noon.

ACT TWO. Interior of a boat-shed on the wharf of the Bartlett place on the California coast. An afternoon six months later.

ACT THREE. Exterior of the Bartlett house – dawn of the following morning.

ACT FOUR. Bartlett's "cabin" – his look-out post – at the top of the house. A night one year later.

Time of the play – About the year 1900

Characters

CAPTAIN ISAIAH BARTLETT, *of the whaling ship, Triton*

SILAS HORNE, *boatswain of the Triton*

BEN CATES

JIMMY KANAKA, *an Islander* } *of the Triton's crew*

BUTLER, *cook of the Triton*

ABEL, *the ship's boy*

SARAH ALLEN BARTLETT, *the captain's wife*

SUE, *their daughter*

NAT, *their son*

DANIEL DREW, *officer of a freight steamer*

DOCTOR BERRY

Gold

ACT ONE

SCENE. *A small, barren coral island on the southern
fringe of the Malay Archipelago. The coral
sand, blazing white under the full glare of the
sun, lifts in the right foreground to a long hum-
muck a few feet above sea-level. A stunted coco
palm rises from the centre of this elevation, its
bunch of scraggly leaves drooping motionlessly,
casting a small circular patch of shadow directly
beneath on the ground about the trunk. About a
hundred yards in the distance the lagoon is seen,
its vivid blue contrasting with the white coral
beach which borders its circular outline. The
far horizon to seaward is marked by a broad
band of purplish haze which separates the bright
blue of the water from the metallic grey-blue of
the sky. The island bakes. The intensity of the
sun's rays is flung back skyward in a quivering
mist of heat-waves which distorts the outlines of
things, giving the visible world an intangible
eerie quality, as if it were floating submerged in
some colourless molten fluid.*

*As the curtain rises, Abel is discovered lying
asleep, curled up in the patch of shade beneath
the coco palm. He is a runty, under-sized boy
of fifteen, with a shrivelled old face, tanned to
parchment by the sun. He has on a suit of dirty
dungarees, man's size, much too large for him,*

5

*which hang in loose folds from his puny frame.
A thatch of brown hair straggles in limp wisps
from under the peaked canvas cap he wears. He
looks terribly exhausted. His dreams are evidently fraught with terror, for he twitches convulsively and moans with fright. Butler enters
hurriedly, panting, from the right, rear. He is a
tall man of over middle age, dressed in the faded
remainder of what was once a brown suit. The
coat, the buttons of which have been torn off,
hangs open, revealing his nakedness beneath. A
cloth cap covers his bald head, with its halo of
dirty thin grey hair. His body is emaciated. His
face, with its round, blue eyes, is weathered and
cracked by the sun's rays. The wreck of a pair of
heavy shoes flop about his bare feet. He looks back
cautiously, as if he were afraid of being followed;
then satisfied that he is not, he approaches the
sleeping boy, and bending down, puts his hand on
Abel's forehead. Abel groans and opens his eyes.
He stares about furtively, as if seeking some one
whose presence he dreads to find.*

ABEL (*in a husky voice*). Where's Capt'n and the
rest, Butts?

BUTLER (*in a hoarse, cracked whisper*). On the
beach — down there.

> (*He makes an exhausted gesture, right, and
> then sinks with a groan at the foot of
> the tree, leaning back against the trunk,*

*trying vainly to hunch his long legs up
so as to be completely in the shade.)*

ABEL. What're they doin'? (*With avid eyes.*)
They ain't found no water yet?

BUTLER (*shaking his head, his eyes closing wearily*).
No. How would they – when there ain't any –
not on this devil's island – dry as a bone, my sonny
– sand and sun – that's all.

ABEL (*remonstratingly – his lips trembling a little*).
Aw – maybe – you don't know no different.

BUTLER. No. Might as well look the devil in
the face, sonny. There's no water here. Not a
damn drop. No – nor a scrap to eat, neither.
Only the damn sun. (*Weakly – touching the skin of
his face with trembling fingers.*) God! My face is
like the raw inside of a wet hide! If it'd only rain!
(*After a pause – kindly.*) But how are you, eh?
Had a good sleep?

ABEL. I was dreamin' awful. (*With a sudden,
shrill agony – his lips twitching.*) I need a drink of
water – something awful! My mouth's burnin'
up. (*With tremulous pleading.*) Say, ain't you got
'nother drink left? – honest, ain't you?

BUTLER (*looking around him cautiously*). Not so
loud! (*Fixing his eyes sternly on the boy.*) This is a
dead secret, mind! You'll swear you won't blab
– not to him?

ABEL. Sure, Butts, sure! Gawd strike me dead!

BUTLER (*takes a pint bottle from the hip-pocket of his pants. It is about half-full of water*). He don't know I've got this, remember! He — and the rest — they'd kill me like a dog — and you too, sonny — remember that!

ABEL. Sure! I ain't goin' to tell 'em, Butts. (*Stretching out his hands frenziedly.*) Aw, give it to me, Butts! Give me a drink, for Christ's sake!

BUTLER. No, you don't! I'll hold it for you. Only a few drops. You'd have it all down your throat. And we've got to be careful. It's got to last 'til the ship comes past that'll pick us up. That's the only hope. (*Holding the bottle at arm's length from the boy.*) Hands down, now — or you don't get a drop! (*The boy lets his hands drop to his sides. Butler puts the bottle carefully to his lips, and allows the boy two gulps — then snatches it away.*) That's all now. More later.

> (*He takes one gulp himself, and making a tremendous effort of will, jerks the bottle from his lips, and corking it quickly, thrusts it back in his pocket and heaves a shuddering sigh.*)

ABEL. Aw, more! Just another swaller —

BUTLER (*determinedly*). No!

ABEL (*crying weakly*). Yuh dirty mut!

BUTLER (*quietly*). There! Don't get riled. It only makes you hotter — and thirstier. (*The boy sinks back exhausted and closes his eyes. Butler begins to talk in a more assured voice, as if the sip of water had renewed his courage.*) That'll save us yet, that bit of water. A lucky notion of mine to think of it – at the last moment. They were just lowering the boats. I could hear you calling to me to hurry and come. They didn't care if I went down with that stinking whaling ship or not, damn them! What did the dirty cook matter to them? But I thought of filling this bottle. It'd been lying there in the galley for two years almost. I'd had it on my hip, full of whisky, that night in Oakland when I was shanghaied. So I filled it out of a bucket before I ran to the boat. Lucky I did, son – for you and me – not for them – damn 'em!

ABEL (*struggling to a sitting posture, evidently strengthened by his drink*). Gee, if the Old Man was wise you got it —

BUTLER. He won't know – nor Horne, nor Cates, nor Jimmy Kanaka, neither. (*As if in self-justification.*) Why should I tell 'em, eh? Did I ever get anything better than a kick or a curse from one of them? (*Vindictively.*) Would they give it to me if they had it? They'd see me in hell first! And besides, it's too late for them. They're mad as hatters right now, the four of them. They ain't had a drop since three nights back, when the water in the cask gave out and we rowed up against this island in the dark. Think of it, and them out

walking and roasting in the sun all day, looking
for water where there ain't any. Wouldn't you be
crazy? (*Suddenly he laughs queerly.*) Didn't you
hear them shouting and yelling like lunatics just
before I came?

ABEL. I thought I heard something – on'y maybe
I was dreamin'.

BUTLER. It's them that are doing the dreaming.
I was with them. I had to go. (*With rising anger.*)
He kicked me awake – and every time I tried to
get away he beat me back. He's strong yet –
(*with threatening vindictiveness.*) – but he can't
last long, damn him! (*Controlling himself, goes on
with his story excitedly.*) Well, we went looking for
water – on this sand pile. Then Jimmy Kanaka
saw a boat sunk half under down inside the reef –
a Malay canoe, only bigger. They got down in
her the best way they could, up to their waists in
water. They thought there might be something
to drink on her. I was trying to sneak off, scared
to go in on account of sharks. All of a sudden
they gave an awful yell. I thought they'd found
something to drink and ran back. They was all
standing about a box they'd forced open, yelling
and cursing and out of their heads completely.
When I looked I seen the box was full of all sorts
of metal junk – bracelets and bands and necklaces
that I guess the Malays wear. Nothing but brass
and copper, and bum imitations of diamonds and

things – not worth a damn; and there they were, shouting with joy and slapping each other on the back. And that hellion of a skipper shouts at me: "Get out of this! No share here for a stinking cook!" he yells. I didn't say nothing but just picked up some of the stuff to make sure. Then I told him straight. "This ain't gold. It's brass and copper – not worth a damn." God, he got wild! I had to run, or he'd knifed me – then and there. That was when I woke you up.

ABEL. And ain't it worth nothin', honest? How'd you know it ain't?

BUTLER. D'you think I ain't learned to know gold in my time? And polished enough copper and brass to know them, too? Just as if it was gold it'd do 'em any good! You can't drink gold, can you? (*With sudden violence.*) It serves 'em right, all that's happened and going to happen. Kicks and smacks in the face if I even winked an eye – two years of it! And me shanghaied when I was drunk – taken away from a good job and forced to cook the swill on a rotten whaler. Oh, I'll pay him back for it! His damn ship is wrecked and lost to him – that's the first of it. I'll see him rot and die – and the three with him! But you and me'll be saved! D'you know why I've let you go halves on this water, instead of hogging it all my-self? It's because you were the only one on board that didn't treat me like a dog – and they kicked and beat you, too. We were in the same boat. And now we'll get even! Them and their dirty box of junk! (*He sinks back, exhausted by this outburst.*)

ABEL (*suddenly, in a piteous voice*). Gee, I wisht I was back home again!

BUTLER. You'll get back. We both will. (*He closes his eyes. After a pause — weakly.*) When I close my eyes, everything gets to rocking under me, like I was in that open boat again. I won't forget these four days in a hurry. Up and down — Nothing but sun and water.

> (*They are both silent, leaning with closed eyes against the bole of the tree, panting exhaustedly. A murmur of men's voices comes from the right, rear, and gradually gets nearer.*)

ABEL (*opening his eyes with a start*). Butts! I hear 'em comin'!

BUTLER (*listening, wide-eyed, for a moment*). Yes, it's them. (*He gets to his feet weakly.*) Come, let's get out of this. (*Abel staggers to his feet. They both move to the left. Butler shades his eyes with his hands and looks toward the beach.*) Look! They're dragging along that box of junk with 'em, the damn fools! (*Warningly.*) They're crazy as hell. Don't give 'em no chance to pick on you, d'you hear? They'd stop at nothing when they're this way.

GOLD

(*There is a scuffling of heavy footsteps in the sand, and Captain Bartlett appears, followed by Horne, who in turn is followed by Cates and Jimmy Kanaka. Bartlett is a tall, huge-framed figure of a man, dressed in a blue double-breasted coat, trousers of the same material, and rubber sea-boots turned down from the knees. In spite of the ravages of hunger and thirst there is still a suggestion of immense strength in his heavy-muscled body. His head is massive, thickly covered with tangled, iron-grey hair. His face is large, bony, and leather-tanned, with a long aquiline nose and a gash of a mouth shadowed by a bristling grey moustache. His broad jaw sticks out at an angle of implacable stubbornness. Bushy grey brows overhang the obsessed glare of his sombre dark eyes. Silas Horne is a thin, parrot-nosed, angular old man, his lean face marked by a lifetime of crass lusts and mean cruelty. He is dressed in grey cotton trousers, and a singlet torn open across his hairy chest. The exposed skin of his arms and shoulders and chest has been blistered and seared by the sun. A cap is on his head. Cates is squat and broad-chested, with thick, stumpy legs and*

13

arms. His square, stupid face, with its greedy pig's eyes, is terribly pock-marked. He is gross and bestial, an unintelligent brute. He is dressed in dungaree trousers and a dirty white sailor's blouse, and wears a brown cap. Jimmy Kanaka is a tall, sinewy, bronzed young Islander. He wears only a loin cloth and a leather belt with a sheath-knife. The last two are staggering beneath the weight of a heavy inlaid chest. The eyes of the three white men are wild. They pant exhaustedly, their legs trembling with weakness beneath them. Their lips are puffed and cracked, their voices muffled by their swollen tongues. But there is a mad air of happiness, of excitement, about their scorched faces.)

BARTLETT (*in a crooning, monotonous voice*). It's heavy, I know, heavy — that chest. Up, bullies! Up with her! (*He flings himself in the shade, resting his back against the tree, and points to the sand at his feet.*) Put 'er there, bullies — there where I kin see!

HORNE (*echoing his words mechanically*). Put 'er there!

CATES (*in thick, stupid tones*). Aye, aye, sir! Down she goes, Jimmy! (*They set the chest down.*)

BARTLETT. Sit down, lads, sit down. Ye've earned your spell of rest.

> (*The three men throw themselves on the sand in attitudes of spent weariness. Bartlett's eyes are fixed gloatingly on the chest. There is a silence suddenly broken by Cates, who leaps to a kneeling position with a choked cry.*)

CATES (*his eyes staring at the Captain with fierce insistence*). I want a drink — water!

> (*The others are startled into a rigid, dazed attention. Horne's lips move painfully in a soundless repetition of the word. There is a pause. Then Bartlett strikes the side of his head with his fist, as if to drive this obsession from his brain. Butler and Abel stand looking at them with frightened eyes.*)

BARTLETT (*having regained control over himself, in a determined voice, deep-toned and menacing*). If ye speak that word ever again, Ben Cates — if ye say it once again — ye'll be food for the sharks! Ye hear?

CATES (*terrified*). Yes, sir.

> (*He collapses limply on the sand again. Horne and the Kanaka relax hopelessly.*)

BARTLETT (*with heavy scorn*). Are ye a child to

take on like a sick woman – cryin' for what ye
know we've not got? Can't ye stand up under a
little thirst like a man? (*Resolutely.*) There'll be
water enough – if ye'll wait and keep a stiff upper
lip on ye. We'll all be picked up to-day. I'll stake
my word on it. This state o' things can't last.
(*His eyes fall on the chest.*) Ye ought to be singin'
'stead o' cryin' – after the find we've made.
What's the lack of water amount to – when ye've
gold before you? (*With mad exultation.*) Gold!
Enough of it in your share alone to buy ye rum,
and wine, and women, too, for the rest o' your life!

CATES (*straightening up to a sitting posture – his
small eyes staring at the box fascinatedly – in a stupid
mumble.*) Aye – aye – rum and wine!

BARTLETT (*half-closing his eyes as if the better to
enjoy his vision.*) Yes, rum and wine and women
for you and Horne and Jimmy. No more hard
work on the dirty sea for ye, bullies, but a full pay-
day in your pockets to spend each day o' the year.
(*The three strain their ears, listening eagerly. Even
Butler and Abel advance a step or two toward him, as
if they, too, were half-hypnotized.*) And Cates grum-
bling because he's thirsty! I'd be the proper one
to complain – if complainin' there was to do!
Ain't I lost my ship and the work o' two years
with her? And what have ye lost, all three, but a
few rags o' clothes? (*With savage emphasis.*) I tell
ye, I be glad the *Triton* went down! (*He taps the*

16

box with his fingers.) They's more in this than ever was earned by all the whalin' ships afloat. They's gold – heavy and solid – and diamonds and emeralds and rubies! – red and green, they be.

CATES (*licking his lips*). Aye, I seen 'em there – and emeralds be green, I know, and sell for a ton of gold!

BARTLETT (*as if he hadn't heard and was dreaming out loud to himself*). Rum and wine for you three, and rest for me. Aye, I'll rest at home 'til the day I die. Aye, woman, I be comin' home now for good. Aye, Nat and Sue, your father be comin' home for the rest o' his life! No more stinkin' blubber on the deck. I'll give up whalin' like ye've always been askin' me, Sarah. Aye, I'll go to meetin' with ye on a Sunday like ye've always prayed I would. We'll make the damn neighbours open their eyes, curse 'em! Carriages and silks for ye – they'll be nothin' too good – and for Sue and the boy. I've been dreamin' o' this in my sleep for years. I never give a damn 'bout the oil – that's just trade – but I always hoped on some voyage I'd pick up ambergris – a whole lot of it – and that's worth gold!

HORNE (*his head bobbing up from his chest – drowsily*). Aye, ambergris! It's costly truck.

BUTLER (*in a whisper to the boy – cautiously*). There! Wasn't I right? Mad as hatters, all of 'em! Come on away!

17

GOLD

ABEL (*staring at the Captain fascinatedly*). No. I wanter see 'em open it.

BUTLER. Look out! You'll be going batty yourself, first thing you know. (*But he also stays.*)

BARTLETT (*his voice more and more that of a somnambulist*). It's time I settled down to home with ye, Sarah, after twenty years o' whalin'. They's plenty o' big trees on my place, bullies, and shade and green grass, and a cool wind off the sea. (*He shakes off the growing drowsiness and glares about him in a rage.*) Hell's fire! What crazy truck be I thinkin' of? (*But he and the others sink back immediately into stupor. After a pause he begins to relate a tale in a droning voice.*) Years ago, when I was whalin' out o' New Bedford — just after I got my first ship, it was — a man come to me — Spanish-looking, he was — and wanted to charter my ship and me go shares. He showed me a map o' some island off the coast of South America somewhere. They was a cross marked on it where treasure had been buried by the old pirates. That was what he said. But I was a fool. I didn't believe him. I didn't see's I could take a chance. He got old Scott's schooner — finally. She sailed and never was heard o' since. But I've never forgot him and his map. And often I've thought if I'd 'a' went that vige — (*He straightens up and shouts with aggressive violence.*) But here she be! Run right into it — without no map nor nothin'. Gold and

diamonds and all – all them things he said was
there – there they be in front o' our eyes! (*To the
now alert Jimmy.*) Open 'er up, Jimmy!

JIMMY (*getting up – in his soft voice*). Aye, Captain. (*He reaches down to lift the lid.*)

BARTLETT (*a sudden change of feeling comes over
him, and he knocks Jimmy's arm aside savagely*).
Hands off, ye dog! I'm takin' care o' this chest,
and no man's hand's goin' to touch it but mine!

JIMMY (*stepping back docilely – in the same un-
moved, soft tone*). Aye, Captain.

(*He squats down to the left of the chest.*)

BARTLETT (*seeming suddenly to notice the cook for the
first time*). So there you be, eh? (*His voice growing
thick with rage.*) I ain't forgot what ye said down
by the shore there! Lucky for ye I didn't catch
ye then! "Brass and copper – junk," ye said –
"not gold! Not worth a damn," ye said! Ye
blasted son o' a liar! No share for ye! I'll not forget. And keep your distance o' me if ye want your
hide! (*Looking at Abel.*) Ye've been tellin' that
boy your lies too, I kin tell by the look o' him.
(*Sternly.*) Come here, boy!

ABEL (*advances with faltering steps*). Y-yes, s-sir?

BARTLETT. Open up that chest! Open it up, ye
brat! (*With a desperate movement of fear Abel
reaches down and flings open the lid of the chest. As
he does so, Bartlett's huge hand fastens on the collar*)

of his coat, and holds him with face bent over the box. Horne, Cates, and Jimmy Kanaka pull themselves close, their necks craning for a look inside. Butler takes a few steps toward them.)

BUTLER (*in a low uncertain tone*). Maybe I was wrong, Captain Bartlett, sir.

BARTLETT (*shaking the terror-stricken boy*). What d'ye see there, ye little swab? What d'ye see there?

ABEL. Aw — leggo — I'm chokin'!

BARTLETT (*grimly*). Ye'll choke in earnest if ye don't answer me. What d'ye see? Is it gold? Answer me — is it gold?

ABEL (*stutteringly*). Yes — sure — gold — I see it!

BARTLETT (*thrusts him away. The boy staggers and falls to the sand. Bartlett turns to Butler triumphantly*). Ye see, ye liar? Gold! Gold! Even a child can tell it at a look. (*With a sombre menace in his tone.*) But ye — don't believe — do ye?

BUTLER (*frightenedly*). Maybe I was wrong, sir. I — didn't — look very careful.

BARTLETT. Come here! (*He stands up, his back against the tree.*) Come here!

BUTLER. Yes, sir. (*But he looks about him shiftily, as if to run away.*)

BARTLETT. Jimmy! (*The Kanaka leaps to his feet.*) Knife him, Jimmy, if he tries to run.

JIMMY (*his hand goes to his knife, his dark eyes light-*

ing up with savagery – in his soft voice). Aye, Captain!

BARTLETT (*to the trembling cook*). Come here!

BUTLER (*goes to him with the courage of desperation*). Yes, sir.

BARTLETT (*pointing to the contents of the chest*). Is it gold – or not?

BUTLER. If I can feel of one —

BARTLETT. Pick one up.

BUTLER (*picks up a heavy anklet encrusted with coloured glass, looks at it for a minute – then feigning great assurance*). I was wrong, Captain. It's gold all right enough – worth all kinds of money, I bet.

BARTLETT (*with mad triumph*). Ha! Ye've come to your senses, have ye? Too late, ye swab! No share for ye! And here's to teach ye for lyin' to me before!

> (*His fist jerks out from his side, and Butler is knocked sprawling on the sand, where he lies groaning for a moment, the anklet still clutched in his hand. The boy gives a gasp of fright and scampers off, left.*)

That'll learn ye! (*He sits down beside the chest. The others crouch close. Bartlett shoves in both of his hands – in a tone of mad gloating.*) Gold! Better'n whaling, ain't she, boys? Better'n ambergris, even if I ever had luck to find any!

GOLD

(Butler staggers to his feet. He examines the anklet with contemptuous scorn and even bites it to make sure. Then he edges stealthily toward the left. A sudden transformation comes over his face and he glowers at the Captain with hatred, his features distorted with fury.)

JIMMY KANAKA *(pointing to Butler).* He got him, Captain!

BARTLETT *(glancing at the cook with contemptuous scorn).* Sneakin' away with that piece o' the gold, be ye? Ye thievin' swine! Ye know right enough it's gold now, don't ye? Well, ye kin keep it – for your share for speakin' the truth that once.

HORNE *(his cupidity protesting).* Don't give it to him, sir! It's so much the less for us that worked for it when he did nothin'!

BUTLER *(overcome by hysterical rage – stammering).* Who asked you for it – eh? Who – wants the damn thing? Not me! No! You damned lunatics! You oughter all be in the asylum? *(Holding the anklet out contemptuously.)* Gold? Ha-ha! This junk? I just bit it to make sure. Gold? Brass, that's what – and pieces of glass! Junk! Not worth a damn. Here! Take it! You can have it! *(He flings it on the sand before them. Bartlett snatches it up protectingly.)*

BARTLETT *(in a frenzy).* Jimmy!

(*But Butler runs off left with a terrified cry. Jimmy springs to his feet and stands with his hand on his knife, waiting for a further order.*)

JIMMY (*eagerly*). I go catch – go stick him, Captain?

BARTLETT (*pausing – with a frown*). No. They's time enough for that – if need be. Sit down. (*Jimmy sits down again with a childish air of sulking. Bartlett stares at the treasure, continuing to frown, as if Butler's action had made him uneasy, bewildered and confused him. He mutters half to himself.*) Queer! Queer! He threw it back as if 'twas a chunk of mud! He knew – and yet he said he didn't want it. Junk, he called it – and he knows it's gold! He said 'twas gold himself a second back. He's queer. Why would he say junk when he knows it's gold? D'ye think – he don't believe?

HORNE. He was mad because you knocked him down.

BARTLETT (*shaking his head grimly*). It ain't the first time I've knocked him down; but he never spoke up to me – like that – before. No, it's somethin' else is wrong with him – somethin'.

HORNE. No share for him, you told him, sir. That's what wrong with him.

BARTLETT (*again shaking his head*). No. His eyes — It's somethin' he's got in his head – somethin'

23

he's hidin'! His share – maybe he thinks he'll get his share anyway, in spite o' us! Maybe he thinks his share wouldn't be all he wants! Maybe he thinks we'll die o' hunger and thirst before we get picked up – and that he'll live – and then – he'll come in for the whole chestful! (*Suddenly springing to his feet in a rage, convinced that he has found the truth.*) Hell's fire! That's it, bullies! That's his sneakin' plan! To watch us die – and steal it from us!

CATES (*rising to his knees and shaking his hand threateningly above his head*). Tell Jimmy to knife him, sir! Tell Jimmy – I ain't got a knife, or I'd do it myself. (*He totters weakly to his feet.*)

JIMMY (*eagerly*). You speak, I stick him, Captain. I stick boy, too.

CATES (*weakening*). I'm weak, but I kin do for him yet. I'm weak — (*His knees sag under him. He pleads piteously.*) If I'd only a drink to put some strength in me! If I'd only a sup o' water, I'd do for him! (*Turning, as if to stagger down toward the beach.*) There must be water. Let's look again. I'll go look —

> (*But the effort he makes is too much for his strength and he falls to the sand, panting with open mouth.*)

BARTLETT (*summoning his strength – sternly*). Put a clapper on that jaw of yours, Cates, or I'll do it for ye!

CATES (*blubbering*). If we don't find water – he'll watch us die.

JIMMY (*insinuatingly*). Better me knife cook fella – kill boy, too!

BARTLETT. Will killin' 'em give us drink, ye fools? (*After a pause, he shakes his head as if to drive off some thought, and mutters.*) No more o' that! (*Suddenly, in a tone of sharp command.*) No more o' that, I say! We're keepin' no right watch for ships. Go aloft on that tree, Jimmy – and damn quick! Take a look and see if ye can sight a sail.

> (*Kanaka shins quickly up the bole of the coco palm to the top and looks out on all sides of him. The others rise painfully to their feet and gaze up at him with awakened hope.*)

JIMMY (*suddenly, in a glad voice*). I see um – see sail, Captain.

CATES (*waving his arms frenziedly*). Sail – ho!

JIMMY. Look plenty like trade schooner, Captain. She no change course she fetch plenty close by here. She make full sail, she got plenty fella wind out there, she come quick.

HORNE (*clapping Cates on the back*). Headin' straight for us, Cates, d'you hear?

BARTLETT. How far d'ye reckon she be?

JIMMY. She's five, six fella mile, Captain.

BARTLETT. Come down. (*The Islander slides down. Bartlett exclaims exultantly.*) Didn't I tell ye? In the nick o' time. When she makes in close we'll go down to the reef and yell and wave at her. They'll see! The luck's with us to-day! (*His eyes fall on the treasure and he starts.*) But now — what's to do with this chest — the gold?

HORNE (*quickly*). You ain't going to tell them on the schooner about it?

CATES. They'd claim to share with us.

HORNE. More like they'd steal it and knife us in the bargain. I know the kind on them schooners.

BARTLETT (*scornfully*). D'ye think I'm cracked? No, we'll bury it here.

CATES (*regretfully*). Leave it behind for anyone to find?

BARTLETT. We'll bury it deep, where hell itself won't find it — and we'll make a map o' this island. (*He takes a sheet of paper and a stub of pencil from his pocket — pointing to the foot of the tree.*) Dig a hole here — you, Horne and Jimmy — and dig it deep. (*The two bend down and commence to hollow out the sand with their hands. Bartlett draws on the paper.*) There's the lagoon — and the reef — and here's this tree — the only one on the island — 't would be hard to miss. (*To Cates, who is peering over his shoulder.*) And here where the tree is, d'ye see, Cates, I'll make a cross where the gold is hid.

26

HORNE (*over his shoulder, without ceasing his work*). How d'ye know the lay o' this island – to find it again?

BARTLETT. By the last reckonin' o' the *Triton's*. It's writ on a page I tore from the log-book. And from there we headed due north in the boat, unless the compass lied – four days – a hundred-and-fifty miles, I reckon. (*Exultantly.*) Oh, all hell'd not stop me from findin' this place again when I know the gold's here. Let us once get home and I'll fit out a small schooner the four of us can sail, and we'll come back here to dig it up. It won't be long, I swear to ye!

HORNE (*straightening up*). This deep enough, sir?

BARTLETT. It looks to be.

JIMMY (*who has straightened up and is looking off left – suddenly points excitedly*). He look, Captain! Cook fella, he look here! Boy he look, too! They look plenty too much, Captain!

> (*All four stand staring off at Butler and the boy, whose presence on the island they have forgotten in their mad excitement.*)

CATES (*in stupid dismay*). They'll know where it's hid, sir!

HORNE. They'll tell 'em on the schooner!

CATES (*wildly*). We've got to do for 'em, Captain! Gimme your knife, Jimmy – your knife —

(He stumbles toward the Islander, who pushes him aside brusquely, looking questioningly toward the Captain.)

BARTLETT *(who has been standing motionless, as if stunned by this forgotten complication — slowly).* There they be watchin' us, the sneakin' dogs! Sit down, an' they won't see. *(They all squat in the sand.)* I was forgettin' they was here. *(Striking his knee with clenched fist.)* We've got to do somethin' damn quick! That schooner'll be up soon where they kin sight her — and they'll wave and yell then — and she'll see 'em!

HORNE. And good-bye to the gold for us!

JIMMY *(eagerly).* You say fella word, Captain, me kill um quick. They no make plenty cry for schooner! They keep damn still plenty too much!

BARTLETT *(looking at the Islander with mad cunning but replying only to Horne).* Aye, it's good-bye to the gold, Horne. That scum of a cook — he's made a mock o' us — sayin' it wasn't gold when he knew it was — he'll tell 'em — he'll get joy o' tellin' 'em!

HORNE. And that scrub of a boy — he's no better. He'll be in with him neck and crop.

CATES *(hoarsely).* Knife 'em — and be done with it — I say!

BARTLETT. Or, if they don't tell the schooner's skipper it'll only be because they're plannin' to come back themselves — before we kin — and dig

28

it up. That cook – there's somethin' queer in his mind – somethin' he was hidin' – pretendin' not to believe. What d'ye think, Horne?

HORNE. I think – time's gettin' short – and talkin' won't do no good. (*Insinuatingly.*) They'd do for us soon enough if *they* was able.

BARTLETT. Aye, murder was plain in his eyes when he looked at me.

HORNE (*lowering his voice to a whisper*). Tell Jimmy – Captain Bartlett – is what I say!

BARTLETT. It's agin the law, Silas Horne!

HORNE. The law don't reach to this island.

BARTLETT (*monotonously*). It's against the law a captain's sworn to keep wherever he sails. They ain't refused duty – nor mutinied.

HORNE. Who'll know they ain't? They're trying to steal what's yours – that's worse'n mutiny. (*As a final persuasion.*) And Jimmy's a nigger – and under no laws. And he's stronger'n you are. You couldn't stop 'im.

BARTLETT. Aye – I couldn't prevent —

JIMMY (*eagerly*). I fix um, Captain, they no tell!

(*Bartlett doesn't answer, but stares at the treasure. Horne makes violent motions to Jimmy to go. The Islander stares at his master's face. Then, seeming to read the direct command there, he grunts*

29

*with satisfaction, and pulling his knife
from its sheath, he goes stealthily off
left. Cates raises himself on his
haunches to watch the Islander's movements. Horne and Bartlett sit still in a
strained immobility, their eyes on the
chest.*)

CATES (*in an excited whisper*). I see 'em! They're
sittin' with their backs this way! (*A slight pause.*)
There's Jimmy. He's crawlin' on his hands behind 'em. They don't notice – he's right behind –
almost atop o' them. (*A pause. Cates gives a fiend-
ish grunt.*) Ugh! (*Butler's muffled cry comes from the
left.*) Right in the middle of the back! The cook's
done! The boy's runnin'!

> (*There is a succession of quick screams from the
> boy, the padding of feet running toward
> them, the fall of a body, and the boy's
> dying groan.*)

HORNE (*with satisfaction*). It's done, sir!

BARTLETT (*slowly*). I spoke no word, remember
that, Silas Horne!

HORNE (*cunningly*). Nor me neither, sir. Jimmy
took it on himself. If blame there is – and who'd
blame him for it? – it's on him.

BARTLETT (*gloomily*). I spoke no word! (*Jimmy
returns noiselessly from the left.*)

JIMMY (*grinning with savage pride*). I fix um fella

plenty, Captain. They no tell. They no open mouth plenty too much!

CATES (*maudlinly*). You're a man, Jimmy – a man with guts to him – even if you're a — (*He babbles incoherently.*)

JIMMY (*as the Captain does not look at him*). I go climb fella tree, Captain? I make look for schooner?

BARTLETT (*rousing himself with an effort*). Yes – go up. (*The Islander climbs the tree.*)

HORNE (*getting to his feet – eagerly*). Where away, Jimmy?

JIMMY. She come, Captain, she come plenty quick.

HORNE (*looking in the direction Jimmy indicates*). I kin see her tops'ls from here, sir. Look!

BARTLETT (*getting to his feet – stares out to sea*). Aye! There she be – and makin' towards us fast. (*In a flash his sombre preoccupation is gone, and he is commander once more. He puts the anklet in his hand into his coat pocket – harshly.*) Come down out o' that? They's work to do. (*Jimmy clambers down.*) Did ye leave – them – lyin' in plain sight on the open sand?

JIMMY. Yes. I no touch um, Captain.

BARTLETT. Then ye'll touch 'em now. Go, bury 'em, cover 'em up with sand. And mind ye make a good job o' it that none'll see. Jump now!

JIMMY (*obediently*). I go, Captain. (*He hurries off left.*)

BARTLETT. Down to the reef with ye, Horne! (*Giving the prostrate Cates a kick.*) Up out o' that, Cates! Go with Horne, and when ye see the schooner hull up, wave to 'em, and yell like mad, d'ye hear?

HORNE. Aye, aye, sir!

BARTLETT. I'll stay here and bury the gold. It's best to be quick about it! They may turn a spy-glass on us when they raise the island from deck! Off with ye! (*He gives Cates another kick.*)

CATES (*groaning*). I'm sick! (*Incoherently.*) Can't – report for duty – this watch. (*With a shout.*) Water!

BARTLETT (*contemptuously*). Ye dog! Give him a hand, Horne.

HORNE (*putting a hand under his shoulder*). Up, man! We're to signal the schooner. There'll be water on board o' her – barrels of it!

CATES (*aroused, scrambles to his feet, violently shaking off Horne's hand*). Water aboard o' her! (*His staring eyes catch the schooner's sails on the horizon. He breaks into a staggering run and disappears down toward the beach, right rear, waving his arms wildly and shouting.*) Ahoy! Ahoy! Water! (*Horne walks out quickly after him. Left alone, Bartlett, after a quick glance around, sinks on his knees beside the chest*)

*and shoves both hands into it. From the chest comes
a metallic clink as he fingers the pieces in his hands
gloatingly.*) Ye're safe now! There's none to tell
left livin'! He's dead — damn him! — that lied
about ye. And ye'll rest safe here till I come back
for ye! (*In a dreaming tone, his eyes fixed before him
in an ecstatic vision.*) No more whalin' on the dirty
seas! Rest at home! Gold! I've been dreamin' o'
it all my life! Aye — we'll rest now, Sarah! Your
father be a rich man, Nat and Sue! (*Shaking himself — savagely.*) Ye fool! What drivel be ye talkin'? Loosin' your senses, be ye? Time ye was
picked up! Lucky! (*He shoves down the lid and
places the chest in the hole. He pushes the sand in on
top of it, whispering hoarsely.*) Lay safe, d'ye hear.
For I'll be back for ye! Aye — in spite of hell I'll
dig ye up again! (*The voices of Horne and Jimmy
can be heard from the distance shouting as*

The Curtain Falls)

ACT TWO

SCENE. *Interior of an old boat-shed on the wharf of the Bartlett place on the California coast. In the rear, a double doorway looking out over the end of the wharf to the bay with the open sea beyond. On the left, two windows, and another door, opening on the dock. Near this door, a cot with blankets and a pillow without a slip. In the centre, front, a table with a bottle and glasses on it, and three cane-bottomed chairs. On the right, a fishing dory. Here and there about the shed all sorts of odds and ends pertaining to a ship — old anchors, ropes, tackle, paint-pots, old spars, etc.*

It is late afternoon of a day six months later. Sunlight filters feebly through the stained, cob-webby window-panes.

As the curtain rises, Bartlett and Silas Horne are discovered. Horne is in working clothes of paint-stained dungaree. If his sufferings on the island have left any marks on his dry wizened face, they are undiscoverable. In Bartlett, however, the evidence is marked. His hair has turned white. There are deep hollows under his cheek-bones. His jaw and tight-lipped mouth express defiant determination, as if he were fighting back some weakness inside himself, a weakness found in his eyes, which have something in them of fear, of a wishing to avoid other eyes. He is dressed much the same as when on the

35

island. He sits by the table, centre, his abstracted gaze bent on the floor before him.

HORNE (*who is evidently waiting for the Captain to say something — after a pause, glancing at him uneasily.*) I'd best be gettin' back aboard the schooner, sir.

(*Receiving no answer he starts for the door on the left.*)

BARTLETT (*rousing himself with an effort*). Wait. (*After a pause.*) The full tide's at dawn to-morrow, ye said?

HORNE. Yes, sir.

BARTLETT. They know we'll be sailin' then, don't they — Cates and Jimmy?

HORNE. Yes, sir. They're all ready. Oh, Cates and Jimmy'll be glad o' the word — and me, too, sir. (*With a greedy grin.*) It's all we've been talking of since ye brought us down here — diggin' up the gold!

BARTLETT (*passionately*). Aye, the gold! We'll have it before long, now, I reckon. That schooner — the way we've fitted her up — she'd take a man safe to the Pole and back! We'll drop anchor here with the chest on board in six months, unless — (*Hesitates.*)

HORNE (*uneasily*). What, sir?

BARTLETT (*brusquely*). The weather, ye fool! Can ye take count before o' storms an' calms?

36

HORNE. We'll trust to luck for that. (*Glancing at the Captain curiously.*) And speakin' o' luck, sir – the schooner ain't been christened yet.

BARTLETT (*betraying a sudden, fierce determination*). She will be!

HORNE. There'd be no luck for a ship sailin' out without a name.

BARTLETT. She'll have a name, I tell ye! A name that'll take all curse away and leave her clean. She'll be named the Sarah Allen, and Sarah'll christen her herself.

HORNE. It oughter been done, by rights, when we launched her a month back.

BARTLETT (*sternly*). I know that as well as ye. (*After a pause.*) She wasn't willin' to do it then. Women has queer notions – when they're sick, like. (*Defiantly – as if he were addressing some one outside of the room.*) But Sarah'll be willin' now! She'll be willin' in spite o' — (*Catching himself and abruptly lowering his voice.*) The schooner'll be christened to-morrow at dawn afore she sails.

HORNE. Yes, sir. (*He again turns to go, as if he were anxious to get away.*)

BARTLETT. Wait! There's somethin' else I want to ask ye. Nat, he's been hangin' round the schooner all his spare time o' late. I seen him talkin' to you and Cates and Jimmy. (*With rising anger.*) I hope ye've remembered what I ordered

ye, all three. Not a word o' it to him! I said I'd
keep him out o' this, for his own good, mind! And
if I thought any of ye — (*His fist is raised threateningly, and he glares savagely at Horne.*)

HORNE (*retreating a step — hastily*). No fear o'
that, sir! We've been keerful. But it's hard. He's
a sharp one, Nat is. And when we tells him the
schooner's fitted out for tradin' in the islands, he
just laughs. He's gettin' the wind on somethin' —
without any o' us sayin' a word.

BARTLETT (*in relieved tones*). Let him s'spect all
he's a mind to — as long as he don't know. It ain't
that I'm afeerd to tell him o' the gold, Silas
Horne. He'll share that, anyway. (*Slowly.*) It's
them — other things — I'd keep him clear of.

HORNE (*immediately guessing what he means — reassuringly*). We was all out o' our heads with
thirst and sun when them things happened, sir.

BARTLETT. Mad? Aye! But I ain't forgot — them
two. (*Harshly.*) I'd rather be you nor me, Silas
Horne. You be too rotten bad to care. And I'd
rather be Cates or Jimmy. Cates be too dull to
remember, and Jimmy be proud as a boy o' what
he done. (*He represses a shudder — then goes on
slowly.*) Do they ever come back to you — when
you're asleep, I mean?

HORNE (*pretending mystification*). Who's that, sir?

BARTLETT (*with sombre emphasis*). That cook and

that boy. They come to me. I'm gettin' to be afeerd o' goin' to sleep – not 'feered o' them, I don't mean. (*With sudden defiant bravado.*) Not all the ghosts out o' hell kin keep me from a thing I've set my mind on. (*Collecting himself.*) But I've waked up talkin' out loud – to them – and I'm afeerd there might be some one hear me. That's why I've been sleepin' down here at the boathouse all alone.

HORNE (*uneasily – with an attempt to be reassuring*). You ain't all cured o' that sun and thirst on the island yet, sir.

BARTLETT (*evidently reassured – roughly*). O' course! D'ye think I'd really believe in things in nightmares? (*With an attempt at conviviality.*) Sit down a bit, Horne, and take a grog.

> (*Horne does so. Bartlett pours out a half-tumbler full of rum for himself and shoves the bottle over to Horne.*)

HORNE. Luck to our vige, sir.

BARTLETT. Aye, luck! (*They drink. Bartlett leans over and taps Horne on the arm.*) Aye, it takes time to get cured o' thirst and sun! Lucky that tradin' schooner picked us up the time she did.

HORNE. If she hadn't – we'd been as dead men – as them two.

BARTLETT (*sombrely – after a pause*). I spoke no word, Silas Horne, d'ye remember?

HORNE. Nor me. Jimmy did it alone. (*Craftily.*) We'd all three swear Bible oaths to that in any court. And even if ye'd given the word, there ain't no good thinkin' more o' it, sir. Didn't they deserve all they got – that thief o' a cook and that boy? Wasn't they plottin' on the sly to steal the gold?

BARTLETT (*his eyes gleaming*). Aye!

HORNE. And when you said he'd get no share of it, didn't he lie to your face that it wasn't gold, thinkin' we'd leave it be and he'd git it all for himself?

BARTLETT (*with sudden rage*). Aye, brass and junk, he said, the lyin' scum! That's what he keeps sayin' when I see him in sleep! He didn't believe – makin' a mock o' me – an' then he owned up himself 'twas gold! He knew! He lied a-purpose! He was a cunnin' rat – a thief ashore afore they shipped him with us, I reckon.

HORNE (*eagerly*). Most like, sir.

BARTLETT (*rising to his feet – with confident defiance*). They deserved no better nor they got. Let 'em rot! (*Pouring out another drink for himself and Horne.*) We'll drink, an' then ye get back to the ship. Tell Cates and Jimmy we sail at dawn – sure! (*He drinks.*)

HORNE. Luck, sir! (*He drinks. There is a knock at the door on the left, followed by Mrs. Bartlett's voice calling feebly,* "ISAIAH! ISAIAH!" *Bartlett starts but makes no answer. He seems suddenly sunk in gloom again. Horne turns to him questioningly.*) It's Mrs. Bartlett, sir. Shall I open the door?

BARTLETT. No. I ain't aimin' to see her – yet awhile. (*Then with sudden reasonless rage.*) Let her in, damn ye!

> (*Horne goes and unhooks the door. Mrs. Bartlett enters. She is a slight, slender little woman of fifty. Sickness, or the inroads of a premature old age, have bowed her shoulders, whitened her hair, and forced her to walk feebly with the aid of a cane. A resolute spirit still flashes from her eyes, however, and there is a look of fixed determination on her face. She stands gazing at her husband. There is something accusing in her stare.*)

BARTLETT (*avoiding her eyes – brusquely*). Well? What is it ye want o' me, Sarah?

MRS. B. I want to speak with you alone, Isaiah.

HORNE. I'll be gettin' back aboard, sir. (*Starts to go.*)

BARTLETT (*in a tone almost of fear*). Wait. I'm goin' with ye. (*Turning to his wife – with a certain rough tenderness.*) Ye oughtn't to walk down the hill here, Sarah. The doctor told ye to rest in the house and save your strength.

MRS. B. I want to speak to you alone, Isaiah. You never come home no more, hardly, so I had to come to ye. (*Accusingly.*) You know it ain't walkin is sappin' my strength, Isaiah.

BARTLETT (*very uneasily*). I've got to work on the schooner, Sarah. That's why I've no time at home.

MRS. B. She'll be sailin' soon?

BARTLETT (*suddenly turning on her defiantly*). To-morrow at dawn!

MRS. B. (*with her eyes fixed accusingly on his*). And you be goin' with her?

BARTLETT (*in the same defiant tone*). Yes, I be! Who else'd captain her?

MRS. B. On a craft without a name.

BARTLETT. She'll have that name.

MRS. B. No.

BARTLETT. She'll have that name, I tell ye.

MRS. B. No.

BARTLETT (*thoroughly aroused, his will tries to break hers, but finds her unbending. He mutters menacingly*). Ye'll see! We'll talk o' that later, you and me. (*With sudden apprehension.*) But not now. They's plenty o' time yet for that. Come on, Horne, we'll get aboard.

> (*Without a further glance at his wife he strides past her and disappears through the doorway, followed by Horne. Mrs.*

*Bartlett sinks down in the chair by the
table. She appears suddenly weak and
crushed. Then from outside comes a
girl's laughing voice. Mrs. Bartlett does
not seem to hear, nor to notice Sue and
Drew when they enter. Sue is a slender,
pretty girl of about twenty, with large
blue eyes, reddish-brown hair, and a
healthy, sun-tanned, out-of-door complexion. In spite of the slightness of her
figure there is a suggestion of great
vitality and nervous strength about her.
Drew is a well-set-up, tall young fellow
of thirty. Not in any way handsome, his
boyish face, tanned to a deep brown, possesses an engaging character of healthy,
cheerful forcefulness that has its com-
pelling charm. There would be no
chance of mistaking him for anything but
the ship's officer he is. It is written on
his face, his walk, his voice, his whole
bearing.*)

SUE (*as they enter*). He'll either be here or on the
schooner, Danny. (*Then she sees her mother, with
startled amazement.*) Ma! Good heavens, what are
you doing here? (*Throwing her arms around her neck
and kissing her.*) Don't you know you shouldn't —

MRS. B. (*with a start — turning to her daughter with
a forced smile*). There, Sue, now! Don't go scold-

in' me. (*Then seeing Drew — in a tone of forced gaiety.*) And if there ain't Danny Drew — back home in port at last! You can kiss an old woman, Danny — without makin' her jealous, I reckon.

DREW (*kissing her — with a smile*). I don't know about that, Ma Bartlett. (*Heartily.*) It certainly seems good to see you again — and be back again myself.

MRS. B. We've been expectin' you right along this past month. Then we read in the paper t'other day where your ship'd reached San Francisco, and we knew you'd be down any day. Sue's been on pins and needles ever since.

SUE (*protestingly*). Ma!

DREW. We were delayed in Valparaiso, waiting for cargo. (*With a grin.*) It's a long time to be away from Sue — four months.

SUE (*laughing*). It seems more like four years!

DREW. You remember, Ma, I left just after the big excitement here — when Captain Bartlett turned up after we'd all heard the *Triton* was wrecked and given him up for lost. That was sure a wonderful surprise when he walked into the house that day.

MRS. B. (*her face clouding — in a tone of deep sorrow*). Yes. (*Drew is surprised and glances at Sue questioningly. She sighs. Mrs. Bartlett gets to her feet with difficulty, assisted by Drew. She forces a smile.*) I've

44

taken on a third leg since you was here, Danny!

SUE. We'll help you back to the house. You can't climb that steep hill alone.

MRS. B. Shucks! I'm sick o' the house. I need sun and fresh air, and to-day's so nice I couldn't stay indoors. I'll take your arm to hold on to, Danny. No, I ain't goin' up to the house yet awhile, so don't you try to bully me into it, Sue. I'm goin' to set in the shade o' this shed out on the wharf and watch your Pa workin' on the schooner. Ain't much time left to see her, Sue. They're sailin' to-morrow at dawn, your Pa says.

SUE. To-morrow! Then – you're going to christen her?

MRS. B. (*with grim determination*). No, I ain't, Sue! (*Catching Drew's glance fixed on her with puzzled curiosity, she immediately attempts to resume her joking tone.*) Shucks! Here's Danny wonderin' what silliness we're talkin' of. It's just this, Danny. Captain Bartlett, he's got a crazy notion in his head that just because his ship was wrecked last vige he'll give up whalin' for life. He's fitted out this little schooner for tradin' in the Islands. More money in that, he says. But I don't agree with no such lunatic notions, and I'm just that stubborn I'm not goin' to set my approval on his craziness by christenin' his ship with my name, like he wants me to. He'd ought to stick to whal-

45

in', like he's done all his life. Don't you think so, Danny?

DREW (*embarrassed*). Why, sure – he's rated one of the smartest whaling skippers here on the coast – and I should think —

MRS. B. Just what I tell him – only he's that stubborn. I'd best get out quick while it's still sunny and warm. It's damp in here for an old body.

> (*Drew helps her to the door on the left, opens it, and the two go out, followed by Sue, who carries a chair. After a pause, Sue and Drew return. Sue carefully shuts the door after them. Her face is troubled.*)

DREW (*looks at her for a minute, then comes and puts his arm around her and kisses her*). What's the trouble, Sue?

SUE (*trying to force a smile*). Nothing, Danny.

DREW. Oh yes there is! No use putting me off that way. Why, I've felt it hanging about in the air ever since I first looked at your mother.

SUE. Yes, she's failed terribly since you saw her last.

DREW. Oh, I don't mean just sickness – only – did you notice how she had to – force herself – to joke about things? She used to be so cheerful natural. (*Scratching his head in honest puzzlement.*)

46

But – that ain't what I mean, either. What is it, Sue? Maybe I can help somehow. You look worried, too. Pshaw! You can tell me, can't you?

SUE. Why, yes, Danny – of course – if I could tell – only I'm just as puzzled as you over what it comes from.

DREW (*persuasively*). Well, you sit down and tell me what's happened since I've been away. Then maybe we can put our heads together and figure out what's wrong, and turn to to get things ship-shape again. (*Sue sits down but does not speak. Drew remarks as if to get her started.*) That schooner's a smart little craft for sailing, I should say. I didn't notice no one about working, though.

SUE. No. They're probably below in the cabin, drinking. That's all they've been doing lately. The schooner's been ready to sail for two weeks – but Pa has kept waiting – I don't know what for. Yes, I do know, too – I think I guess. He's been waiting for Ma to give in and christen the ship with her name. But she won't give in. You heard her.

DREW. Well, I suppose she does take it to heart that he'd give up the business he's been in all his life to go in for something new – at his age.

SUE. He mortgaged the house to get money to buy and fit out this schooner. You know he lost most everything when the *Triton* was wrecked.

47

He'd only had her two years, and she cost him a pile of money. Then, too, he's lost a lot all his life – since he and Ma moved out here from the East – investing in all sorts of silly mining ventures – gold mines that always turned out to be only holes in the ground. As far back as I can remember he's never seemed to care about the whaling business – the oil. Ambergris was what he was after. Finding one chunk of that meant more to him than a full cargo of oil.

DREW (*with a grin*). "Old Ambergris." That's what they call him along the coast – behind his back, of course. I reckon he was sort of prospecting the Pacific Ocean looking for an ambergris mine. (*Apologetically*.) Sounds as if I was making fun of him, but you remember how you'n' me 'n' Nat used to laugh about it together.

SUE. It's past a laughing matter now, Danny.

DREW. And what do you reckon the real trouble is?

SUE. Something between him and Ma – something that only the two of them know. It all seemed to start one morning after you'd left – about a week after he'd come home with those three awful men. During that first week he acted all right – just like he used to – only he'd get talking kind of wild now and then about being glad the *Triton* was lost, and promising we'd all be millionaires once he started making trips on the

48

schooner. Ma didn't seem to mind his going in
for trading then. Then, the night of the day he
bought the schooner, something must have happened between them. Neither of them came down
to breakfast. I went up to Ma, and found her so
sick we sent for the doctor. He said she'd suffered
a great shock of some kind, although she wouldn't
tell him a word. I found Pa down in this shed.
He'd moved that cot down here, and said he'd
have to sleep here after that because he wanted to
be near the schooner. It's been that way ever since.
He's slept down here and never come up to the
house except at meal-times. He's never been alone
with Ma one second since then, I don't believe.
And she – she's been trying to corner him, to get
him alone. I've noticed it, although she does her
best to hide it from Nat and me. And she's been
failing, growing weaker and sicker looking every
day. (*Breaking down.*) Oh, Danny, these last
months have been terrible! I'm so glad you're
back again.

DREW (*soothing her*). There! It'll all come out right·

SUE. I'm sure that's why she's crept down here
to-day. She's bound she'll see him alone before he
sails.

DREW. Well, maybe it's for the best. Maybe
when they've had it out, things'll clear up.

SUE. Yes, perhaps. But I can't help feeling –
it'll only make it worse.

DREW (*frowning*). Seems to me it must be all your Pa's fault, Sue — whatever it is. Have you tried to talk to him?

SUE. Yes — a good many times; but all he's ever said was: "There's things you wouldn't take interest in, Sue. You'll know when it's time to know." — and then he'd break off by asking me what I'd like most to have in the world if he had piles of money. And then, one time, he seemed to be terribly afraid of something, and he said to me: "You hustle up and marry Danny, Sue. You marry him and get out of this."

DREW (*with an affectionate grin*). That does sound crazy — any man wanting to get rid of you that way. (*A note of entreaty in his voice.*) But I surely wish you'd take his advice, Sue! (*He kisses her.*)

SUE (*with intense longing*). Oh, I wish I could, Danny.

DREW. I've quite considerable saved now, Sue, and it won't be so long before I get my own ship, I'm hoping, now that I've got my master's certificate. I was hoping at the end of this voyage —

SUE. So was I, Danny — but it can't be this time. With Ma so weak, and no one to take care of her but me — (*Shaking her head — in a tone of decision.*) I couldn't leave home now, Danny. It wouldn't be right. I couldn't feel really happy — until this thing — whatever it is — is settled between Pa and Ma and they're just as they used to be again. (*Pleadingly*.) You understand, don't you, Danny?

DREW (*soberly*). Why — surely I do, Sue. (*He pats her hand*.) Only, it's hard waiting. (*He sighs*.)

SUE. I know. It's just as hard for me.

DREW. I thought maybe I could help; but this isn't anything anyone outside your family could mix in. (*Sue shakes her head. He goes on gloomily after a pause*.) What's the matter with Nat? Seems as if he ought to be able to step in and talk turkey to your Pa.

SUE (*slowly*). You'll find Nat changed, too, Danny — changed terribly. He's caught the disease — whatever it is. You know how interested in his work he's been ever since they put him in the designing department down in the shipyard?

DREW. Yes.

SUE (*with emphasis*). Well, all that's changed. He hates it now, or at least he says he does. And when he comes home, he spends all his time prowling around the dock here, talking with those three awful men. And what do you think he told me only the other day? That he was bound he'd throw up his job and make this voyage on the schooner. He even asked me to ask Pa to let him go.

DREW. Your Pa doesn't want him to, eh?

SUE. Why, of course not! Leave a fine position he worked so hard to get just for this crazy notion!

Pa'd never let him. He's even ordered him to keep off the schooner and not to talk to those men.

DREW. Funny Nat'd like to go to sea. He's always seemed to want to fight shy of it.

SUE. The terrible part is, he's got Ma worried to death — as if she wasn't upset enough already. She's so afraid he'll go — that Pa'll let him at the last moment. She's always pleading with Nat not to think of it — so that he keeps out of her way, too. Poor Ma! She's only got me to talk to.

DREW. Maybe I can help after all. I can talk to Nat.

SUE (*shaking her head*). He's not the same Nat, Danny.

DREW (*trying to be consoling*). Pshaw, Sue! I think you just get to imagining things. (*As he finishes speaking, the door in the rear opens and Nat appears. He is a tall, loose-framed boy of eighteen, who bears a striking resemblance to his father. His face, like his father's, is large and bony, with deep-set black eyes, an aquiline nose, and a wide, thin-lipped mouth. There is no suggestion in Nat, however, of the older man's physical health and great strength. He appears an indoor product, undeveloped in muscle, with a sallow complexion and stooped shoulders. His thick hair is a deep black. His voice recalls his father's, hollow and penetrating. He is dressed in a grey flannel shirt and corduroy trousers. Drew calls out to him heartily.*) Hello, Nat! Speak of the Devil! Sue and I were just talking about you. (*He goes toward Nat, his hand outstretched.*)

NAT (*comes toward them, meets Drew, and shakes his hand with evident pleasure*). Hello, Danny! You're a sight for sore eyes! (*His manner undergoes a sudden change. He casts a quick, suspicious glance from Drew to his sister.*) You were talking about me? What about?

SUE (*quickly – with a warning glance at Drew*). About your work down at the shipyard.

NAT (*disgustedly*). Oh, that. (*In a tone of reasonless irritation.*) For God's sake, Sue, let me alone about my work. Don't I have to live with the damn thing all day, without your shoving it in my face the minute I get home? I want to forget it – get away!

DREW. Go to sea, eh?

NAT (*suspiciously*). Maybe. Why? What do you mean?

DREW (*warned by a glance from Sue, says carelessly*). Well, that's where you'd be apt to go, isn't it?

NAT (*suspiciously*). That isn't what you were thinking, Danny. (*Turning to his sister – angrily.*) What have you been telling Danny?

SUE. I was talking about the schooner – telling him that she sails to-morrow.

NAT (*dumbfounded*). To-morrow? (*Overcome by*

53

sudden, nervous excitement.) It can't be. How do you know? Who told you?

SUE. Ma. Pa told her.

NAT. Then she's been talking to him – telling him not to take me, I'll bet. (*Angrily.*) Oh, I wish Ma'd mind her own business!

SUE. Nat!

NAT. Well, Sue, how would you like it? I'm not a little boy any more. I know what I want to do. I want to go with them. I want to go more than I've ever wanted anything else in my life before. He – he doesn't want me. He's afraid I — But I think I can force him to — (*He glances at Drew's amazed face and stops abruptly – sullenly.*) Where is Pa?

SUE. He's aboard the schooner.

NAT (*disappointedly*). Then it's no good trying to see him now. I'll have to wait.

DREW. Sound's funny to hear you talking about going to sea. Why, you always used —

NAT (*wearily*). I know. This is different.

DREW. You want to see the Islands, I suppose?

NAT (*suspiciously*). Maybe. Why not?

DREW. What group is your Pa heading for first?

NAT (*more suspiciously*). You'll have to ask him. Why do you want to know? (*Abruptly.*) You better be getting up to the house, Sue – if we're to

54

have any supper. Danny must be hungry. (*He turns his back on them. They exchange meaning glances.*)

SUE (*with a sigh*). It must be getting late. Come on, Danny. You can see Pa later on. (*They go toward the door in the rear.*) Aren't you coming, Nat?

NAT. No. I'll wait. (*Impatiently.*) Go ahead. I'll be up before long.

DREW. See you later, then, Nat.

NAT. Yes.

> (*They go out, rear. Nat paces up and down in a great state of excitement. The door on the left is opened and Bartlett enters. His eyes are wild, as if he had been drinking heavily, but he shows no other effects. Father and son stand looking at one another for a second. Nat takes a step backward as if in fear, then straightens up defiantly.*)

BARTLETT (*slowly*). Is this the way ye mind my orders, boy? I've told ye time an' again not to be sneakin' and spyin' around this wharf.

NAT. I'm not sneaking and spying. I wanted to talk to you, Pa.

BARTLETT (*sits down by the table*). Well, here I be.

NAT. Sue said the schooner sails to-morrow.

BARTLETT. Aye!

NAT (*resolutely*). I want to go with you, Pa.

BARTLETT (*briefly — as if dismissing the matter*). Ye can't. I've told ye that before. Let this be the last time ye ask it.

NAT. But why? Why can't I go?

BARTLETT. Ye've your own work to do – good work. Attend to that and leave me to mine.

NAT. But you always wanted me to go on voyages to learn whaling with you.

BARTLETT. This be different.

NAT (*with excited indignation*). Yes, this is different! Don't I know it? Do you think you can hide that from me? It is different, and that's why I want to go.

BARTLETT. Ye can't, I say.

NAT (*pleadingly*). But why not, Pa? I'm not a boy. I can do a man's work on a ship, or anywhere else.

BARTLETT (*roughly*). Let's have done with talk! Your place is here, with Sue and your Ma, and here you'll stay.

NAT (*angrily*). That isn't any reason. But I know your real one. You're afraid —

BARTLETT (*half-rising to his feet*). Ye say that to me? (*Recovering himself with an effort and settling down again.*) Keep a clapper on your jaw, boy.

That's talk I'll not put up with. (*With a touch of uneasiness — forcing a scornful laugh.*) Afeerd! Afeerd o' what? Did ye ever know me to be afeerd?

NAT. Afraid of what I know, of what I might find out if I went with you.

BARTLETT (*with the same forced, uneasy scorn*). And what d'ye think ye'd find out, Nat?

NAT. First of all that it's not a trading venture you're going on. Oh, I'm not a fool! That story is all right to fool the neighbours and girls like Sue. But I know better.

BARTLETT. What d'ye know?

NAT. You're going for something else.

BARTLETT. What would that be?

NAT. I don't know — exactly. Something — on that island.

BARTLETT. What?

NAT. I don't know. But I could guess a lot of things. (*With sudden excitement.*) Ambergris! That's it! Is that it? It must be. That's what you've been hunting for years.

BARTLETT. Aye — and never found! (*He gets to his feet with a forced burst of laughter.*) Ambergris! Ye fool of a boy! Ye got that notion out o' some fool book ye've been reading, didn't ye? And I thought ye'd growed to be a man! (*More and more*

57

wild in his forced scorn.) Ye'll be tellin' me next it's buried treasure I be sailin' after – pirates' gold buried on that island – all in a chest – and a map to guide me with a cross marked on it where the gold is hid! And then they be ghosts guardin' it, ben't they – spirits o' murdered men? They always be, in the books. (*He laughs scornfully*.)

NAT (*gazing at him with fascinated eyes*). No, not that last. That's silly – but I did think you might have found —

BARTLETT (*laughing again*). Treasure? Gold? (*With forced sternness*.) Nat, I be ashamed of ye. Ye've had schoolin', and ye've been doin' a man's work in the world, and doin' it well, and I'd hoped ye'd take my place here to home when I be away, and look after your Ma and Sue. But ye've owned up to bein' little better nor a boy in short britches, dreamin' o' pirates' gold that never was 'cept in books.

NAT. But you – you're to blame. When you first came home you did nothing but talk mysteriously of how rich we'd all be when the schooner got back.

BARTLETT (*roughly*). But what's that to do with silly dreams? It's in the line o' trade I meant.

NAT. But why be so mysterious about trade? There's something you're hiding. You can't say no, because I feel it.

BARTLETT (*insinuatingly – with a crafty glance at*

58

his son). Supposin' in one of them Eastern trading ports I'd run across a bit o' business with a chance for a fortune in it for a man that wasn't afeerd of the law, and could keep his mouth shut?

NAT (*disappointed*). You mean illegal trading?

BARTLETT. I mean what I mean, Nat — and I'd be a fool to tell an overgrown boy, or two women — or any man in the world, for the matter o' that — what I do mean.

NAT (*turning toward the door in the rear — disgustedly*). If it's only that, I don't want to hear it. (*He walks toward the door — stops and turns again to his father.*) No, I don't believe it. That's not like you. You're not telling the truth, Pa.

BARTLETT (*rising to his feet — with a savage sternness in which there is a wild note of entreaty*). I've listened to your fool's talk enough. Get up to the house where ye belong! I'll stand no more o' your meddling in business o' mine. I've been patient with ye, but there's an end to that! Take heed o' what I'm sayin', if ye know what's good for ye! I'd rather see ye dead to-night than sail on that schooner at dawn. I'd kill ye with my own hands first! (*With a sort of sombre pride.*) I'll stand alone in this business and finish it out alone if I go to hell for it. Ye hear me?

NAT (*alarmed by this outburst — submissively*). Yes, Pa.

BARTLETT. Then see that ye heed. (*After a pause*

59

— as Nat lingers.) They'll be waitin' for ye at the house.

NAT. All right. I'll go. (*He turns to the doorway on the left, but before he gets to it, the door is pushed open and Mrs. Bartlett enters. Nat stops, startled*). Ma!

MRS. BARTLETT (*with a forced smile*). Run along, Nat. It's all right. I want to speak with your Pa.

BARTLETT (*uneasily*). You'd best go up with Nat, Sarah. I've work to do.

MRS. BARTLETT (*fixing her eyes on her husband*). I want to talk with you alone, Isaiah.

BARTLETT (*grimly — as if he were accepting a challenge*). As ye like, then.

MRS. BARTLETT (*dismissing Nat with a feeble attempt at a smile*). Tell Sue I'll be comin' up directly, Nat.

NAT (*hesitates for a moment, looking from one to the other uneasily*). All right, Ma. (*He goes out.*)

BARTLETT (*waits for Nat to get out of hearing*). Won't ye set, Sarah? (*She comes forward and sits by the table. He sits by the other side.*)

MRS. BARTLETT (*shuddering as she sees the bottle on the table*). Will drinkin' this poison make you forget, Isaiah?

BARTLETT (*gruffly*). I've naught to forget — least-ways naught that's in your mind. But they's things

60

about the stubborn will o' woman I'd like to forget. (*They look at each other across the table. There is a pause. Finally he cannot stand her accusing glance. He looks away, gets to his feet, walks about, then sits down again, his face set determinedly – with a grim smile.*) Well, here we be, Sarah – alone together for the first time since —

MRS. BARTLETT (*quickly*). Since that night, Isaiah.

BARTLETT (*as if he hadn't heard*). Since I come back to you, almost. Did ye ever stop to think o' how strange it be we'd ever come to this? I never dreamed a day'd come when ye'd force me to sleep away from ye, alone in a shed like a mangy dog!

MRS. BARTLETT (*gently*). I didn't drive you away, Isaiah. You came o' your own will.

BARTLETT. Because o' your naggin' tongue, woman – and the wrong ye thought o' me.

MRS. BARTLETT (*shaking her head, slowly*). It wasn't me you ran from, Isaiah. You ran away from your own self – the conscience God put in you that you think you can fool with lies.

BARTLETT (*starting to his feet – angrily*). Lies?

MRS. BARTLETT. It's the truth, Isaiah, only you be too weak to face it.

BARTLETT (*with defiant bravado*). Ye'll find I be strong enough to face anything, true or lie! (*Then protestingly.*) What call have ye to think evil o' me, Sarah? It's mad o' ye to hold me to account for

61

things I said in my sleep — for the damned nightmares that set me talkin' wild when I'd just come home and my head was still cracked with the thirst and the sun I'd borne on that island. Is that right, woman, to be blamin' me for mad dreams?

MRS. BARTLETT. You confessed the rest of what you said was true — of the gold you'd found and buried there.

BARTLETT (*with a sudden fierce exultation*). Aye — that be true as Bible, Sarah. When I've sailed back in the schooner, ye'll see for yourself. There be a big chest o' it, yellow and heavy, and fixed up with diamonds, emeralds and sech, that be worth more, even, nor the gold. We'll be rich, Sarah — rich like I've always dreamed we'd be! There'll be silks and carriages for ye — all the woman's truck in the world ye've a mind to want — and all that Nat and She'll want, too.

MRS. BARTLETT (*with a shudder*). Are you tryin' to bribe me, Isaiah — with a treasure that's been cursed by God?

BARTLETT (*as if he hadn't heard*). D'ye remember long ago, back East, just after we was married, and I was skipper o' my first whalin' ship, how that foreigner come to me with the map o' the pirates' gold and asked me to charter the ship? D'ye remember o' how I'd talk to ye o' findin' ambergris, a pile o' it on one vige that'd make us rich? Ye used to take interest then, and all th'

62

vige with me ye'd be hopin' I'd find it, too.

MRS. BARTLETT. That was my sin o' greed that I'm bein' punished for now.

BARTLETT (*again as if he hadn't heard*). And now when it's come to us at last — bigger nor I ever dreamed on — ye drive me away from ye and say it's cursed.

MRS. BARTLETT (*inexorably*). Cursed with the blood o' the man and boy ye murdered!

BARTLETT (*in a mad rage*). Ye lie, woman! I spoke no word!

MRS. BARTLETT. That's what you kept repeatin' in your sleep, night after night that first week you was home, till I knew the truth, and could bear no more. "I spoke no word!" you kept sayin', as if 'twas your own soul had you at the bar of judgment. And "That cook, he didn't believe 'twas gold," you'd say, and curse him.

BARTLETT (*wildly*). He was lyin', the thief! Lyin' so's he and the boy could steal th' gold. I made him own up he was lyin'. What if it's all true, what ye heard? Hadn't we the right to do away with two thieves? And we was all mad with thirst and sun. Can ye hold madmen to account for the things they do?

MRS. BARTLETT. You wasn't so crazed but you remember.

BARTLETT. I remember I spoke no word, Sarah — as God's my judge!

MRS. BARTLETT. But you could have prevented it with a word, couldn't you, Isaiah? That heathen savage lives in the fear of you. He'd not have done it if —

BARTLETT (*gloomily*). That's woman's talk. There be three o' us can swear in any court I spoke no word.

MRS. BARTLETT. What are courts? Can you swear it to yourself? You can't, and it's that's drivin' you mad, Isaiah. Oh, I'd never have believed it of you for all you said in sleep, if it wasn't for the way you looked and acted out of sleep. I watched you that first week, Isaiah, till the fear of it had me down sick. I had to watch you, you was so strange and fearful to me. At first I kept sayin', 'twas only you wasn't rid o' the thirst and the sun yet. But then, all to once, God gave me sight, and I saw 'twas guilt written on your face, on the queer stricken way you acted, and guilt in your eyes. (*She stares into them.*) I see it now, as I always see it when you look at me. (*She covers her face with her hands with a sob.*)

BARTLETT (*his face haggard and drawn — hopelessly, as if he were too beaten to oppose her further — in a hoarse whisper*). What would ye have me do, Sarah?

MRS. BARTLETT (*taking her hands from her face —*

her eyes lighting up with religious fervour). Confess
your sin, Isaiah! Confess to God and men, and
make your peace and take your punishment. Forget that gold that's cursed and the voyage you be
settin' out on, and make your peace. (*Passionately.*)
I ask you to do this for my sake and the children's,
and your own most of all! I'll get down on my
knees, Isaiah, and pray you to do it, as I've prayed
to God to send you his grace! Confess and wash
your soul of the stain o' blood that's on it. I ask
you that, Isaiah — and God asks you — to make
your peace with Him.

BARTLETT (*his face tortured by the inward struggle —
as if the word strangled him*). Confess and let some
one steal the gold! (*This thought destroys her influ-
ence over him in a second. His obsession regains possession of him instantly, filling him with rebellious
strength. He laughs harshly.*) Ye'd make an old
woman o' me, would ye, Sarah? — an old, Sunday
go-to-meetin' woman snivvelin' and prayin' to
God for pardon! Pardon for what? Because two
sneakin' thieves are dead and done for? I spoke no
word, I tell ye — but if I had, I'd not repent it.
What I've done I've done, and I've never asked
pardon o' God or men for aught I've done, and
never will. Confess, and give up the gold I've
dreamed of all my life that I've found at last! By
thunder, ye must think I'm crazed.

MRS. BARTLETT (*seeming to shrivel up on her chair*

as she sees she has lost — weakly). You be lost, Isaiah — no one can stop you.

BARTLETT (*triumphantly*). Aye, none'll stop me. I'll go my course alone. I'm glad ye see that, Sarah.

MRS. BARTLETT (*feebly trying to get to her feet*). I'll go home.

BARTLETT. Ye'll stay, Sarah. Ye've had your say, and I've listened to ye; now I'll have mine and ye listen to me. (*Mrs. Bartlett sinks back in her chair exhaustedly. Bartlett continues slowly.*) The schooner sails at dawn on the full tide. I ask ye again and for the last time, will ye christen her with your name afore she sails?

MRS. BARTLETT (*firmly*). No.

BARTLETT (*menacingly*). Take heed, Sarah, o' what ye're sayin'! I'm your husband ye've sworn to obey. By right I kin order ye, not ask.

MRS. BARTLETT. I've never refused in anything that's right — but this be wicked wrong.

BARTLETT. It's only your stubborn woman's spite makes ye refuse. Ye've christened every ship I've ever been skipper on, and it's brought me luck o' a kind, though not the luck I wanted. And we'll christen this one with your own name to bring me the luck I've always been seekin'.

MRS. BARTLETT (*resolutely*). I won't, Isaiah.

BARTLETT. Ye will, Sarah, for I'll make ye. Ye force me to it.

MRS. BARTLETT (*again trying to get up*). Is this the way you talk to me who've been a good wife to you for more than thirty years?

BARTLETT (*commandingly*). Wait! (*Threateningly.*) If ye don't christen her afore she sails, I'll take Nat on the vige along with me. (*Mrs. Bartlett sinks back in her chair, stunned.*) He wants to go, ye know it. He's asked me a hundred times. He s'pects — 'bout the gold — but he don't know for sartin. But I'll tell him the truth o' it, and he'll come with me, unless —

MRS. BARTLETT (*looking at him with terror-stricken eyes — imploringly*). You won't do that, Isaiah? You won't take Nat away from me and drag him into sin? I know he'll go if you give him the word, in spite of what I say. (*Pitifully.*) You be only frightenin' me! You can't be so wicked cruel as that.

BARTLETT. I'll do it, I take my oath — unless —

MRS. BARTLETT (*with hysterical anger*). Then I'll tell him myself — of the murders you did, and —

BARTLETT (*grimly*). And I'll say 'twas done in fair fight to keep them from stealin' the gold! I'll tell him your's is a woman's notion, and he'll believe me, not you. He's his father's son, and he's set to go. Ye know it, Sarah. (*She falls back in the chair hopelessly staring at him with horrified eyes. He turns away and adds after a pause.*) So ye'll christen the Sarah Allen in the mornin' afore she sails, won't ye, Sarah?

MRS. BARTLETT (*in a terrified tone*). Yes – if it's needful to save Nat – and God'll forgive me when He sees my reason. But you – Oh, Isaiah! (*She shudders and then breaks down, sobbing.*)

BARTLETT (*after a pause, turns to her humbly as if asking her forgiveness*). Ye mustn't think hard o' me that I want your name. It's because it's a good woman's name, and I know it'll bring luck to our vige. I'd find it hard to sail without it – the way things be.

MRS. BARTLETT (*getting to her feet – in a state of feverish fear of him*). I'm goin' home.

BARTLETT (*going to her*). I'll help ye to the top o' the hill, Sarah.

MRS. BARTLETT (*shrinking from him in terror*). No. Don't you touch me! Don't you touch me!

> (*She hobbles quickly out of the door in the rear, looking back frightenedly over her shoulder to see if he is following as*

The Curtain Falls)

ACT THREE

SCENE. *Dawn of the following morning — exterior of the Bartlett home, showing the main entrance, facing left, toward the harbour. On either side of the door, two large windows, their heavy green shutters tightly closed. In front of the door, a small porch, the roof supported by four white columns. A flight of three steps goes up to this porch from the ground. Two paths lead to the steps through the straggly patches of grass, one around the corner of the house to the rear, the other straight to the left to the edge of the cliff where there is a small projecting iron platform, fenced in by a rail. The top of a steel ladder can be seen. This ladder leads up the side of the cliff from the shore below to the platform. The edge of the cliff extends from the left corner front, half-diagonally back to the right, rear-centre.*

In the grey half-light of the dawn, Horne, Cates, and Jimmy Kanaka are discovered. Horne is standing on the steel platform looking down at the shore below. Cates is sprawled on the ground near by. Jimmy squats on his haunches, his eyes staring out to sea as if he were trying to pierce the distance to the warm islands of his birth. Cates wears dungarees, Jimmy dungaree trousers and a black jersey; Horne the same as in ACT TWO.

CATES (*with sluggish indifference*). Ain't she finished with it yet?

69

HORNE (*irritably*). No, damn her! I kin see
'em all together on the wharf at the bow o' the
schooner. That old crow o' a woman o' his! Why
the hell don't she christen her and be done with it
and let us make sail?

CATES (*after a pause*). Funny, ain't it – his order-
in' us to come up here and wait till it's all done.

HORNE (*angrily*). That's her doin', too. She
thinks we ain't good enough to be where she is.
(*After a pause.*) But there's nothin' funny to me
that he does no more. He's still out o' his head,
d'ye know that, Cates?

CATES (*stupidly*). I ain't noticed nothin' diff'rent
'bout him.

HORNE (*scornfully*). He axed me if I ever seen
them two in my sleep – that cook and the boy o'
the *Triton*. Said he did often.

CATES (*immediately protesting uneasily as if he had
been accused*). They was with us in the boat b'fore
we fetched the island, that's all 'bout 'em I remember. I was crazy, after.

HORNE (*looking at him with contempt*). So was we
all crazy, for the matter o' that. I'll not call ye a
liar, Cates, but – a hell o' a man ye be! You wasn't
so out o' your head that ye forgot the gold, was ye?

CATES (*his eyes glistening*). That's diff'rent. Any
man'd remember that, even if he was crazy.

HORNE (*with a greedy grin*). Aye. That's the one

thing I see in my sleep. (*Gloatingly.*) We'll dig it up soon now. In three months we'd ought to be there – an' then we'll be rich, by Christ! (*There is the faint sound of cries from the beach below. Horne starts and turns to look down again.*) They must 'a' finished it. (*Cates and Jimmy come to the edge to look down.*)

JIMMY (*suddenly – with an eager childish curiosity*). That fella wife Captain she make strong fella spell on ship, we sail fast, plenty good wind?

HORNE (*contemptuously*). Aye, that's as near as ye'll come to it. She's makin' a spell. Ye stay here, Jimmy, and tell us when the Old Man is comin'. (*Jimmy remains looking down. Horne motions Cates to follow him, front – then in a low voice, disgustedly.*) Did ye hear that damn fool nigger?

CATES (*grumblingly*). Why the hell is the Old Man givin' him a full share? One piece o' it'd be enough for a nigger like him.

HORNE (*craftily*). There's a way to get rid o' him – if it comes to that. He knifed them two, ye remember.

CATES. Aye.

HORNE. The two o' us can take oath to that in any court.

CATES. Aye.

HORNE (*after a calculating look into his companion's greedy eyes – meaningly*). We're two sane men,

71

Cates — and the other two to share is a lunatic and a nigger. The skipper's showed me where there's a copy o' his map o' the island locked up in the cabin — in case anything happens to him I'm to bring back the gold to his woman, he says. (*He laughs harshly.*) Bring it back! Catch me! The fool! I'll be open with ye, Cates. If I could navigate and find the island myself I wouldn't wait for a cracked man to take me there. No, be damned if I would! Me and you'd chance it alone some way or other.

CATES (*greedily*). The two o' us — share and share alike! (*Then shaking his head warningly.*) But he's a hard man to git the best on.

HORNE (*grimly*). And I be a hard man, too. And he's not right in his head. We'll keep our eyes peeled for a chance. Something may turn up — and maybe —

JIMMY (*turning to them*). Captain, he come.

> (*Cates and Horne separate hastily. Bartlett climbs into sight up the ladder to the platform. He is breathing heavily, but his expression is one of triumphant exultation..*)

BARTLETT (*motions with his arms*). Down with ye and git aboard. The schooner's got a name now — a name that'll bring us luck. We'll sail on this tide.

HORNE. Aye — aye, sir.

BARTLETT. I got to wait here till they climb up the path. I'll be aboard afore long. See that ye have her ready to cast off by then.

HORNE. Aye – aye, sir. (*He and Cates disappear down the ladder. Jimmy lingers, looking sidewise at his Captain.*)

BARTLETT (*noticing him – gruffly but almost kindly*). What are ye waitin' for?

JIMMY (*volubly*). That old fella wife belong you, Captain, she make strong fella spell for wind blow plenty? She catch strong devil charm for schooner, Captain?

BARTLETT (*scowling*). What's that, ye brown devil? (*Then suddenly laughing harshly.*) Yes – a strong spell to bring us luck. (*Roughly.*) Git aboard, ye dog! Don't let her find ye here with me.

> (*Jimmy disappears hurriedly down the ladder. Bartlett remains at the edge looking down after him. There is a sound of voices from the right and presently Mrs. Bartlett, Sue, Drew and Nat enter, coming around the house from the rear. Nat and Drew walk at either side of Mrs. Bartlett, who is in a state of complete collapse, so that they are practically carrying her. Sue follows, her handkerchief to her eyes. Nat keeps his eyes on the ground, his expression fixed and gloomy. Drew casts a glance of angry*)

indignation at the Captain, who, after one indifferent look at them, has turned back to watch the operations on the schooner below.)

BARTLETT (*as they reach the steps of the house — intent on the work below — makes a megaphone of his hands and shouts in stentorian tones*). Look lively there, Horne!

SUE (*protestingly*). Pa!

BARTLETT (*wheels about. When he meets his daughter's eyes he controls his angry impatience and speaks gently*). What d'ye want, Sue?

SUE (*pointing to her mother who is being assisted through the door — her voice trembling*). You mustn't shout. She's very sick.

BARTLETT (*dully, as if he didn't understand*). Sick?

SUE (*turning to the door*). Wait. I'll be right back.

(*She enters the house. As soon as she is gone all of Bartlett's excitement returns. He paces up and down with nervous impatience. Nat comes out of the house.*)

NAT (*in a tone of anxiety*). Ma seems bad. We can't do anything. I'm going for the doctor. (*As his father doesn't seem to hear him — tapping him on the shoulder, his voice breaking.*) Why did you make her do it, Pa? It was too much for her strength. Wouldn't anyone else or any other name have done just as well?

74

GOLD

BARTLETT (*impatiently*). No. It had to be.

NAT. When she spoke the words — and fell back in a faint — I thought she was dead.

BARTLETT (*vaguely*). Weakness. She'll be all right again after a rest. (*He draws Nat's attention to the schooner.*) Smart lines on that schooner, boy. She'll sail hell bent in a breeze. I knowed what I was about when I bought her.

NAT (*staring down fascinatedly*). How long will the voyage take?

BARTLETT (*preoccupied*). How long?

NAT (*insinuatingly*). To get to the island.

BARTLETT. Three months at most — with fair luck. (*Exultantly*). And I'll have luck now!

NAT. Then in six months you may be back — with *it*?

BARTLETT. Aye, with — (*Stopping abruptly, turns and stares into his son's eyes — angrily*). With what? What boy's foolishness be ye talkin'?

NAT (*pleading fiercely*). I want to go, Pa! There's no good in my staying here any more. I can't think of anything but — Oh, why don't you be fair and let me sail with you!

BARTLETT (*sternly, to conceal his uneasiness*). Keep clear o' this, boy, I've warned ye!

SUE (*appearing in doorway — indignantly*). Nat! Haven't you gone for the doctor yet?

75

NAT (*shamefacedly*). 1 forgot.

SUE. Forgot!

NAT (*starting off*). I'm going, Sue. (*Then over his shoulder.*) You won't sail before I come back, Pa? (*Bartlett does not answer. Nat stands miserably hesitating.*)

SUE. Nat! For heaven's sake!

(*Nat hurries off around the corner of the house, rear. Sue comes to her father who is watching her with a queer, humble, hunted expression.*)

BARTLETT. Well, Sue?

SUE (*her voice trembling*). Oh, Pa, how can you do such terrible things. How could you drag Ma out of bed at dawn to christen your old boat – when you knew how sick she's been!

BARTLETT (*avoiding her eyes*). It's only weakness. She'll get well o' it soon.

SUE. Pa! How can you say things like that – as if you didn't care! (*Accusingly.*) The way you've acted ever since you've been home almost, anyone would think – you *hated* her!

BARTLETT (*wincing*). No!

SUE. Oh, Pa, what is it that has come between you? Can't you tell me? Can't I help to set things right again?

BARTLETT (*mumblingly*). Nothin' – nothin' ye kin

76

help – nor me. Keep clear o' it, Sue. Danny – ye think o' him, that's enough for ye.

SUE. But things can't go on like this. Don't you see how it's killing Ma?

BARTLETT. She'll forget her stubborn notions, now I be sailin' away.

SUE. But you're not – not going for a while now, are you?

BARTLETT. Ain't I been sayin' I'd sail at dawn to-day? They're makin' her ready to cast off. I'm waitin' for Horne to hail.

SUE (*looking at him for a moment with shocked amazement*). But – you can't mean – right now!

BARTLETT (*keeping his face averted*). Aye – or we'll miss this tide.

SUE (*putting her hands on his shoulders and trying to look into his face*). Pa! You can't mean that! (*His face is set with his obsessed determination. She lets her hands fall with a shudder.*) You can't be as cruel as that! Why, I thought, of course, you'd put off — (*Wildly.*) You have, haven't you, Pa? You did tell those men you couldn't sail when you saw how sick Ma was, didn't you – when she fainted down on the wharf?

BARTLETT (*implacably*). I said I was sailin' by this tide – and sail I will, by thunder!

SUE. Pa! (*Then pleadingly.*) When the doctor comes and you hear what he says —

BARTLETT (*roughly*). I ain't stoppin' on his word nor any man's. I know what's best to do. (*Intensely.*) That schooner's been fit to sail these two weeks past. I been waitin' on her stubborn will (*he gestures toward the house*), eatin' my heart out day and night. Then I swore I'd sail to-day. I tell ye, Sue, I got a feelin' in my bones if I don't put out now I never will. Aye, I feel it deep down inside me. (*In a tone of superstitious awe.*) And when she christened the schooner — jest to the minute, mind ye! — a fair breeze sprung up and come down out o' the land to blow her out to sea — like a sign o' good luck.

SUE (*aroused to angry indignation*). What kind of a man have you become — to think of such things now! Oh, I can't believe you're the same man who used to be my father!

BARTLETT. Sue!

SUE. To talk cold-bloodedly of sailing away on a long voyage when Ma's inside — dying for all you seem to know or care! Oh, I hate you when you're like this! You're not the father I love! You've changed into some one else — hateful and cruel — and I hate him, I hate him! (*She breaks down, sobbing hysterically.*)

BARTLETT (*who has listened to her with a face suddenly stricken by fear and torturing remorse*). Sue! Ye don't know what ye be sayin', do ye?

SUE. I do! You're not the same to me any more

78

– or to any of us. I'm afraid of you. And when you coldly propose to go away – now – I hate you, yes I do! And I hate those three awful men who make you act this way. I hate the schooner! I wish she and they were at the bottom of the sea!

BARTLETT (*frenziedly – putting his hand over her mouth to stop her words*). Stop, girl! Don't ye dare —

SUE (*shrinking away from him – frightenedly*). Pa!

BARTLETT (*bewilderedly, pleading for forgiveness*). Don't heed that, Sue – I didn't mean – ye git me so riled – I'd not hurt ye for all the gold in the world. But don't ye talk wrong o' things ye can't know on.

SUE. Oh, Pa, what kind of things must they be – when you're ashamed to tell them!

BARTLETT. I ain't ashamed. It ain't that. On'y they be things a girl's no call to meddle in. They be men's business and I be man enough to carry 'em out alone. Ye'll know all they be to know – and your Ma and Nat, too – when I come back from this vige. And the sooner I sail, the quicker I'll be back to ye. Oh, ye'll be glad enough then – when ye see with your own eyes! Ye'll bless me then 'stead o' turning agin me! (*Hesitating for a second – then sombrely.*) On'y now – till it's all over and done – ye'd best keep clear o' it.

SUE (*passionately*). I don't care – I don't want to know anything about it. What I do know is that

79

you can't sail now. Oh, Pa, don't you see you can't? Haven't you any heart at all? Can't you see how bad Ma is?

BARTLETT. It's the sight o' me sickens her. She'll git better with me away from her.

SUE. No. She needs you. She doesn't want you to go. She called your name just a while ago – the only word she's spoken since she christened the ship. Come in to her, Pa! Tell her you won't go!

BARTLETT (*desperately*). I got to git away from her, I tell ye, Sue! She's been houndin' me ever since I got back – houndin' me with her stubborn tongue till she's druv me mad, a'most! Ye've been on'y givin' thought to her, not me. They's my side to it, too!

SUE. I'll talk to her, Pa. She can't realize she's hurting you or she wouldn't — And then everything will be just the same as it used to be again.

BARTLETT (*shaking his head*). They be too much between. The only chance for that be my plan – to sail away and come back with – what I be seekin'. Then she'll give over her stubborn naggin' – if she's human woman. It's for her sake as much as my own I'm goin' – for her and you and Nat. (*With a sudden return of his old resolution.*) I've made up my mind, I tell ye, and in the end ye'll know I be right. (*A hail in Horne's voice comes thinly up from the shore below. Bartlett starts, his eyes gleaming.*) Ye hear? It's Horne hailin' me to come. They be ready to cast off. I'll git aboard. (*He starts for the ladder.*)

SUE. Pa! After all I've said – without one word of good-bye to Ma! (*Hysterically.*) Oh, what can I do, what can I say to stop you! She hasn't spoken but that one call for you. She hardly seems to breathe. If it weren't for her eyes I'd believe she was dead – but her eyes look for you. She'll die if you go, Pa!

BARTLETT. No!

SUE. You might just as well kill her now in cold blood as murder her that way!

BARTLETT (*shaken – raising his hands as if to put them over his ears to shut out her words – hoarsely*). No! Ye lie! She'll live till I git back and all'll be as it was again!

DREW (*appearing in the doorway, his face working with grief and anger – harshly*). Captain Bartlett! (*Then lowering his voice as he sees Sue.*) Mrs. Bartlett is asking to see you, Captain, before you go.

SUE. There! Didn't I tell you, Pa!

BARTLETT (*struggling with himself – dully*). She's wantin' to hound me again, that be all.

SUE (*seeing him weakening – grasps his hand persuasively*). Pa! Come with me. She won't hound you. How silly you are! Come! (*Hesitatingly, head bowed, he follows her toward the door.*)

BARTLETT (*as he comes to Drew he stops and looks*

into the young man's angry, accusing face. He mutters half-mockingly). So ye, too, be agin me, Danny?

DREW (*unable to restrain his indignation*). What man that's a real man wouldn't be against you, sir?

SUE (*frightenedly*). Danny! Pa!

BARTLETT (*in a sudden rage draws back his fist threateningly. Drew stares into his eyes unflinchingly – Bartlett controls himself with an effort and lets his arm fall to his side – scornfully*). Big words from a boy, Danny. I'll forget them this time – on account o' Sue. (*He turns to her.*) I'm goin' in to her to please ye, Sue – but if ye think any words that she kin say'll change my mind, ye make a mistake – for I be sailin' out as I planned I would in spite o' all hell! (*He walks resolutely into the house. Sue follows him after exchanging a hopeless glance with Danny.*)

DREW (*to himself – with a shudder*). He's mad, damn him!

> (*He paces up and down. Horne appears on the ladder from below, followed by Cates.*)

HORNE (*coming forward and addressing Drew*). Is the skipper about?

DREW (*curtly*). He's in the house. You can't speak to him now.

HORNE. She's ready to cast off. I hailed him from below, but I 'spect he didn't hear. (*As Drew*

82

makes no comment – impatiently.) If he don't shake a leg, we'll miss the tide. There's a bit o' fair breeze, too.

DREW (*glancing at him resentfully*). Don't count on his sailing to-day. It's just as likely he'll change his mind.

HORNE (*angrily*). Change his mind again? After us waitin' and wastin' time for weeks! (*To Cates in a loud tone so Drew can hear.*) What did I tell ye, Cates? He's crazy as hell.

DREW (*sharply*). What's that?

HORNE. I was tellin' Cates the skipper's not right in his head. (*Angrily.*) What man in his senses'd do the way he does?

DREW (*letting his resentment escape him*). That's no lie, damn it!

HORNE (*surprised*). Aye, ye've seen it, too, have ye? (*After a pause.*) Now I axe ye, as a sailor, how'd ye like to be puttin' out on a vige with a cracked man for skipper?

> (*Sue comes out of the door, stops with a shudder of disgust as she sees the two sailors, and stands listening. They do not notice her presence.*)

DREW. It seems to me a crazy voyage all round. What kind of trading is it you're to do?

HORNE (*suspiciously*). Ye'll have to ask the skipper that.

DREW (*with a scornful shrug*). I was forgetting it's such a dead secret. That the craziest part, eh? (*With sudden interest as if a new idea had come to him.*) But you know all about it, don't you – what the Captain plans to do on this voyage – and all that?

HORNE (*dryly*). Aye, as well as himself – but I'm tellin' no man.

DREW. And I'm not asking. What do you suppose I care about any sneaking trade deal in the Islands he may have up his sleeve? What I want to find out is: Do you know enough about this business to make this one voyage alone and attend to everything – in case the Captain can't go?

HORNE (*exchanging a quick glance with Cates – trying to hide his eagerness*). Aye, I could do as well as any man alive. I've been sailin' this sea for twenty year or more and I know the Island trade inside and out. He could trust me for it – and I'd make more money for him than he's likely to make with his head out o' gear. (*Then scowling.*) On'y trouble is, who'd captain her if he ain't goin'?

DREW (*disappointedly*). Then you don't know navigation enough for that?

HORNE. I've never riz above bo'sun. (*Then after a pause in which he appears to be calculating something – curiously.*) Why d'ye ask me them questions? (*Insinuatingly – almost in a whisper.*) It can't be done 'less we got an officer like you aboard.

DREW (*angrily*). Eh? What're you driving at?
D'you think I —

SUE (*who has been listening with aroused interest*).
Danny! (*She comes down to him. Horne and Cates
bob their heads respectfully and move back near the
platform. Horne watches Sue and Drew out of the
corner of his eye.*) Danny, I've been listening to
what you were saying, but I don't understand.
What are you thinking of?

DREW (*excitedly*). I was thinking — Listen, Sue!
Seems to me from what I saw your Pa's out of his
right mind, and, being that way, he's sure bound
to go unless some one or something steps in to
stop him. D'you think your Ma — ?

SUE (*shaking her head — sadly*). No, I'm afraid
anything she says will only make things worse.

DREW. Then you've no hope — ? No more have
I. Something's got to be done to keep him home
in spite of himself. Even leaving your Ma out of
it, he's not in any fit state to take a ship to sea;
and I was thinking if we could fix it some way so
that fellow Horne could take her out on this
voyage —

SUE. But, Danny, Pa'd never give in to that.

DREW. I wasn't thinking he would. It'd have to
be done on the sly. We — you'd have to give the
word — and keep him in the house somehow — and
then when he did come out it'd be too late. The
schooner'd be gone.

SUE (*disturbed, but showing that his plan has caught her mind*). But – would it be fair? – he'd never forgive ——

DREW. When he's back in his right mind again, he would. (*Earnestly.*) I'm not fond of lying and tricks myself, Sue, but this is a case where you can't pick and choose. You can't let him sail, and wreck his ship and himself in the bargain, likely. Then, there's your Ma ——

SUE. No, no, we can't let him. (*With a glance at Horne and Cates.*) But I don't trust those men.

DREW. No more do I; but it would be better to chance them than —— (*Suddenly interrupting himself – with a shrug of his shoulders.*) But there's no good talking of that. I was forgetting. None of them can navigate. They couldn't take her out.

SUE. But didn't I hear him say – if they had an officer on board – like you ——

DREW. Yes, but where'll you find one at a second's notice?

SUE (*meaningly*). And you told me, didn't you, that you'd just got your master's papers. Then you're a captain by rights.

DREW (*looking at her with stunned astonishment*). Sue! D'you mean ——

SUE (*a light coming over her face*). Oh, Danny, we could trust you! He'd trust you! And after he'd calmed down I know he wouldn't mind so much.

Oh, Danny, it'll break my heart to have you go, to send you away just after you've come back. But I don't see any other way. I wouldn't ask – if it wasn't for Ma being this way – and him –– Oh, Danny, can't you see your way to do it – for my sake?

DREW (*bewilderedly*). Why, Sue, I – I never thought –– (*Then as he sees the look of disappointment which comes over her face at his hesitancy – resolutely.*) Why sure, Sue, I'll do it – if you want me to. I'll do it if it can be done. But we've got to hustle. You stand in the door, Sue. You've got to keep him in the house some way if he aims to come out. And I'll talk to them.

(*Sue goes to the doorway. Drew goes over to Horne and Cates.*)

SUE (*after listening*). He's still in with Ma. It's all right.

DREW (*to Horne, with forced joviality*). How would you like me for skipper on this one voyage?

HORNE (*craftily*). Ye got your skipper's papers all reg'lar?

DREW. Yes, that part of it's all right and square. Listen here. Miss Sue's decided her father isn't in a fit state to captain this trip. It'd mean danger for him and the schooner – and for you.

HORNE. That's no lie.

CATES (*to Horne protestingly*). But if we git ketched
87

the Old Man'll take it out o' our hides, not his'n.

HORNE (*savagely*). Shut up, ye fool! (*To Drew, craftily.*) Cates is right, jest the same. Ye are as good as his married son and she's his daughter. He'd not blame you if things went wrong. He'd take it out on us.

DREW (*impatiently*). I'll shoulder all that risk, man!

SUE (*earnestly*). No harm will come to any of you, I promise you. This is all my plan, and I'll tell my father I'm alone to blame.

HORNE (*in the tone of one clinching a bargain*). Then we'll chance it. (*Warningly.*) But it's got to be done smart, sir. Ye'd best look lively.

DREW. I've got to get my dunnage. I'll be right back and we'll tumble aboard. (*He goes to the door.*) Hold him, Sue, on some excuse if he's coming. Only a second now and it'll all be safe. (*He goes into the house. She follows him in.*)

CATES (*with stupid anger*). This is a hell o' a mess we're gettin' in, if ye axe me.

HORNE. And I tell ye it's a great stroke o' luck. It couldn't o' come out better.

CATES. He'll be aboard to spy on us.

HORNE. Let him! What does he know? He thinks we're goin' tradin', and there's no one to tell him diff'rent but me.

CATES. He'll know better afore long. He'll s'pect —

HORNE. 'Bout the gold? He ain't that kind. He's a soft young swab o' a lady steamer's mate. Leave me to fool him. And when the time comes to git rid o' him, I'll find a means some way or other. But can't ye see, ye fool, it's luck to have him with us till we git clear o' civilized ports? He kin navigate and he's got skipper's papers that'll come in handy if there's any trouble. And if anythin' goes wrong at the start and we're brung back, him and the girl'll take the blame.

CATES (*stupidly*). S'long as he don't git no share o' the gold —

HORNE (*contemptuously*). Share, ye dumbhead! I'd see him in hell first – and send him there myself.

(*Drew comes out of the house carrying his bag which he hands to Cates. Sue follows him.*)

DREW. Look lively now! Let's hustle aboard and get her under way.

HORNE. Aye – aye, sir. (*He and Cates clamber hurriedly down the ladder.*)

SUE (*throwing her arms around his neck and kissing him*). Good-bye, Danny. It's so fine of you to do this for us! I'll never forget —

DREW (*tenderly*). Ssssh! It's nothing, Sue.

SUE (*tearfully*). Oh, Danny, I hope I'm doing right! I'll miss you so dreadfully! But you'll come back just as soon as you can —

DREW. Of course!

SUE. Danny! Danny! I love you so!

DREW. And I guess you know I love you, don't you? (*Kisses her.*) And we'll be married when I come back this time *sure?*

SUE. Yes — yes — Danny — sure!

DREW. I've got to run. Good-bye, Sue.

SUE. Good-bye, dear.

> (*They kiss for the last time and he disappears down the ladder. She stands at the top, sobbing, following him with her eyes. Nat comes around the house from the rear and goes to the front door.*)

NAT (*seeing his sister*). Sue! He hasn't gone yet, has he?

> (*She doesn't hear him. He hesitates in the doorway for a moment, listening for the sound of his father's voice from inside. Then, very careful to make no noise, he tiptoes carefully into the house. Sue waves her hand to Drew who has evidently now got aboard the ship. Then she covers her face with her hands, sobbing. Nat comes out of the house again and goes to his sister. As she sees him ap-*)

proaching, she dries her eyes hastily, trying to smile.)

SUE. Did you get the doctor, Nat?

NAT. Yes, he's coming right away, he promised. (*Looking at her face.*) What – have you been crying?

SUE. No.

> (*She walks away from the edge of the cliff, drawing him with her.*)

NAT. Yes, you have. Look at your eyes.

SUE. Oh, Nat, everything's so awful! (*She breaks down again.*)

NAT (*trying to comfort her in an absent-minded way*). There, don't get worked up. Ma'll be all right as soon as the doctor comes. (*Then curiously.*) Pa's inside with her. They were arguing – have they made it up, d'you think?

SUE. Oh, Nat, I don't know. I don't think so.

NAT. The strain's been too much for him – waiting and hiding his secret from all of us. What do you suppose it is, Sue – ambergris?

SUE (*wildly*). I don't know and I don't care! (*Noticing the strange preoccupied look in his eyes – trying to bring him back to earth – scornfully.*) Ambergris! Are you going crazy? Don't you remember you've always been the first one to laugh at that silly idea?

NAT. Well, there's something — (*Starts for the*

platform. Sue does her best to interpose to hold him back.) Are they all ready on the schooner. He'll have to hurry if she's going to sail on this tide. (*With sudden passion.*) Oh, I've got to go! I can't stay here! (*Pleadingly.*) Don't you think, Sue, if you were to ask him for me he'd — You're the only one he seems to act sane with or care about any more.

SUE. No! I won't! I can't!

NAT (*angrily*). Haven't you any sense? Wouldn't it be better for every one if I went in his place?

SUE. No. You know that's a lie. Ma would lose her mind if you went.

NAT. And I'll lose mine if I stay! (*Half-aware of Sue's intention to keep him from looking down at the schooner — irritably.*) What are you holding my arm for, Sue? I want to see what they're doing. (*He pushes her aside and goes to the platform — excitedly.*) Hello, they've got the fores'l and mains'l set. They're setting the stays'l. (*In amazement.*) Why — they're casting off! She's moving away from the wharf! (*More and more excitedly.*) I see four of them on board! Who — who is that, Sue?

SUE. It's Danny.

NAT (*furiously*). Danny! What right has he — when I can't! Sue, call Pa! They're sailing, I tell you, you little fool!

SUE (*trying to calm him — her voice trembling*). Nat!

Don't be such a donkey! Danny's only going a little way — just trying the boat to see how she sails while they're waiting for Pa.

NAT (*uncertainly*). Oh. (*Then bitterly.*) I was never allowed to do even that — his own son! Look, Sue, that must be Danny at the stern waving.

SUE (*brokenly*). Yes.

> (*She waves her handkerchief over her head — then breaks down, sobbing again. There is the noise of Bartlett's voice from inside and a moment later he appears in the doorway. He seems terribly shattered, at the end of his tether. He hesitates uncertainly, looking about him wildly as if he didn't know what to do or where to go.*)

SUE (*after one look at his face, runs to him and flings her arms about his neck*). Pa! (*She weeps on his shoulder.*)

BARTLETT. Sue, ye did wrong beggin' me to see her. I knowed it'd do no good. Ye promised she'd not hound me — "Confess," she says — when they be naught to tell that couldn't be swore to in any court. "Don't go on this vige," she says, "there be the curse o' God on it." (*With a note of baffled anguish.*) She kin say that after givin' the ship her own name! (*With wild, haggard defiance.*) But curse or no curse, I be goin'!

93

(*He moves toward the platform, Sue clinging to his arm.*)

SUE (*frightenedly*). Pa! Go back in the house, won't you?

BARTLETT. I be sorry to go agin your will, Sue, but it's got to be. Ye'll know the reason some day — and be glad o' it. And now good-bye to ye. (*With a sudden strange tenderness he bends and kisses his daughter. Then as she seems about to protest further, his expression becomes stern and inflexible.*) No more o' talk, Sue! I be bound out. (*He takes her hand off his arm and strides to the platform. One look down at the harbour and he stands transfixed — in a hoarse whisper.*) What damned trick be this? (*He points to the schooner and turns to Nat bewilderedly.*) Ain't that my schooner, boy — the Sarah Allen — reachin' toward the p'int?

NAT (*surprised*). Yes, certainly. Didn't you know? Danny's trying her to see how she sails while they're waiting for you.

BARTLETT (*with a tremendous sigh of relief*). Aye. (*Then angrily.*) He takes a lot o' rope to himself without askin' leave o' me. Don't he know they's no time to waste on boy's foolin'? (*Then with admiration.*) She sails smart, don't she, boy? I knowed she'd show a pair o' heels.

NAT (*with enthusiasm*). Yes, she's a daisy! Say, Danny's taking her pretty far out, isn't he?

BARTLETT (*anxiously*). He'd ought to come about

94

now if he's to tack back inside the p'int. (*Furiously.*) Come about, damn ye! The swab! That's what comes o' steamer trainin'. I'd sooner trust Sue to sail her nor him. (*Waves his arm and shouts.*) Come about!

NAT (*bitterly*). He seems to be heading straight for the open sea. He's taking quite a sail, it seems to me.

BARTLETT (*as if he couldn't believe his eyes*). He's passed the p'int – and now – headin' her out to sea – so'east by east. By God, that be the course I charted for her! (*Sue bursts out sobbing. He wheels on her, his mouth fallen open, his face full of a stupid despair.*) They be somethin' wrong here. What be it, Sue? What be it, Nat? (*His voice has begun to quiver with passion.*) That schooner – she's sailin' without me — (*He suddenly springs at Nat and grabs him by the throat – with hoarse fury, shaking him.*) What be it, ye whelp? It's your doin' – because I wouldn't let ye go. Answer me!

SUE (*rushing to them with a scream*). Pa!

> (*She tugs frantically at his hands. Bartlett lets them fall to his side, stepping back from Nat who sinks weakly to the ground, gasping for breath. Bartlett stands looking at him wildly.*)

Nat didn't know, Pa. It's all my fault. I had to do it. There was no other way —

BARTLETT (*raging*). What d'ye mean, girl? What

is it ye've done? Tell me, I say! Tell me or I'll —

SUE (*unflinchingly*). You had to be stopped from going some way. You wouldn't listen to reason. So I asked Danny if he wouldn't make the trip in your place. He's just got his captain's papers — and oh, Pa, you can trust him, you know that! That man Horne said he knows about everything you wanted done, and he promised to tell Danny, and Danny'll come back —

BARTLETT (*chokingly*). So — that be it — (*Shaking his clenched fist at the sky as if visualizing the fate he feels in all of this.*) Curse ye! Curse ye!

> (*He subsides weakly, his strength spent, his hand falls limply at his side.*)

MRS. BARTLETT (*appears in the doorway. Her face is pale with anguish. She gives a cry of joy when she sees her son.*) Nat! (*Then with a start of horror as her eyes fall on her husband.*) Isaiah! (*He doesn't seem to hear.*) Then — you ain't sailed yet?

SUE (*going to her — gently*). No, Ma, he isn't going to sail. He's going to stay home with you. But the schooner's gone. See.

> (*She points and her mother's eyes turn seaward.*)

BARTLETT (*aloud to himself — in a tone of groping superstitious awe and bewildered fear*). They be somethin' queer — somethin' wrong — they be a curse in this somewhere —

MRS. BARTLETT (*turning accusing eyes on him — with a sort of fanatical triumph*). I'm glad to hear you confess that, Isaiah. Yes, there be a curse — God's curse on the wicked sinfulness o' men — and I thank God He's saved you from the evil of that voyage, and I'll pray Him to visit His punishment and His curse on them three men on that craft you forced me to give my name —

> (*She has raised her hand as if calling down retribution on the schooner she can dimly see.*)

SUE (*terrified*). Ma!

BARTLETT (*starting toward his wife with an insane yell of fury*). Stop it, I tell ye!

> (*He towers over her with upraised fist as if to crush her.*)

SUE. Pa!

NAT (*starting to his feet from where he has been sitting on the ground — hoarsely*). Pa! For God's sake!

MRS. BARTLETT (*gives a weak, frightened gasp*). Would you murder me too, Isaiah?

> (*She closes her eyes and collapses in Sue's arms.*)

SUE (*tremblingly*). Nat! Help me! Quick! We must carry her to bed.

> (*They take their mother in their arms, carrying her inside the house.*)

GOLD

BARTLETT (*while they are doing this, rushes in his mad frenzy to the platform over the edge of the cliff. He puts his hands to his mouth, megaphone-fashion, and yells with despairing rage*). Ahoy! Ahoy! *Sarah Allen!* Put back! Put back! (*as*

The Curtain Falls)

ACT FOUR

SCENE. *About nine o'clock of a moonlight night one year later — Captain Bartlett's "cabin," a room erected on the top of his house as a look-out post. The interior is fitted up like the cabin of a sailing vessel. On the left, forward, a porthole. Farther back, the stairs of the companionway. Still farther, two more portholes. In the rear, left, a marble-topped sideboard. In the rear, centre, a door opening on stairs which lead to the lower house. A cot with a blanket is placed against the wall to the right of door. In the right wall, five portholes. Directly under them, a wooden bench. In front of the bench, a long table with two chairs placed, one in front, one to the left of it. A cheap, dark-coloured rug is on the floor. In the ceiling, midway from front to rear, a skylight extending from opposite the door to above the left edge of the table. In the right extremity of the skylight is placed a floating ship's compass. The light from the binnacle sheds down over this and seeps into the room, casting a vague globular shadow of the compass on the floor. Moonlight creeps in through the portholes on the right. A lighted lantern is on the table.*

As the curtain rises, Sue and Doctor Berry are discovered sitting by the table. The doctor is a man of sixty or so, hale and hearty-looking, his white hair and moustache setting off his ruddy complexion. His blue eyes have a gentle

99

expression, his smile is kindly and sympathetic. His whole manner toward Sue is that of the old family doctor and friend, not the least of whose duties is to play father-confessor to his patients. She is dressed in deep mourning. She looks much older. Her face is pale and plainly marked by the ravages of suffering and grief. But there is an excited elation in her face at present, her eyes are alight with some unexpected joy.

SUE (*excitedly*). And here is Danny's letter, Doctor – to prove it's all true. (*She takes a letter from the bosom of her dress and holds it out to him.*)

DOCTOR (*takes it with a smile, patting her hand*). I can't say how glad I am, Susan. Coming after we'd all given him up for lost – it's like a miracle. Eh, well, I can hardly believe —

SUE (*smiling happily*). Read what he says. Then you won't doubt.

DOCTOR (*hesitating – playfully*). I don't know that it's right for me – love-letters at my age!

SUE. Go ahead. I want you to read it. (*He reaches in his pocket for his spectacles. Sue continues gratefully.*) As if I could have any secrets from you after all you've done for us since Ma died. You've been the only friend — (*She stops, her lips trembling.*)

DOCTOR. Tut-tut. (*He adjusts his spectacles and peers at her over them.*) Who wouldn't be of all the service he could to a brave girl like you – and

I who've known you since you were so high! Eh, well, my dear girl, this past year – with your mother's death – the state your father's in – and then the news of the schooner being reported lost – one damn thing on top of another! You've borne the whole brunt of it on your shoulders and stood up like a major. I'll tell Danny when he comes he ought to get down on his knees and thank God for getting such a wife!

sue (*flushing*). You're too good. I don't deserve it. It was just a case where some one had to carry things on.

doctor. Not many could have stood it – living in this house with him the way he is – even if he was their father.

sue (*glancing up at the skylight – apprehensively*). Ssshh! He might hear you.

doctor (*listening intently*). Not him. There he goes pacing up and down up there in the night, looking out to sea for that ship that will never come back! And your brother Nat is getting just as bad. (*Shaking himself.*) Brrr! This house of mad dreams! It's the crowning wonder to me you haven't lost your balance too – spending nearly all of your time in this crazy cabin – afraid to go out – afraid of what he might do —

sue. Don't you think Pa'll come to realize the schooner is lost as time goes by and she doesn't come back?

DOCTOR. If he was going to realize that, the report of the facts five months ago would have convinced him. There it was, plain as the nose on your face. British freighter reports finding derelict schooner. Steams near enough to read the name on the stern – *Sarah Allen*, Harbourport. Well, who could get around that evidence except a man with an obsession? No, your father won't let himself look the facts in the face. If he did, probably the shock of it would kill him. That darn dream of his has become his life. No, Susan, as time goes on he'll believe in it harder and harder. After observing him for the past year – and I speak for his own sake, too, as his good friend for twenty years or more – my final advice is the same: Send him to an asylum.

SUE (*with a shudder*). No, Doctor.

DOCTOR (*shaking his head*). You'll have to come to it in time. He's getting worse. No one can tell – he might get violent —

SUE. How can you say that? You know how gentle and sane he is with me – just like he used to be in the old days.

DOCTOR. You're his last connecting link with things as they are – but that can't last. On the other hand, I think that if we got him away from the sea, from this house, especially from this crazy cabin and the ship's deck he had built up there – (*he nods upward*) – that perhaps —

SUE (*with conviction*). No. It would kill him to leave it.

DOCTOR. Eh, well, my dear, one thing you've got to realize: Your father and Nat must be separated somehow. Nat's going to pieces. He's lost his job, he moons about this house, he takes no interest in anything but this craziness. I'll bet he doesn't believe that schooner is lost any more than your father does.

SUE. You mean he still hopes it may not be true. That's only natural. He's in San Francisco now tracing down the report again. He saw in the papers where the British freighter that found the derelict was in port again and he went to talk with the people on board. I'm hoping he'll come back fully convinced, with the whole thing out of his mind.

DOCTOR (*shaking his head – gravely*). I've watched him and talked with him — Why, even your father seems to realize, in his twisted way, that he has a bad effect on Nat.

SUE. Yes, as I've told you before, he hasn't spoken to Nat alone since the schooner sailed a year ago. And Nat sneaks about trying to spy on him – and I have to be always on the watch to keep them apart — It's terrible.

DOCTOR. You've got to persuade Nat to go away, Susan.

SUE. He won't heed me – but I was thinking

that now Danny is coming back, I'd get him —

DOCTOR. There's another thing. You can't continue to play slave to these two after you're married.

SUE (*miserably*.) We'll have to wait a while longer —

DOCTOR (*roughly*). Rats! You can't sacrifice any more of your life and Danny's to mad dreams.

SUE (*helplessly*). I don't know — (*Then brightening.*) That'll all be decided when the time comes. Just now it's enough to know Danny's alive and coming back. Read his letter, Doctor. You've been holding it in your hand all this time.

DOCTOR. Yes, yes, let's see. (*He takes the letter from the envelope.*)

SUE. Poor Danny! He's been through terrible things.

DOCTOR. Hmm! Rangoon.

SUE. Yes, he's still in the hospital there. You'll see.

DOCTOR (*reads the letter — grunts with astonishment — angrily*). By Gad! The damn scoundrels!

SUE (*shuddering*). Yes, wasn't it hideous — those awful men stabbing him and leaving him for dead in that out-of-the-way native settlement! The natives nursed him back to life, have you got that far yet? And then he was laid up for four months there waiting for a vessel to touch and take him back to civilization. And then, think of it, getting the fever on top of all that and nearly dying in the hospital in Rangoon!

DOCTOR. A terrible time of it! He's lucky to be alive. Hmm. I see he foresaw the wreck of the schooner. Those brutes couldn't navigate. (*Folding the letter and putting it back.*) He doesn't seem to have found out what the purpose of that mad trip was. Horne hid it from him to the last, he says. Well, it's queer – damn queer. But I'm glad to know those wretches have gone to their final accounting.

SUE (*with a shudder*). I was always afraid of them. They looked like – murderers. (*At a noise from below they both start. Steps can be heard climbing the stairs. Sue jumps to her feet frightenedly.*) Why – do you hear – who can that be? (*There is a soft rap on the door. The Doctor jumps to his feet. Sue turns to him with a half-hysterical laugh.*) Shall I open? I don't know why – but I'm afraid.

DOCTOR. Tut-tut! I'll see who it is. (*He opens the door and Nat is discovered on the stairs outside.*) Why hello, boy. You gave us a scare. Susan thought it was a ghost knocking.

NAT (*comes into the room. He has aged, grown thin, his face gaunt and drawn from continual mental strain, his eyes moody and preoccupied. He glances up at the skylight apprehensively, then turns to Sue*). I didn't find you downstairs, so I — (*Then to the Doctor.*) Yes, you do grow to look for ghosts in this house, don't you? (*Again glancing upward.*) He's up there as usual, I suppose — looking for a ship that'll *never, never come now*!

DOCTOR (*with a grunt of approval*). I'm glad to hear you acknowledge that.

SUE (*who is just recovering from her fright*). But Nat, I didn't expect you — Did you find out — ?

NAT. Yes, I talked with several of the men who were on board at the time. They said they steamed in so close to the schooner it was easy to read the name with the naked eye. All agreed — *Sarah Allen*, Harbourport. They even remembered how her taffrail was painted. There's no chance for mistake. The *Sarah Allen* is gone. (*With great emphasis.*) And I'm glad — damn glad! I feel as if a weight of lead had been taken off my brain. I feel free again, and I can go back to work — but not here. I've got to go away — start new altogether.

SUE (*happily, coming and putting her arms around him*). It's so good to hear you talk like your old self again.

DOCTOR (*earnestly*). Yes, Nat, by Gad, that's sound sense. Get out of this.

NAT (*giving him a queer look*). I suppose you thought I was doomed, eh? — like him. (*He makes a motion upward — then with an uncertain laugh.*)

106

A doctor's always looking for trouble where there isn't any. (*In a tone of finality.*) Well, it's all over, anyway.

SUE (*snatching the letter from the table*). Oh, I was forgetting, Nat. Read this. I got it yesterday.

NAT (*turns it over in his hands suspiciously*). Who from?

SUE. Open it and see.

NAT (*does so and turns over the pages to read the signature — he gives a start — hoarsely*). Danny! It can't be! But it's his writing, sure enough! (*He exclaims with a sudden wild exultation.*) Then they must have been lying to me!

SUE. No, the *Sarah Allen* was wrecked all right, but that was afterwards. He wasn't on board then. Read it. You'll see.

> (*Nat sinks back on a chair, evidently depressed by this information. He starts to read the letter with unconcealed indifference, then becomes engrossed, excited, the paper trembling in his hands. The Doctor shakes his head at Sue, indicating his disapproval of her giving him the letter. Nat finishes and springs to his feet — angrily.*)

NAT. The stupid fool! He let Horne pull the wool over his eyes in fine shape. He deserved all he got for being so dumb!

SUE (*indignantly*). Nat!

NAT (*unheedingly*). Oh, if I could only have gone in his place! I knew the kind Horne was. He couldn't have played that trick on me. I'd have forced the secret out of him if I had to — (*He raises his clenched fist in a gesture of threat like his father's — then lets it fall and sits down again — disgustedly.*) But what's the use? And what's the use of this? (*Tosses the letter contemptuously on the table.*) He might just as well not have written. We're no wiser than we were before.

SUE (*snatching up the letter — deeply hurt*). Aren't you even glad to hear Danny's alive?

NAT (*turning to her at once — with remorseful confusion*). Yes — yes — of course, Sue — I don't have to say that, do I? What I mean is, he never found out from Horne — and we're no wiser.

DOCTOR (*briskly — with a significant glance at Sue*). Well, Susan — Nat — I've got to run along — (*Meaningly.*) I'll be over again to-morrow, Susan.

SUE. Yes, do come. (*Goes with him to the door.*) Can you see your way?

DOCTOR. Yes. Good night.

SUE. Good night.

(*She closes the door and comes back to Nat. The Doctor's footsteps die out.*)

NAT (*savagely*). That damned old fool! What

is he doing, sneaking around here all the time?
I've grown to hate the sight of him.

SUE. Nat! You can't mean that. Think of how
kind he's been.

NAT. Yes — kindness with a purpose.

SUE. Don't be silly. What purpose could he
have except wanting to help us?

NAT. To find out things, of course, you simple-
ton. To pump Pa when he's not responsible for
what he's saying.

SUE (*indignantly*). Nat!

NAT. Much good it's done him! I know Pa.
Sane or not, he won't tell *that* to anyone — not
even you or me, Sue. (*With sudden fury.*) I'm
going away — but before I go I'm going to make
him tell me! He won't refuse this time when he
knows I'm leaving for good. He'll be glad then.
He's been so afraid I'd find out, so scared to speak
to me even — locking himself up here. But I'll
make him tell — yes, I will!

SUE. Careful, Nat. He'll hear you if you shout
like that.

NAT. But we have a right to know — his own
children. What if he dies without ever speaking?

SUE (*uneasily*). Be sensible, Nat. There's nothing to tell except in your imagination. (*Taking his
arm — persuasively.*) Come on downstairs. I'll get

you something to eat. You must be starved, aren't you?

NAT. No – I don't know – I suppose I ought to be. (*He gets to his feet and glances around with a shudder.*) What a place for him to build to wait in – like the cabin of a ship sunk deep under the sea – like the *Sarah Allen*'s cabin as it is now, probably. (*With a shiver.*) There's a chill comes over you. No wonder he's mad. (*He listens.*) Hear him. A year ago to-day she sailed. I wonder if he knows that. Back and forth, always staring out to sea for the *Sarah Allen*. Ha-ha! God! It would be funny if it didn't make your flesh creep. (*Brusquely.*) Come on. Let's leave him and go down where there's light and warmth.

> (*They go down the stairs, closing the door behind them. There is a pause. Then the door of the companionway above is heard being opened and shut. A gust of wind sweeps down into the room. Bartlett stamps down the stairs. The madness which has taken almost complete possession of him in the past year is clearly stamped on his face, particularly in his eyes which seem to stare through and beyond objects with a hunted, haunted expression. His movements suggest an automaton obeying invisible wires. They are quick, jerky, spas-*

modic. He appears to be labouring under a state of extraordinary excitement. He stands for a second at the foot of the stairs, peering about him suspiciously. Then he goes to the table and sits down on the edge of a chair, his chin supported on his hands.)

BARTLETT (*takes a folded piece of paper from his pocket and spreads it out on the table in the light of the lantern – pointing with his finger – mumblingly*). Where the cross be – ye'll not forget that, Silas Horne. Ye had a copy o' this – no chance for a mistake, bullies – the gold's there, restin' safe – back to me and we'll share it fair and square. A year ago to-day – ye remember the orders I wrote ye, Horne. (*Threateningly.*) Ye'll not be gone more nor a year or I'll – and if ye make port home here at night, hang a red and a green light at the mainm'st-head so I'll see ye comin'. A red and a green — (*He springs up suddenly and goes to a porthole to look out at the sea – disappointedly.*) No light be there – but they'll come. The year be up to-day and ye've got to come or I'll — (*He sinks back on the chair, his head in his hands. Suddenly he starts and stares straight in front of him as if he saw something in the air – with angry defiance.*) Aye, there ye be again – the two o' ye! Makin' a mock o' me! Brass and junk, ye say, not worth a damn! Ye don't believe, do ye? I'll show ye! (*He springs to his feet and makes a motion as if grabbing some one by the throat and shaking them — savagely.*) Ye lie! Is it gold or no? Answer me! (*With a mocking laugh.*) Aye, ye own up to it now, right enough. Too late, ye swabs! No share for ye! (*He sinks back on the chair again — after a pause, dully.*) Jimmy's gone. Let them rot. But I spoke no word, Silas Horne, remember! (*Then in a tone of fear.*) Be ye dyin', Sarah? No, ye must live — live to see your ship come home with the gold — and I'll buy ye all in the world ye set your heart on. No, not ambergris, Sarah — gold and diamonds and sech! We're rich at last! (*Then with great anguish.*) What woman's stubborn talk be this? Confess, ye say? But I spoke no word, I swear to ye! Why will ye hound me and think evil o' what I done? Men's business, I tell ye. They would have killed us and stolen the gold, can't ye see? (*Wildly.*) Enough o' talk, Sarah! I'll sail out in spite o' ye!

> (*He gets to his feet and paces up and down the room. The door in the rear is opened and Nat re-enters. He glances at his father, then looks down the stairs behind him cautiously to see if he is followed. He comes in and closes the door behind him carefully.*)

NAT (*in a low voice*). Pa! (*Then as his father does not appear to notice his presence — louder.*) Pa!

BARTLETT (*stops short and stares at his son as if he*

were gradually awakening from a dream — slowly).
Be that ye, Nat?

NAT (*coming forward*). Yes. I want to talk with
you.

BARTLETT (*struggling to bring his thoughts under
control*). Talk? Ye want to talk — to me? Men's
business — no room for a boy in it — keep clear o'
this.

NAT (*defiantly*). That's what you've always said.
But I won't be put off any longer. I won't, do you
hear?

BARTLETT (*angrily*). I've ordered ye not to set
foot in this cabin o' mine. Git below where ye
belong. Where's Sue? I told her to keep ye away.

NAT. She can't prevent me this time. I've made
up my mind. Listen, Pa. I'm going away to-
morrow.

BARTLETT (*uncertainly*). Goin' away?

NAT. Yes, and I'm never coming back. I'm going to start a new life. That's why I want a final
talk with you — before I go.

BARTLETT (*dully*). I've naught to say to ye.

NAT. You will have. Listen. I've absolute proof
the *Sarah Allen* is lost.

BARTLETT (*fiercely*). Ye lie!

NAT (*curiously*). Why do you say that? You know
it's true. It's just that you *won't believe*.

BARTLETT (*wanderingly – the word heading his mind into another channel*). Believe? Aye, he wouldn't believe. Brass and junk, he said, not worth a damn – but in the end I made him own up 'twas gold.

NAT (*repeating the word fascinatedly*). Gold?

BARTLETT. A year ago to-day she sailed. Ye lie! Ye don't believe either, do ye? – like him. But I'll show ye! I'll make ye own up as I made him! (*With mad exultation.*) She's comin' home to-night as I ordered Horne she must! I kin feel her makin' for home, I tell ye! A red an' a green at the mainm'st-head if ye make port o' night, I ordered Horne. Ye'll see!

(*He goes to look out of a porthole. Nat, as if under a spell, goes to another.*)

NAT (*turning away disappointedly – making an effort to throw off his thoughts – without conviction.*) Nonsense. There's nothing there – no lights – and I don't believe there ever will be.

BARTLETT (*his wild eyes fixed on his son's with an intense effort of will as if he were trying to break down his resistance*). Ye'll see, I tell ye – a red and a green! It ain't time yet, boy, but when it be they'll be plain in the night afore your eyes.

(*He goes and sits down by the table. Nat follows him and sits down in the other chair. He sees the map and stares at it fascinatedly.*)

NAT. What is this — the map of the island? (*He reaches out his hand for it.*)

BARTLETT (*snatching it up — with a momentary return to reason — frightenedly*). Not for ye, boy. Keep clear o' this for your own good. (*Then with a crazed triumph.*) Aye! Ye'd believe this soon enough, wouldn't ye?

NAT (*intensely*). I've always believed there was something — and a moment ago you mentioned gold. (*Triumphant in his turn.*) So you needn't try to hide the secret any longer. I know now. It's gold — gold you found on that island — gold you fitted out the *Sarah Allen* to sail back for — gold you buried where I saw that cross marked on the map! (*Passionately.*) Why have you been afraid to confide in me, your own son? Why didn't you let me sail back in your place? Were you afraid I'd give the secret away? Did you think I wouldn't believe — ?

BARTLETT (*with a mad chuckle*). Aye, ye believe now, right enough.

NAT. I always believed, I tell you. (*Pleadingly.*) And now that I know so much why can't you tell me the rest? I must know! I have a right to be heir to the secret. Why don't you confess —

BARTLETT (*interrupting — his brain catching at the word*). Confess? Confess, did ye say, Sarah? To Nat, did ye mean? Aye, Sarah, I'll tell him all and leave it to him to say if I did wrong. (*His gleaming eyes fixed on his son's.*) I'll tell ye, boy, from start to finish o' it. I been eatin' my heart to tell some one – some one who'd believe – some one that'd say I did no wrong. Listen, boy, ye know o' our four days in an open boat after the *Triton* went down. I told ye o' that when I come home. But what I didn't tell ye was they was six o' us in that boat, not four.

NAT. Six? There were you and Horne and Cates and Jimmy —

BARTLETT. The cook o' the *Triton* and the ship's boy. We'd been on the island two days – an island barren as hell, mind – without food or drink. We was roasted by the sun and nigh mad with thirst. Then, on the second day, I seed a Malay canoe – a proper war canoe such as the pirates use – sunk down inside the reef. I sent Jimmy down to go over her thinkin' they might be some cask o' water in her the sea'd not got to. (*With impressive emphasis.*) He found no water, boy, but he did find – d'ye know what, boy?

NAT (*exultantly*). The gold, of course!

BARTLETT (*laughing harshly*). Ha-ha! Ye do believe right enough, don't ye! Aye, the gold – in a chest. We hauled her up ashore and forced the lid open. (*Gloatingly.*) And there it was afore our eyes in the sun – gold bracelets and rings and ornaments o' all sorts fixed up fancy with diamonds and emeralds and rubies and sech – red and green – shinin' in the sun! (*He stops impressively.*)

NAT (*fascinatedly*). Diamonds and — But how did they get there?

BARTLETT. Looted treasure o' some Chinese junk, likely. What matter how it come about? There it was afore our eyes. And then, mind ye, that thief o' a cook came runnin' up from where he'd been shirkin' to look at what we'd found. "No share for ye, ye swab," I yelled at him; and then he says: "It ain't gold – brass and junk," he says and run off for fear o' me. Aye, he run off to the boy and told him to jine with his sneakin' plan to steal the gold from us!

NAT (*savagely*). But why didn't you stop him? Why didn't you — ?

BARTLETT. I be comin' to that, boy, and ye'll see if I did wrong. We carried the chest to the shade o' a palm and there was that thief o' a cook an' the boy waitin'. I collared 'em both and made 'em look at the gold. "Look and tell me if it's gold or no," I says. (*Triumphantly.*) They was afeerd to lie. Even that thief o' a cook owned up 'twas gold. Then when I turned 'em loose, because he knowed he'd git no share, he shouted again: "Brass and junk. Not worth a damn."

NAT (*furiously*). But why did you allow — Why didn't you —

BARTLETT (*with mad satisfaction*). Aye, ye be seein' the way o' it, boy. It was just then we sighted the schooner that picked us up after. We made a map and was buryin' the gold when we noticed them two thieves sneakin' about to see where we'd hide it. I saw 'em plain, the scum! That thief o' a cook was thinkin' he'd tell the folks on the schooner and go shares with them — and leave us on the island to rot; or he was thinkin' he and the boy'd be able to come back and dig it up afore I could. We had to do somethin' quick to spile their plan afore the schooner come. (*In a tone of savage satisfaction.*) And so — though I spoke no word to him — Jimmy knifed 'em both and covered 'em up with sand. But I spoke no word, d'ye hear? Their deaths be on Jimmy's head alone.

NAT (*passionately*). And what if you had? They deserved what they got.

BARTLETT. Then ye think I did no wrong?

NAT. No! Any man — I'd have done the same myself.

BARTLETT (*gripping his son's hand tensely*). Ye be true son o' mine, Nat. I ought to told ye before. (*Exultantly.*) Ye hear, Sarah? Nat says I done no wrong.

NAT. The map! Can I see it?

BARTLETT. Aye.

> (*He hands it to Nat, who spreads it out on the table and pores over it.*)

118

GOLD

NAT (*excitedly*). Why, with this I – we – can go back – even if the *Sarah Allen* is lost.

BARTLETT. She ain't lost, boy – not her. Don't heed them lies ye been hearin'. She's due now. I'll go up and look. (*He goes up the companionway stairs. Nat does not seem to notice his going, absorbed in the map. Then there is a loud muffled hail in Bartlett's voice.*) Sarah Allen, ahoy!

        (*Nat starts, transfixed – then rushes to one of the portholes to look. He turns back, passing his hand over his eyes, frowning bewilderedly. The door above is flung open and slammed shut and Bartlett stamps down the stairs.*)

BARTLETT (*fixing Nat hypnotically with his eyes – triumphantly*). What did I tell ye? D'ye believe now she'll come back? D'ye credit your own eyes?

NAT (*vaguely*). Eyes? I looked. I didn't see —

BARTLETT. Ye lie! The *Sarah Allen*, ye blind fool, come back from the Southern Seas as I swore she must! Loaded with gold as I swore she would be! – makin' port! – droppin' her anchor just when I hailed her.

NAT (*feebly, his will crumbling*). But – how do you know? – some other schooner —

BARTLETT. Not know my own ship – and the signal I'd ordered Horne to make!

NAT (*mechanically*). I know – a red and a green at the mainm'st-head.

119

BARTLETT. Then look out if ye dare! (*He goes to a porthole.*) Ye kin see it plain from here. (*Commandingly.*) Will ye believe your eyes? Look!

> (*Nat comes to him slowly — looks through the porthole — and starts back, a possessed expression coming over his face.*)

NAT (*slowly*). A red and a green — clear as day!

BARTLETT (*his face is now transfigured by the ecstasy of a dream come true*). They've lowered a boat — the three — Horne an' Cates and Jimmy Kanaka. They're rowin' ashore. Listen. I hear the oars in the locks. Listen!

NAT (*staring into his father's eyes — after a pause during which he appears to be straining his hearing to the breaking point — excitedly*). I hear!

BARTLETT. Listen! They've landed. They'll be comin' up the path now. (*In a crooning, monotonous tone.*) They move slowly — slowly. It be heavy, I know — that chest. (*After a pause.*) Hark! They're below at the door in front.

NAT. I hear!

BARTLETT. Ye'll see it now in a moment, boy — the gold. Up with it, bullies! Up ye come! Up, bullies! It's heavy, heavy!

NAT (*madly*). I hear them! They're on the floor below! They're coming! I'll open the door. (*He springs to the door and flings it open, shouting.*) Welcome home, boys!

(Sue is discovered outside just climbing up the stairs from below. She steps inside, then stops, looking with amazement and horror from father to brother. Nat pushes her roughly aside to look behind her down the stairs.)

SUE. Nat!

NAT *(turning to his father).* I'll go down to the wharf. They must be there or —

(The rest of his words are lost as he hurries down the stairs. Bartlett steps back, shrinking away from his daughter, and sinks on a chair by the table with a groan, his hands over his eyes.)

SUE *(comes to him and shakes him by the shoulder — alarmed).* Pa! What has happened? What is the matter with Nat? What have you told him? *(With bitter despair.)* Oh, can't you see you're driving him mad, too?

BARTLETT *(letting his hands fall and staring at her haggardly — falteringly, as if reason were slowly filtering back into his brain).* Sue — ye said — drivin' him mad, *too!* Then ye think I be — ? *(He staggers to his feet. Sue breaks down, sobbing. Bartlett falters on.)* But I seen her — the *Sarah Allen* — the signal lights —

SUE. Oh, Pa, there's nothing there! You know it! She was lost months ago.

121

BARTLETT. Lost? (*He stumbles over to a porthole and looks out. His body sags as if he were going to fall. He turns away and cries hopelessly in a tone of heart-rending grief.*) Lost! Aye, they be no *Sarah Allen* there — no lights — nothin'!

SUE (*pleading fiercely*). Pa, you've got to save Nat! He won't heed anyone else. Can't you tell him the truth — the whole truth whatever it is — now when I'm here and you're yourself again — and set him free from this crazy dream!

BARTLETT (*with wild grief*). Confess, ye mean? Sue, ye be houndin' me like your Ma did to her dyin' hour! Confess — that I spoke the word to Jimmy — in my mind! Confess — brass and junk — not worth a damn! (*In frenzied protest.*) No! Ye lie!

SUE. Oh, Pa, I don't know what you mean. Tell Nat the truth! Save him!

BARTLETT. The truth? It's a lie! (*As Sue tries to bar his way to the companionway — sternly.*) Out o' my way, girl!

> (*He pulls himself feebly up the stairs. The door is heard slamming above. Sue sits down in a chair in a hopeless, exhausted attitude. After a pause Nat re-enters. He is panting heavily from his exertions. His pale face is set in an expression of despair.*)

NAT (*looking about the room wildly*). Where is he?

Sue! (*He comes forward and falls on his knees beside her chair, hiding his face in her lap like a frightened child. He sobs hoarsely.*) Sue! What does it all mean? I looked. There was nothing there – no schooner – nothing.

SUE (*soothing him as if he were a little boy*). Of course there wasn't. Did you expect there would be, you foolish boy? Come, you know better than that. Why, Nat, you told the doctor and I that you were absolutely convinced the *Sarah Allen* was lost.

NAT (*dully*). Yes, I know – but I don't believe – like him —

SUE. Sshhhh! You know the state Pa is in. He doesn't realize what he's saying half the time. You ought to have better sense than to pay any attention —

NAT (*excitedly*). But he told me all he's been hiding from us – all about the gold!

SUE (*looking at him with alarm – mystified*). Gold? (*Then forcing a smile.*) Don't be silly, Nat. It doesn't exist except in his poor, deranged mind.

NAT (*fiercely*). That's a lie, Sue! I saw the map, I tell you – the map of the island with a cross marked on it where they buried the gold.

SUE. He showed a map to you – a real map? (*Gently.*) Are you sure you're not just imagining that, too?

NAT. I had it in my hands, you fool, you! There — on the table. (*He springs to his feet, sees the map on the table, and snatches it up with an exclamation of joy — showing it to Sue.*) See! Now will you believe me! (*She examines the map perplexedly. Nat paces up and down — excitedly.*) I tell you it's all true. You can't deny it now. It's lucky for us I forced him to confess. He might have died keeping the secret and then we'd have lost — I'll tell you what I'm going to do now, Sue. I'm going to raise the money somewhere, somehow, and fit out another schooner and this time I'll sail on her myself. No trusting to Danny or anyone else! Yes, Sue, we'll come into our own yet, even if the *Sarah Allen* is lost — (*He stops — then in accents of bewildered fear.*) But — she can't be lost — I saw the lights, Sue — red and green — as plain as I see you now — (*He goes to one of the portholes again.*)

SUE (*who has been watching him worriedly, puts the map back on the table, gets up and, assuming a brisk, matter-of-fact tone, she goes over and takes him by the arm*). Come downstairs, Nat. Don't think any more about it to-night. It's late and you're worn out. You need rest and a good sleep.

NAT (*following her toward the door — confusedly*). But Sue — I saw them — (*From above in the night comes the muffled hail in Bartlett's voice.*) Sarah Allen, ahoy!

GOLD

(*Nat stops, tortured, his hands instinctively
raised up to cover his ears. Sue gives a
startled cry. The door above is slammed
and Bartlett comes down the stairs, his
face revealing that the delusion has
again full possession of his mind.*)

BARTLETT (*pointing his finger at his son and fixing
him with his eyes — in ringing, triumphant tones.*)
The *Sarah Allen*, boy — in the harbour below — a
red and a green plain afore my eyes! What did I
tell ye, boy? Come back from the Southern Seas
as I swore she must! Loaded with gold as I swore
she would be!

(*Nat again seems to crumble — to give way to
the stronger will. He takes a step toward his father, his eyes lighting up.
Sue looks at his face — then rushes to her
father.*)

SUE (*putting her hands to her father's head and forcing him to look down into her face — intensely.*) Pa!
Stop, do you hear me! It's all mad! You're driving Nat mad, too! (*As she sees her father hesitate,
the wild light dying out of his eyes, she summons all her
power to a fierce pleading.*) For my sake, Pa! For
Ma's sake! Think of how she would feel if she
were alive and saw you acting this way with Nat!
Tell him! Tell him now — before me — tell him
it's all a lie!

BARTLETT (*trying in an agony of conflict to get hold*
125

GOLD

of his reason — incoherently). Yes, Sue — I hear ye — confess — aye, Sarah, your dyin' words — keep Nat clear o' this — but — red and green — I seen 'em plain — (*Then suddenly after a tremendous struggle, lifting his tortured face to Nat's — in tones of despair.*) Nothin' there, boy! Don't ye believe! No red and green! She'll never come! Derelict and lost, boy, the *Sarah Allen*. (*After another struggle with himself.*) And I lied to ye, boy. I gave the word — in my mind — to kill them two. I murdered 'em in cold blood.

SUE (*shrinking from him in horror*). Pa! You don't know what you're saying.

BARTLETT. The truth, girl. Ye said — confess —

NAT (*bewilderedly*). But — it was right. They were trying to steal —

BARTLETT (*overcome by the old obsession for a moment — savagely.*) Aye, that's it! The thievin' scum! They was tryin' — (*He stops short, throwing his head back, his whole body tense and quivering with the effort he makes to force this sustaining lie out of his brain — then, broken but self-conquering, he looks again at Nat — gently.*) No, Nat. That be the lie I been tellin' myself ever since. That cook — he said 'twas brass — But I'd been lookin' for ambergris — gold — the whole o' my life — and when we found that chest — I *had* to believe, I tell ye! I'd been dreamin' o' it all my days! But he said brass and junk, and told the boy — and I

126

give the word to murder 'em both and cover 'em up with sand.

NAT (*very pale – despairingly*). But he lied, didn't he? It is gold – real gold – isn't it?

BARTLETT (*slowly takes the studded anklet from his pocket and holds it out to Nat. The latter brings it to the light of the lantern. Bartlett sits on a chair, covering his face with his hands – in a tone of terrible suffering*). Ye'll tell me, boy – if it's gold or no. I've had it by me all this time – but I've been afeerd to show —

NAT (*in a tone of wild scorn*). Why, it's brass, of course! The cheapest kind of junk – not worth a damn!

> (*He flings it savagely into a corner of the room. Bartlett groans and seems to shrink up and turn into a figure of pitiable feebleness.*)

SUE (*pityingly*). Don't, Nat.

> (*She puts her arms around her father's shoulders protectingly.*)

NAT (*in a stifled voice*). What a damned fool I've been!

> (*He flings himself down on the cot, his shoulders heaving.*)

BARTLETT (*uncovers his grey face on which there is now settling an expression of strange peace – stroking*

GOLD

his daughter's hand). Sue — don't think hard o' me.
(*He takes the map.*) An end to this!

> (*He slowly tears it into small pieces, seeming
> to grow weaker and weaker as he does
> so. Finally as he lets the fragments
> filter through his fingers, his whole
> frame suddenly relaxes. He sighs, his
> eyes shut, and sags back in his chair, his
> head bent forward limply on his chest.*)

SUE (*alarmed*). Pa! (*She sinks to her knees beside
him and looks up into his face.*) Pa! Speak to me!
It's Sue! (*Then turning toward her brother — terri-
fiedly.*) Nat! Run — get the doctor — (*Nat starts
to a sitting position. Sue tries with trembling hands
to feel of her father's pulse, his heart — then begins
to sob hysterically.*) Oh, Nat — he's dead, I think
he's dead!

(The Curtain Falls)

'Marco Millions'

'Marco Millions'

A Play

by

Eugene O'Neill

Foreword

THIS play is an attempt to render poetic justice to one long famous as a traveller, unjustly world-renowned as a liar, but sadly unrecognized by posterity in his true eminence as a man and a citizen — Marco Polo of Venice. The failure to appraise Polo at a fair valuation is his own fault. He dictated the book of his travels but left the traveller out. He was no author. He stuck to a recital of what he considered facts and the world called him a liar for his pains. Even in his native Venice, he was scoffingly nicknamed 'the millionaire,' or 'Marco Millions.' They could not take seriously his impressive statistics about the 'millions' of this and the 'millions' of that in the East. Polo, the man of brass tacks, became celebrated as an extravagant romancer and ever since has travelled down the prejudiced centuries, a prophet without honour, or even notoriety, save in false whiskers. This has moved me to an indignant crusade between the lines of his book, the bars of his prison, in order to whitewash the good soul of that maligned Venetian.

'Marco Millions'

Characters

CHRISTIANS (in the order in which they appear).

A TRAVELLER
MARCO POLO
DONATA
NICOLO POLO, *Marco's father*
MAFFEO POLO, *Marco's uncle*
TEDALDO, *Legate of Syria (afterward Pope Gregory X)*
A DOMINICAN MONK
A KNIGHT-CRUSADER
A PAPAL COURIER
PAULO LOREDANO, *Donata's father, a gentleman from Venice*

Ladies and gentlemen of Venice, soldiers, people of Acre, musicians, servants, etc.

HEATHEN (in the order in which they appear):

A MAGIAN TRAVELLER
A BUDDHIST TRAVELLER
A MAHOMETAN CAPTAIN OF GHAZAN'S ARMY
THE ALI BROTHERS, *Mahometan merchants*
A PROSTITUTE
A DERVISH
TWO BUDDHIST MERCHANTS
TWO TARTAR MERCHANTS
A MONGOL PRIEST
EMISSARY FROM KUBLAI
KUBLAI, THE GREAT KAAN

9

'MARCO MILLIONS'

PRINCESS KUKACHIN, *his granddaughter*
CHU-YIN, *a Cathayan sage*
GENERAL BAYAN
A MESSENGER FROM PERSIA
GHAZAN, KHAN OF PERSIA
A BUDDHIST PRIEST
A TAOIST PRIEST
A CONFUCIAN PRIEST
A MOSLEM PRIEST
A TARTAR CHRONICLER

People of Persia, India, Mongolia, Cathay, courtiers, nobles, ladies, wives, warriors of Kublai's court, musicians, dancers, Chorus of Mourners.

Part One

PROLOGUE

A sacred tree in Persia near the confines of India toward the close of the thirteenth century.

ACT ONE

ACT TWO

11

'MARCO MILLIONS'
ACT THREE

SCENE I: The Grand Throne Room in the Imperial Palace at Cambaluc, one year later – and later the Dining Room of the Polo Home in Venice at the same time.

SCENE II: The Grand Throne Room at Cambaluc – one year later.

EPILOGUE

The theatre.

'Marco Millions'

PROLOGUE

SCENE. *A sacred tree on a vast plain in Persia near the confines of India. Votive offerings, pieces of cloth torn from clothing, bangles, armlets, ornaments, tapers, have been nailed on the trunk or tied to the branches. The heavy limbs spread out to a great distance from the trunk. Beneath them is deep cool shade, contrasting with the blinding glare of the noon sun on the sandy plain in the background. A merchant carrying in each hand a strapped box that resembles a modern sample case, plods wearily to the foot of the tree. He puts the boxes down and takes out a handkerchief to mop his forehead. He is a white Christian, middle-aged, average-looking, with a moustache and beard beginning to show grey. His clothes in the style of the Italian merchant class of the thirteenth century are travel-worn. He sighs, tired and hot.*

CHRISTIAN. Phoo!

> (*From the left a Magian, a Persian, dressed in the fashion of a trader, comes in. He carries a small, square bag. He also is hot, weary, and dust-covered. In age and appearance, making allowance for the difference in race, he closely resembles the Christian. He and the latter*

13

*stare at each other, then bow perfunc-
torily. The Magian sets down his bag
and wipes his brow.)*

CHRISTIAN *(sympathetically)*. Hot as hell!

MAGIAN *(grimly)*. Hotter!

*(They both chuckle. A Buddhist, a Kashmiri
travelling merchant, comes in, puffing
and sweating, from the right. He has a
pack strapped on his back. He resembles the other two in the essential character of his body and face. He stops on
seeing them. After eyeing him for an
appraising second, the two bow and the
Buddhist comes forward to set his pack
beside the bags of the others.)*

BUDDHIST *(with relief)*. Phoo! *(Then breaking
the ice.)* The sun would cook you!

MAGIAN. It is hot certainly.

CHRISTIAN *(as they all sit down to rest, looks from
one to the other — jovially)*. Funny! You'd think
we three had an appointment here. Your faces
look familiar. Haven't I seen you somewhere
before?

MAGIAN. In the house of the courtesans at
Shiraz. You were drunk.

BUDDHIST. I happened to be there that night,
too. You danced and sang lewd songs.

CHRISTIAN *(a bit embarrassed, but grinning)*.

14

Humn — oh, yes — I remember. It was my birth-day and I'd taken a drop too much — a very un-usual thing for me. (*Then abruptly changing the subject.*) How are conditions down your way?

BUDDHIST (*pursing his lips*). Slow. I come from Delhi. There is a new import tax and trade is very unsettled. We make prayer beads.

MAGIAN (*gloomily*). And I, for my sins, am hawk-ing a novelty, a block-printed book, for an Arab house. It contains one thousand Arabian lies, with one over for good measure, all full of lechery — at least so they instructed me to tell people to get them to buy.

CHRISTIAN. Did your trip take you down around Ispahan way?

MAGIAN. I just came from there. It is a sad city now. All the bazaars have been closed by an im-perial edict in mourning for Queen Kukachin.

CHRISTIAN (*bounding to his feet as if a wasp had stung him*). Is Queen Kukachin dead? (*Stunned.*) Why, I've got a letter of introduction to her from the head of my firm — Marco Polo of Polo Brothers and Son, Venice. He acted as her official escort, and took her from Cathay to Persia to be married! Why, I was counting on selling her and her hus-band a whole fleet load of goods!

MAGIAN (*suddenly, pointing off left*). What makes that cloud of dust? (*They all stare and begin to grow worried.*)

15

CHRISTIAN. It doesn't look like camels.

BUDDHIST (*fearfully*). It has a strange look!

CHRISTIAN. It's coming directly this way.

MAGIAN. These plains are haunted by evil spirits.

CHRISTIAN (*very frightened, but striving to put up a brave front*). I've heard those rumours. And I know for a fact that people are sometimes possessed by devils, but I don't believe —

BUDDHIST (*suddenly, pointing to the tree*). I am going to offer a prayer for protection to this tree sacred to Buddha.

CHRISTIAN ⎰ (*in chorus — irritably*). Sacred to
MAGIAN ⎱ Buddha?

BUDDHIST. Certainly! Do you not know the legend of how the Holy Sakya picked a twig to cleanse his teeth, and then throwing it away, it took root, and sprang up into this mighty tree to testify for ever to his miraculous power?

CHRISTIAN (*resentfully*). You're absolutely all wrong! This tree was the staff of our first father, Adam. It was handed down to Moses who used it to tap water out of stones and finally planted it. The cross our Lord was crucified on was made of this wood. And ever since this tree has been sacred to Him!

MAGIAN (*cuttingly*). You have both of you been duped by childish lies! This tree is sacred to the

16

founder of the one true religion, Zoroaster, who brought a shoot of the Tree of Life down from Paradise and planted it here!

BUDDHIST (*scornfully*). You are a pair of super-stitious sheep!

CHRISTIAN. You are a couple of idolatrous dogs!

MAGIAN. The two of you are blasphemous hogs!

> (*They glare at each other insultingly, their hands on their daggers. Suddenly they hear a noise from the left. Their eyes at once are turned in that direction and, forgetting personal animosities, they give a startled exclamation at what they see.*)

BUDDHIST. They are pulling a chariot!

CHRISTIAN. They must be slaves. See how the driver lashes them!

BUDDHIST. But what can that be on the wagon? —like a coffin!

CHRISTIAN. It must be treasure!

MAGIAN. No. It is a coffin. (*Trembling.*) Ssst! I have a foreboding of evil.

> (*They prostrate themselves, their faces to the ground. A moment later, preceded by shouts, a cracking of whips, and the dull stamping of feet, a double file of thirty men of different ages, stripped to the waist, harnessed to each other waist-to-*

waist and to the long pole of a two-wheeled wagon, stagger in, straining forward under the lashes of two soldiers who run beside them and the long whips of the Captain and a Corporal who are riding on the wagon, the Captain driving. As they reach the middle of the shade they stop. Lashed on the wagon is a coffin covered with a white pall.)

CAPTAIN *(a brutal, determined-looking man of forty, bellows).* Halt! *(The files of bleeding and sweating men collapse in panting, groaning heaps. The Soldiers sprawl down beside them. The Captain springs off the wagon.)* Phoo! This shade is grateful. *(He looks at the tree — then in an awed tone.)* This must be the Holy Tree which was once the staff of Mahomet and, passing down through generations, was buried in the grave of Abu Abdallah where it struck root and grew by the will of Allah into this tree. *(He makes obeisance and prays to the tree as do the Soldiers. He gets up and takes a gulp of water — then, looking around, notices the three merchants — with startled surprise, drawing his sword.)* Ho! What are you? Get up! *(They do so fearfully. He stares at them and laughs coarsely with relief.)* By all the demons, you startled me! But you traders are like fleas, one finds you everywhere! *(Then with a scowl.)* Three dogs of unbelievers, too! *(Sharply.)* Give an account of yourselves!

18

BUDDHIST. I was proceeding westward on a business venture, good sir.

MAGIAN. And I to the northward.

CHRISTIAN. And I to the court of Ghazan Khan to present this letter to Queen Kukachin. But I hear she's dead.

> (*He hands him the letter but the Captain backs away superstitiously.*)

CAPTAIN. Allah forbid I touch what belongs to a corpse. (*Then with forced laughter.*) You need not journey farther. She is in there! (*His voice has dropped, he points toward the coffin. The others stare at it, dumbfounded and awed. The Captain goes on dryly.*) You cannot cheat her now, Christian! (*Then lowering his voice as if afraid he will be overheard.*) And yet, to look at her face you would think her only sleeping.

CHRISTIAN (*astonished*). What? Can you look at her?

CAPTAIN. Her coffin is glass. Her body was anointed by Egyptians so that she preserves the appearance of life. This was done by command of her grandfather Kublai, the Great Kaan. She is being taken home to Cathay for burial — and under penalty of torture I must transport her over the first stage by dark to-night! (*Suddenly lamenting.*) But Allah afflicted me! When I reached the last village with my camels foundering, I found the accursed villagers had driven off their beasts to

19

escape requisition. But the dogs could not balk me. I hitched them to the pole instead. (*He looks at the moaning figures with a cruel appraising eye.*) But will they last till night? Hi, there! Water to revive them!

> (*The Soldiers carry around jugs of water which the panting men reach out for avidly, then sink back. But three of the more elderly men are too spent to move.*)

CHRISTIAN (*timorously — anxious to change the subject*). Was the Queen very beautiful?

CAPTAIN (*with bravado*). Would you care to see? You had a letter to her. It can do no harm — and it is a very great wonder!

CHRISTIAN (*reassuringly, because he is now extremely curious*). Dead Queens in the West usually lie in state.

CAPTAIN. You pull back the cloth then, since that is your custom.

> (*The Christian goes to the wagon and gingerly pulls back the pall from the head of the coffin — then retreats with an exclamation as Kukachin's face, that of a beautiful Tartar princess of twenty-three, is revealed inside the glass. Her calm expression seems to glow with the intense peace of a life beyond death, the eyes are shut as if she were asleep. The men stare, fascinated.*)

20

CHRISTIAN (*after a pause — crossing himself awedly*). Are you certain she's dead?

CAPTAIN (*in an awed whisper*). In the palace I commanded the company who guarded her coffin at night. I could not take my eyes from her face. It seemed that any moment she must awake and speak!

> (*While they have been speaking, unnoticed by them, it has grown dark. An unearthly glow, like a halo, lights up the face of Kukachin. From the branches of the tree comes a sound of sweet sad music as if the leaves were tiny harps strummed by the wind. The face of Kukachin becomes more and more living. Finally her lips part and her eyes open to look up at the tree.*)

(*Kneeling down to pray.*) Allah, be pitiful!

BUDDHIST. Buddha, protect Thy servant!

MAGIAN. Mithra, All-Powerful One!

CHRISTIAN. Jesus, have mercy!

> (*A voice which is Kukachin's, and yet more musical than a human voice, comes from the coffin as her lips are seen to move.*)

KUKACHIN. Say this, I loved and died. Now I am love, and live. And living, have forgotten. And loving, can forgive. (*Here her lips part in a smile of beautiful pity.*) Say this for me in Venice!

(*A sound of tender laughter, of an intoxicating, supernatural gaiety, comes from her lips and is taken up in chorus in the branches of the tree as if every harp-leaf were laughing in music with her. The laughter recedes heavenward and dies as the halo of light about her face fades and noonday rushes back in a blaze of baking plain. Everyone is prostrate, the harnessed wretches in the exhausted attitudes of sleep, the others visibly trembling with superstitious horror.*)

CHRISTIAN (*the first to recover — with bewilderment*). Venice! It must have been a message she wished me to take back to Marco Polo!

CAPTAIN (*his terror going and rage taking its place, leaps to his feet*). It was the voice of some Christian devil you summoned! It bewitched even me until Allah drove it back to hell! (*He draws his sword.*) Cover her face, accursed sorcerer!

CHRISTIAN (*pulls the covering over the head of the coffin with indecent haste*). I pledge you my word, good Captain —!

CAPTAIN (*to his Soldiers*). Attention! Kick them up! We must get away from here! (*With blows and kicks the Soldiers get their human beasts to their feet. There are groans and curses and cries of pain. But three cannot be roused. The Captain growls savagely at the Christian to keep up his courage.*) Pig of an infidel! (*Then glaring at the Buddhist and Magian.*) You too! You were in league with him! (*He grips his sword.*)

ALL THREE (*kneeling — pitiably*). Mercy! Spare us!

A CORPORAL (*comes up and salutes*). We cannot get three of them up, sir.

CAPTAIN (*raging*). Lash them!

CORPORAL. They are dead, sir.

CAPTAIN (*glumly*). Oh. (*Then an idea comes — with cruel satisfaction.*) Three, did you say? That is fortunate. Allah has provided! Cut them out and put these in their places!

> (*At a sign, the Soldiers fall upon the three merchants, strip off their upper clothes, untie the dead men, and hitch them in their places. All the time the three set up miserable screams of protest, punctuated by the blows and kicks they receive. The others look on with exhausted indifference.*)

CHRISTIAN (*making himself heard above the tumult*). My letter! It was to the Queen! When Polo Brothers hear of this outrage they'll get the Kaan to flay you alive!

CAPTAIN (*taken aback a moment — then craftily*). Show me your letter again!

CHRISTIAN (*holding it out with frantic eagerness*). Here! Now set me free!

CAPTAIN (*takes it and calmly tears it up*). I cannot read, but I think you are lying. At any rate, now you have no letter! (*The Christian sets up a wailing cry and receives a blow. The Captain and Corporals spring up on the wagon.*) And now forward march!

(*With a great cracking of whips and shouts of pain the wagon is pulled swiftly away. On the ground under the sacred tree three bodies lie in crumpled heaps. The same sweet sad music comes from the tree again as if its spirit were playing on the leaves a last lamenting farewell to the dead Princess. It rises softly and as softly dies away until it is nothing but a faint sound of wind rustling the leaves.*)

Curtain.

ACT ONE

SCENE ONE

SCENE. *Twenty-three years earlier. A fresh boy's voice is heard singing a love song in a subdued tone. The light slowly reveals the exterior of Donata's home on a canal, Venice. Marco Polo, a boy of fifteen, youthfully handsome and well made, is standing in a gondola beneath a barred window of the house, a guitar over his shoulder. The song finished, he waits anxiously. A hand is thrust out to him through the bars. He kisses it passionately. It is hurriedly withdrawn. Donata's face appears pressed against the bars. She is a girl of twelve, her face pale and pretty in the moonlight.*

DONATA (*coyly and tenderly*). You mustn't, Mark.

MARCO. There's no harm in that – just kissing your hand!

DONATA (*demurely*). It's a sin, I'm sure of it.

MARCO (*with a quick movement of his own hand, captures hers through the bars*). Then I'll have to steal it, and that's a worse sin. (*He pulls her willing hand down toward his lips.*)

DONATA. You're hurting my fingers.

MARCO (*boldly now*). Then I know how to cure them. (*He kisses them one by one.*) There!

25

DONATA (*tenderly*). You silly boy! Why do you do that?

MARCO (*very seriously*). You know, Donata.

DONATA. Know what? (*Softly.*) Go on and tell me, Mark.

MARCO (*blurts out gruffly*). I love you, that's what! I've loved you ever since I can remember. And you've known it right along, too, so there's no good pretending.

DONATA (*softly*). I wasn't sure.

MARCO (*recklessly*). And how about you? Do you love me? You've got to answer me that!

DONATA. You know – without my saying it.

MARCO. Please say it!

DONATA (*in a whisper*). I love you. There, silly!

MARCO. And you'll promise to marry me when I come back?

DONATA. Yes, but you'll have to ask my parents.

MARCO (*easily*). Don't worry about them. They'll be glad, and my folks, too. It'll bring the two firms into closer contact.

DONATA (*practically*). Yes, I think so, too.

> (*A pause. Songs and music come from near and far-off in the night about them. Marco has gained possession of her two hands now and his face is closer to the bars of her window.*)

26

MARCO (*with a sigh*). It's beautiful to-night. I wish I hadn't got to go away.

DONATA. I wish, too! Must you really!

MARCO. Yes. And I want to, too — all but leaving you. I want to travel and see the world and all the different people, and get to know their habits and needs from first-hand knowledge. You've got to do that if you want to become really big and important. That's what Father says — and Uncle.

DONATA. But won't this trip so very far away be full of danger?

MARCO (*boastfully*). I can take care of myself. Uncle says taking chances — *necessary* chances, of course — is the best schooling for a real merchant; and Father has a saying that where there's nothing risked, there's nothing gained. And they ought to know, oughtn't they, after spending nine years at the court of the Great Kaan and travelling there and back?

DONATA. Is that where you're going?

MARCO. Yes. He's the richest king in the world and Uncle and Father are personal friends of his. They did a lot of work for him. I'll be on the right side of him from the start, and Father and Uncle both say there's millions to be made in his service if you're not afraid of work and keep awake to opportunity.

DONATA. I'm sure you'll succeed. But I wish you weren't going for so long.

MARCO. I'll miss you as much as you miss me. (*Huskily.*) I hate to leave you, Donata — but I've got to make my own way — so that we can marry —

DONATA (*hurriedly*). Yes — of course — only come back as soon as you can.

MARCO. But you'll wait, won't you, no matter how long?

DONATA (*solemnly*). Yes, I swear to, Mark.

MARCO. And I swear by God I'll come back and marry you, and I'll always be true and never forget or do anything —

DONATA (*startled by a noise from within*). Ssshh! There's some one moving inside. You'll have to go. Here. (*She hands him a locket.*) It's a medallion of me painted by an artist who owed Father for spices and couldn't pay with money. Will you keep looking at this all the time you're away and never forget me?

MARCO (*kissing it passionately*). Every day!

DONATA. And you'll write to me?

MARCO. I promise. Every chance I get.

DONATA (*hesitatingly*). Will you write me — a poem? I won't care how short it is if it's only a poem.

MARCO. I'll try, Donata. I'll do my best.

DONATA. I'll just love it to death, Mark! (*Startledly.*) Ssshh! I hear it again. It must be Father. I've got to sneak back.

MARCO (*desperately*). Won't you kiss me – let me really kiss you – just once – for good-bye?

DONATA. I mustn't.

MARCO. Just once – when I'm going so far away? (*Desperately.*) I – I – I'll die if you don't!

DONATA. Well – just once. (*The moonlight fades into darkness as their lips meet. Then from the darkness are their voices heard in hushed tones.*) Good-bye, Mark.

MARCO. Good-bye, Donata.

> (*The sentimental singing voices and guitars are heard from all corners of the night in celebration of love. The sound gradually grows fainter and fainter, receding into the distance, as if Marco were already leaving Venice behind him.*)

DARKNESS

ACT ONE

SCENE TWO

SCENE. *Six months later. The tolling of a church bell is first heard. Then the interior of the Papal Legate's palace at Acre is revealed — a combination of church and government building.*

The Legate, Tedaldo, a man of sixty with a strong, intelligent face, is seated on a sort of throne placed against the rear wall. On his right, stands a warrior noble, a Knight-Crusader, in full armour, leaning on his sword. On his left, a Dominican Monk, his adviser. On the left of the room is an altar with candles burning. On the right, an open portal with a sentry pacing up and down, spear in hand.

The two elder Polos, Nicolo and Maffeo, stand in attitudes of patient servility before the throne. Marco's father, Nicolo, is a small thin middle-aged man, with a dry, shrewd face. Maffeo, Marco's uncle, is about the same age, but he is tall and stout with a round, jovial face and small, cunning eyes. There is a strong general resemblance between both of them and Marco. Marco is sitting on a stool in the foreground, his body all screwed up into an awkward intensity, striving with all his might to compose a poem to Donata, but constantly distracted in spite of himself.

TEDALDO (*bored but tolerantly*). What can I do except advise you to be patient? I'm sure the Conclave of Cardinals must soon select a Pope.

NICOLO. Two years in session! (*Then suddenly —consoled.*) Well, it's a new world's record, anyway.

MAFFEO (*shaking his head*). This uncertainty is bad for trade.

TEDALDO (*with a bored yawn*). No doubt. (*Then rather impatiently.*) Then, when your business so evidently calls you to the East, why delay longer? Why not simply explain to the Great Kaan, Kublai, that there was no Pope to whom you could deliver his message?

NICOLO. He mightn't understand. His instructions to us were pretty emphatic.

MAFFEO. To request the Pope to send him a hundred wise men of the West —

TEDALDO (*dryly*). This Kublai is an optimist!

MAFFEO. —to argue with his Buddhists and Taoists and Confucians which religion in the world is best.

MONK (*outraged*). Impudent ignoramus! Does he imagine the Church would stoop to such bickering?

TEDALDO (*with a weary smile*). I begin to think Kublai is a humorist, too.

MAFFEO (*craftily*). It'd pay to convert him. He's

31

the richest king in the world. He rules over millions of subjects, his empire covers millions of square miles of great undeveloped natural resources, his personal wealth in cash and jewels and goods alone easily runs into millions of millions!

MARCO (*stares at his uncle — then mutters, fascinatedly.*) Millions! (*Then, shaking away this interruption, bends to his writing again.*)

TEDALDO (*wearily*). I am bored with your millions, Messrs. Polo. Even if they are true, it is too much effort to conceive them. (*They bow humbly and retire backward. His eyes following them listlessly Tedaldo sees Marco, who at this moment is scratching himself, twisting and turning his legs and feet, tearing his hair in a perfect frenzy of balked inspiration. Tedaldo smiles and addresses him in an affectionate, humorous tone.*) God's mercy on you, Master Marco! Are you suddenly possessed by a devil — or is it only these infernal Mahometan fleas the Almighty sends us for our sins?

MARCO (*coming out of his fit — sheepishly*). I'm only writing something.

MAFFEO. Mark is surprisingly quick at figures.

NICOLO. But still heedless. A dreamer! (*To Marco, with a condescending paternal air.*) What are you writing, son? (*He and Maffeo draw near Marco.*)

MARCO (*more confused*). Nothing, sir — just — something. (*He tries to hide it.*)

MAFFEO. Why are you so mysterious? Come, let's see.

MARCO. No — please, Uncle.

MAFFEO (*with a sudden cunning motion, he snatches it from Marco's hand, glances at it and bursts into laughter*). Look, Nicolo, look!

MARCO (*rebelliously*). Give that back!

NICOLO (*sternly*). Behave yourself, Mark! (*To Maffeo.*) What is it?

MAFFEO. See for yourself. (*He hands it to him.*) Did you know you'd hatched a nightingale? (*He laughs coarsely. Nicolo reads, a scornful grin coming to his lips.*)

TEDALDO. Surely it cannot be a song he has written?

NICOLO (*going to him — laughing*). A rhyme! A love poem, no less!

TEDALDO (*severely, as he takes the poem*). Do not mock at him! Rather be grateful if a thistle can bring forth figs. (*Marco remains sullenly apart, shamefaced and angry, his fists clenched. Tedaldo reads — frowns — laughs — then smilingly to Nicolo.*) Your fear that this is a poem is — hum — exaggerated! (*He reads with amusement as Marco squirms.*)

> 'You are lovely as the gold in the sun
> Your skin is like silver in the moon
> Your eyes are black pearls I have won.
> I kiss your ruby lips and you swoon,

M 33

Smiling your thanks as I promise you
A large fortune if you will be true,
While I am away earning gold
And silver so when we are old
I will have a million to my credit
And in the meantime can easily afford
A big wedding that will do us credit
And start having children, bless the Lord!'

(*There is a roar of laughter in which Tedaldo joins.
Marco looks about for a hole into which to crawl.
Tedaldo addresses him amusedly but with kindness.*)
Come, Marco. Here is your poem. Your lady is
a bit too mineral, your heaven of love a trifle mone-
tary — but, never mind, you will be happier as a
Polo than as a poet. Here. (*He gives it to Marco.
The latter fiercely crumples it up and throws it on the
floor and stamps on it.*)

NICOLO (*approvingly*). Sensibly done, my boy.

TEDALDO (*looking searchingly at Marco's face —
gently*). Perhaps I was too critical. Your poem
had merits of its own. I am sure it would touch
your lady's heart.

MARCO (*with a great bluster of manliness*). Oh, I
don't mind your making fun. I can take a joke.
It *was* silly. Poetry's all stupid, anyway. I was
only trying it for fun, to see if I could. You won't
catch me ever being such a fool again!

MONK (*as a noise of shouting comes toward them*).
Ssstt! What's that?

(*The Knight hurries to the portal.*)

KNIGHT. Some one is running here, and a crowd behind. I hear them shouting 'Pope.'

MONK. Then the Conclave has chosen!

POLOS (*joyfully*). At last!

> (*The cries of many voices. The Sentinel and Knight admit the Messenger but push back the others.*)

MESSENGER (*exhausted — falls on his knees before Tedaldo, holding out a sealed paper*). I come from the Conclave. You were chosen. Your Holiness — (*He falls fainting. The crowds cheer and sweep in.*)

TEDALDO (*rising — pale and trembling*). What does he say?

MONK (*has picked up the document — joyfully*). See! The official seal! You are the Pope! (*He kneels humbly.*) Your Holiness, let me be the first —

> (*He kisses Tedaldo's hand. All are kneeling now, their heads bowed. The bells of the churches begin to ring.*)

TEDALDO (*raising his hands to heaven — dazed*). Lord, I am not worthy! (*Then to those about him — tremblingly.*) Leave me. I must pray to God for strength — for guidance!

CROWD (*in a clamour*). Your blessing!

(Tedaldo, with a simple dignity and power, blesses them. They back out slowly, the Monk and Knight last. The Polos group together in the foreground, holding a whispered conference. Tedaldo kneels before the altar.)

MAFFEO. Now that he's the Pope, if we could get an answer from him, we could start right away.

NICOLO. We couldn't hope for better weather.

MAFFEO. He seems to have taken a fancy to Mark. You speak to him, Mark.

MARCO *(unwillingly).* He's praying.

MAFFEO. He'll have time enough for that, but with us time is money. *(Giving the unwilling Marco a push.)* This will test your nerve, Mark! Don't shirk!

MARCO *(gritting his teeth).* All right. I'll show you I'm not scared! *(He advances boldly toward the altar, stands there for a moment awkwardly as Tedaldo remains oblivious — then he falls on his knees — humbly but insistently.)* Your Holiness. Forgive me, Your Holiness —

TEDALDO *(turns to him and springs to his feet — imperiously).* I wish to be alone! *(Then as Marco is shrinking back — more kindly.)* Well, what is it? I owe you a recompense, perhaps — for an injury.

MARCO *(stammeringly).* Your Holiness — if you could give us some answer to deliver to the Great

36

Kaan — we could start now — with such favourable weather —

TEDALDO (*amused in spite of himself*). On the last day one of your seed will interrupt Gabriel to sell him another trumpet! (*Then sardonically to the elder Polos.*) I have no hundred wise men — nor one! Tell the Great Kaan he must have been imposed upon by your patriotic lies, or he could never make such a request.

POLOS (*terrified*). But, Your Holiness, we dare not repeat — He'd have us killed!

TEDALDO. I will send him a monk or two. That is quite sufficient to convert a Tartar barbarian!

MAFFEO. But, Your Holiness, he's not a barbarian! Why, every plate on his table is solid gold!

TEDALDO (*smiling*). And has he millions of plates, too? (*Then with a sudden whimsicality.*) But if the monks fail, Master Marco can be my missionary. Let him set an example of virtuous Western manhood amid all the levities of paganism, shun the frailty of poetry, have a million to his credit, as he so beautifully phrased it, and I will wager a million of something or other myself that the Kaan will soon be driven to seek spiritual salvation somewhere! Mark my words, Marco will be worth a million wise men — in the cause of wisdom! (*He laughs gaily, raising his hand over Marco's head.*) Go with my blessing! But what need have you for a blessing? You were born with

37

success in your pocket! (*With a last gesture he turns, going quickly out of the door in rear.*)

MAFFEO (*as he goes — approvingly*). Mark is making a good impression already!

NICOLO. Well, he's got a head on him!

MARCO (*beginning to swell out a bit matter-of-factly*). Never mind about me. When do we start?

POLOS (*hurriedly*). At once. Let's go and pack. (*They go out left.*) Come, Mark! Hurry!

MARCO. I'm coming. (*He waits, looks after them, picks up the crumpled poem, starts to hide it in his jacket, stops, mutters with brave self-contempt.*) Aw! You damn fool!

> (*He throws the poem down again, starts to go, hesitates, suddenly turns back, picks it up, crams it into his doublet and runs wildly out of the door. The scene fades into darkness. For a time the church bells, which have never ceased ringing, are heard acclaiming the new Pope; but the Polos proceed speedily on their journey and the sound is soon left behind them.*)

DARKNESS

38

ACT ONE

SCENE. *Light comes, gradually revealing the scene. In the rear is the front of a Mahometan mosque. Before the mosque is a throne on which sits a Mahometan ruler. On the right, the inevitable warrior – on his left, the inevitable priest – the two defenders of the State. At the ruler's feet his wives crouch like slaves. Everything is jewelled, high-coloured, gorgeous in this background. Squatted against the side walls, forming a sort of semi-circle with the throne at C., counting from left to right consecutively, are a mother nursing a baby, two children playing a game, a young girl and a young man in a loving embrace, a middle-aged couple, an aged couple, a coffin. All these Mahometan figures remain motionless. Only their eyes move, staring fixedly but indifferently at the Polos, who are standing at centre. Marco is carrying in each hand bags which curiously resemble modern sample cases. He sets these down and gazes around with a bewildered awe.*

NICOLO (*turning on him – genially*). Well, son, here we are in Islam.

MARCO (*round-eyed*). A man told me that Noah's Ark is still somewhere around here on top of a mountain. (*Eagerly.*) And he proved it to me, too.

39

Look! (*He shows them a piece of wood.*) He broke this off of the Ark. See, it's got Noah's initials on it!

MAFFEO (*grimly*). How much did you pay him for it?

MARCO. Ten soldi in silver.

NICOLO (*dashing it out of Marco's hand – bitterly*). Muttonhead! Do you suppose Almighty God would allow infidels to cut up Noah's Ark into souvenirs to sell to Christians?

MAFFEO (*teasingly*). Your son and your money are soon parted, Brother. (*Then placatingly.*) But he's only a boy. He'll learn. And before we go farther, Nicolo, we had better read him from the notes we made on our last trip all there is to remember about this corner of the world.

NICOLO (*they take out note-books closely resembling a modern business man's diary and read*). We're now passing through Kingdoms where they worship Mahomet.

MAFFEO. There's one kingdom called Musul and in it a district of Baku where there's a great fountain of oil. There's a growing demand for it. (*Then speaking.*) Make a mental note of that.

MARCO. Yes, sir.

NICOLO. Merchants make great profits. The people are simple creatures. It's very cold in winter. The women wear cotton drawers. This they

40

do to look large in the hips, for the men think that a great beauty.

> (*The two Mahometan Merchants enter from the left. Maffeo recognizes them immediately — in a swift aside to his brother.*)

MAFFEO. There's those damned Ali brothers. They'll cut under our prices with their cheap junk as usual. (*The Ali brothers have seen the Polos and a whispered aside, evidently of the same nature, passes between them. Then simultaneously the two firms advance to meet each other, putting on expressions of the utmost cordiality.*) Well, well. You folks are a welcome sight!

ONE ALI. My dear, dear friends! Praise be to Allah! (*They embrace.*)

MAFFEO (*with a cunning smirk*). Selling a big bill of goods hereabouts, I'll wager, you old rascals?

THE OLDER ALI (*airily*). My dear friend, don't speak of business. But you, you are on a venture to the court of the Great Kaan, we hear?

MAFFEO. What lies get around! Nothing in it — absolutely nothing!

NICOLO. For Heaven's sake, let's not talk business! Let's have a nice friendly chat. (*The four squat together in a circle.*)

MAFFEO (*with a wink*). I'll tell you a good one an Armenian doily-dealer told me down in Bagdad.

(They all bend their heads toward him with expectant grins. He looks around – then begins in a cautious lowered tone.) Well, there was an old Jew named Ikey and he married a young girl named Rebecca –

> *(He goes on telling the rest of the story with much exaggerated Jewish pantomime but in a voice too low to be heard. In the meantime, Marco has slipped off, full of curiosity and wonder, to look at this strange life. He goes first to the left, stops before the mother and baby, smiles down at it uncertainly, then bends down to take hold of its hand.)*

MARCO. Hello! *(Then to the mother.)* He's fat as butter! *(Both remain silent and motionless, staring at him from a great distance with indifferent calm. Marco is rebuffed, grows embarrassed, turns away to the children, who, frozen in the midst of their game of jackstraws, are looking at him. Marco adopts a lofty condescending air.)* Humh! Do you still play that game here? I remember it – when I was a kid. *(They stare silently. He mutters disgustedly.)* Thickheads! *(And turns to the lovers, who, with their arms about each other, cheek to cheek, stare at him. He looks at them, fascinated and stirred, and murmurs enviously.)* She's pretty. I suppose they're engaged – like Donata and me. *(He fumbles and pulls out the locket which is hung around his neck on a ribbon.)* Donata's prettier. *(Then, with embarrassment, he holds it out for them to see.)* Don't you think she's

42

pretty? She and I are going to be married some day. (*They do not look except into his eyes. He turns away, hurt and angry.*) Go to the devil, you infidels! (*He stuffs the locket back – stops before the throne – tries to stare insolently at the king but, awed in spite of himself, makes a grudging bow and passes on, stops before the family group, sneers and passes on, stops before the old couple and cannot restrain his curiosity.*) Would you tell me how old you are?

> (*He passes on, rebuffed again, stops as if fascinated before the coffin, leans out and touches it with defiant daring, shudders superstitiously and shrinks away, going to the merchant group who are roaring with laughter as Maffeo ends his story.*)

THE OLDER ALI (*to Nicolo*). Your son?

NICOLO. Yes, and a chip of the old block.

THE OLDER ALI. Will he follow in your footsteps?

NICOLO (*jocosely*). Yes, and you'd better look out then! He's as keen as a hawk already.

THE OLDER ALI (*with a trace of a biting smile*). He greatly resembles a youth I saw back on the road buying a piece of Noah's Ark from a wayside sharper.

MAFFEO (*hastily coming to the rescue as Nicolo cannot hide his chagrin – boastfully*). It wasn't Mark. Mark would have sold him the lions of St. Mark's for good mousers!

(*The Prostitute enters from the right. She is painted, half-naked, alluring in a brazen, sensual way. She smiles at Marco enticingly.*)

MARCO (*with a gasp*). Look! Who's that?

(*They all turn, and, recognizing her, laugh with coarse familiarity.*)

MAFFEO (*jokingly*). So here you are again. You're like a bad coin — always turning up.

PROSTITUTE (*smiling*). Shut up. You can bet it isn't old fools like you that turn me.

NICOLO (*with a lecherous grin at her*). No? But it's the old who have the money.

PROSTITUTE. Money isn't everything, not always. Now I wouldn't ask money from him. (*She points to Marco.*)

NICOLO (*crossly and jealously*). Leave him alone, you filth!

MAFFEO (*broad-mindedly*). Come, come, Nicolo. Let the boy have his fling.

PROSTITUTE (*her eyes on Marco*). Hello, Handsome.

MARCO (*bewildered*). You've learned our language?

PROSTITUTE. I sell to all nations.

MARCO. What do you sell?

PROSTITUTE (*mockingly*). A precious jewel. Myself. (*Then desirously.*) But for you I'm a gift. (*Putting her hands on his shoulders and lifting her lips.*) Why don't you kiss me?

MARCO (*terribly confused — strugglingly*). I – I don't know – I mean, I'm sorry but – you see I promised some one I'd never – (*Suddenly freeing himself – frightened.*) Leave go! I don't want your kisses.

> (*A roar of coarse taunting laughter from the men. Marco runs away, off L.*)

NICOLO (*between his teeth*). What a dolt!

MAFFEO (*slapping the Prostitute on the bare shoulder*). Better luck next time. He'll learn!

PROSTITUTE (*trying to hide her pique – forcing a cynical smile*). Oh, yes, but I won't be a gift then. I'll make him pay, just to show him!

> (*She laughs harshly and goes out L. A pause. All four squat again in silence.*)

THE OLDER ALI (*suddenly*). Many wonders have come to pass in these regions. They relate that in old times three kings from this country went to worship a Prophet that was born and they carried with them three manner of offerings – Gold and Frankincense and Myrrh – and when they had come to the place where the Child was born, they marvelled and knelt before him.

MAFFEO. That's written in the Bible. The child

was Jesus Christ, our Lord. (*He crosses himself, Nicolo does likewise.*)

THE OLDER ALI. Your Jesus was a great prophet.

NICOLO (*defiantly*). He was the Son of God!

BOTH ALIS (*stubbornly*). There is no God but Allah!

> (*A strained pause. A dervish of the desert runs in shrieking and begins to whirl. No one is surprised except the two Polos, who get up to gape at him with the thrilled appreciation inspired by a freak in a sideshow. Marco comes back and joins them.*)

MAFFEO (*with appreciation*). If we had him in Venice we could make a mint of money exhibiting him. (*Nicolo nods.*)

MARCO. I'll have to write Donata all about this. (*Wonderingly.*) Is he crazy?

MAFFEO (*in a low aside to him*). My boy, all Mahometans are crazy. That's the only charitable way to look at it.

> (*Suddenly the call to prayer sounds from Muezzins in the minarets of the mosque. The Dervish falls on his face. Everyone sinks into the attitude of prayer except the Polos who stand embarrassed, not knowing what to do.*)

MARCO. Are they praying?

46

NICOLO. Yes, they call it that. Much good it does them!

MAFFEO. Ssshh! Come! This is a good time to move on again. Marco! Wake up!

> (*They go quickly out* R., *Marco following with the sample cases. The scene fades quickly into darkness as the call of the Muezzins is heard again.*)

DARKNESS

47

ACT ONE

SCENE FOUR

SCENE. *The slowly-rising light reveals an Indian snake-charmer squatted on his haunches at* C. *A snake is starting to crawl from the basket in front of him, swaying its head to the thin, shrill whine of a gourd. Otherwise, the scene, in the placing of its people and the characters and types represented, is the exact duplicate of the last except that here the locale is Indian. The background for the ruler's throne is now a Buddhist temple instead of a mosque. The motionless staring figures are all Indians. Looming directly above and behind the ruler's throne is an immense Buddha. The Polos stand at centre as before, Marco still lugging the sample cases. He is seventeen now. Some of the freshness of youth has worn off. They stare at the snake-charmer, the two older men cynically. Marco gasps with enthralled horror.*

MARCO. Look at that deadly snake!

MAFFEO (*cynically*). He's a fake, like everything else here. His fangs have been pulled out.

MARCO (*disillusioned*). Oh! (*He turns away. The snake-charmer glares at them, stops playing, pushes his snake back into the box and carries it off, after spitting on the ground at their feet with angry disgust. Marco sits on one of the cases and glances about with a*

48

forced scorn; looks finally at the Buddha — in a superior tone.) So that is Buddha!

NICOLO (*begins to read from his note-book*). These people are idolaters. The climate is so hot that if you put an egg in their rivers it will be boiled.

MAFFEO (*taking up the reading from his book in the same tone*). The merchants make great profits. Ginger, pepper, and indigo. Largest sheep in the world. Diamonds of great size. The Kings have five hundred wives apiece.

MARCO (*disgustedly*). It's too darn hot here!

MAFFEO (*warningly*). Sshhh! Don't let the natives hear you. Remember any climate is healthy where trade is brisk.

MARCO (*walks sullenly off to left. At the same moment two merchants, this time Buddhists, come in. The same interplay goes on with them as with the Ali Brothers in the previous scene, only this time it is all done in pantomime until the loud laughter at the end of Maffeo's story. As Maffeo tells the story, Marco is looking at the people, but this time he assumes the casual, indifferent attitude of the worldly-wise. He makes a silly gesture to attract the baby's attention, passes by the two children with only a contemptuous glance, but stops and stares impudently at the lovers — finally spits with exaggerated scorn*). Where do you think you are — home with the light out? Why don't you charge admission? (*He stalks on — pauses before the middle-aged couple who have a bowl of rice between them —*

49

*in astonishment as though this evidence of a humanity
common with his struck him as strange.)* Real rice!
*(He ignores the throne, passes quickly by the old people
with a glance of aversion and very obviously averts his
head from the coffin. As he returns to the group at centre, Maffeo has just finished his story. There is a roar
of laughter. Grinning eagerly.)* What was it, Uncle?

MAFFEO *(grinning teasingly).* You're too young.

MARCO *(boastfully).* Is that so?

NICOLO *(severely).* Mark!

> *(The Prostitute, the same but now in Indian
> garb, has entered from left and comes up
> behind Marco.)*

PROSTITUTE. A chip of the old block, Nicolo!

NICOLO *(angrily).* You again!

MARCO *(pleased to see her, but embarrassed).* Why,
hello!

PROSTITUTE *(cynically).* I knew you'd want to
see me. *(She raises her lips.)* Will you kiss me
now? *(As he hesitates.)* Forget your promise. You
know you want to.

MAFFEO *(grinning).* There's no spirit in the
youngsters nowadays. I'll bet he won't.

PROSTITUTE *(her eyes on Marco's).* How much
will you bet?

MAFFEO. Ten —

(Marco suddenly kisses her.)

PROSTITUTE *(turning to Maffeo)*. I win, Uncle.

MARCO *(with a grin)*. No. I kissed you before he said ten what.

MAFFEO. That's right! Good boy, Mark!

PROSTITUTE *(turning to Marco — cynically)*. You're learning, aren't you? You're becoming shrewd even about kisses. You need only me now to make you into a real man — for ten pieces of gold.

MARCO *(genuinely overcome by a sudden shame)*. No, please — I — I didn't mean it. It was only in fun.

PROSTITUTE *(with a sure smile)*. Later, then — when we meet again. *(She walks off L.)*

MARCO *(looks after her. As she evidently turns to look back at him, he waves his hand and grins — then abashed)*. She's pretty. It's too bad she's — what she is.

MAFFEO. Don't waste pity. Her kind are necessary evils. All of us are human.

(A long pause.)

THE OLDER BUDDHIST MERCHANT *(suddenly)*. The Buddha taught that one's loving-kindness should embrace all forms of life, that one's compassion should suffer with the suffering, that one's sympathy should understand all things, and last that one's judgment should regard all persons and things as of equal importance.

NICOLO (*harshly*). Who was this Buddha?

THE OLDER BUDDHIST MERCHANT. The Incarnation of God.

NICOLO. You mean Jesus?

THE OLDER BUDDHIST MERCHANT (*unheedingly*). He was immaculately conceived. The Light passed into the womb of Maya, and she bore a son who, when he came to manhood, renounced wife and child, riches and power, and went out as a beggar on the roads to seek the supreme enlightenment which would conquer birth and death; and at last he attained the wisdom where all desire has ended and experienced the heaven of peace, Nirvana. And when he died he became a God again.

> (*The temple bells begin to ring in chorus. All except the Polos prostrate themselves before the Buddha.*)

MARCO (*to his uncle – in a whispered chuckle*). Died and became a God? So that's what they believe about that stone statue, is it?

MAFFEO. They're all crazy, like the Mahometans. They're not responsible.

MARCO (*suddenly*). I saw two of them with a bowl of rice –

MAFFEO. Oh, yes. They eat the same as we do. (*Then abruptly.*) Come on! This is our chance to make a start. Don't forget our cases, Mark.

> (*They go out* L. *followed by Marco with the sample cases. The scene fades into darkness. The clamour of the temple bells slowly dies out in the distance.*)

DARKNESS

ACT ONE

SCENE FIVE

SCENE. *From the darkness comes the sound of a small
Tartar kettledrum, its beats marking the rhythm
for a crooning, nasal voice, rising and falling in
a wordless chant.*

*The darkness gradually lifts. In the rear is
a section of the Great Wall of China with an
enormous shut gate. It is late afternoon, just before sunset. Immediately before the gate is a rude
throne on which sits a Mongol ruler with warrior
and sorcerer to right and left of him. At the sides
are Mongol circular huts. The motionless figures
sit before these. The Minstrel, squatting at centre, is the only one whose body moves. In the
back of the throne and above it is a small idol
made of felt and cloth. The clothes of the ruler
and his court are of rich silk stuffs, lined with
costly furs. The squatting figures of the people
are clothed in rough robes.*

*The Polos stand at centre, Marco still lugging
the battered sample cases. He is now nearly
eighteen, a self-confident young man, assertive
and talkative. All the Polos are weary and their
clothes shabby and travel-worn.*)

MARCO (*setting down the bags with a thump and
staring about with an appraising contempt*). Welcome to that dear old Motherland, Mongolia!

54

MAFFEO (*wearily takes out his guide-book and begins to read in the monotone of a boring formula*). Flocks – goats – horses – cattle. The women do all the buying and selling. Business is all in cattle and crops. In short, the people live like beasts.

NICOLO (*reading from his book*). They have two Gods – a God of Heaven to whom they pray for health of mind, and a God of Earth who watches over their earthly goods. They pray to him also and do many other stupid things.

MARCO (*bored*). Well – let them!

> (*He walks away and makes the circuit of the figures, but now he hardly glances at them. The Two Tartar Merchants enter and there is the same pantomime of greeting between them and the Polos as with the Buddhist Merchants in the previous scene. Marco joins them. It is apparent the whole company is extremely weary. They yawn and prepare to lie down.*)

MAFFEO. We'll have time to steal a nap before they open the Gate.

MARCO (*with an assertive importance*). Just a moment! I've got a good one an idol-polisher told me in Tibet. This is the funniest story you ever heard! It seems an Irishman got drunk in Tangut and wandered into a temple where he mistook one of the female statues for a real woman and —

> (*He goes on, laughing and chuckling to himself, with endless comic pantomime. The two Tartar Merchants fall asleep. Nicolo stares at his son bitterly, Maffeo with contemptuous pity. Finally Marco finishes to his own uproarious amusement.*)

NICOLO (*bitterly*). Dolt!

MAFFEO (*mockingly. With a yawn*). Youth will have its laugh!

> (*Marco stops open-mouthed and stares from one to the other.*)

MARCO (*faintly*). What's the matter?

NICOLO (*pettishly*). Unless your jokes improve you'll never sell anything.

MAFFEO. I'll have to give Marco some lessons in how to tell a short story. (*Warningly.*) And until I pronounce you graduated, mum's the word, understand! The people on the other side of that wall may look simple but they're not.

> (*The Prostitute enters, dressed now as a Tartar. She comes and puts her hand on Marco's head.*)

PROSTITUTE. What has this bad boy been doing now?

56

MAFFEO. He's getting too witty! (*He rests his head on his arms and goes to sleep.*)

PROSTITUTE. Shall I expect you again to-night?

MARCO. No. You've got all my money. (*Suddenly gets to his feet and faces her – disgusted.*) And I'm through with you, anyway.

PROSTITUTE (*with a scornful smile*). And I with you – now that you're a man. (*She turns away.*)

MARCO (*angrily*). Listen here! Give me back what you stole! I know I had it on a ribbon around my neck last night and this morning it was gone. (*Threateningly.*) Give it to me, you, or I'll make trouble!

PROSTITUTE (*takes a crumpled paper from her bosom*). Do you mean this?

MARCO (*tries to snatch it*). No!

PROSTITUTE (*she unfolds it and reads*).

'I'll have a million to my credit
And in the meantime can easily afford
A big wedding that will do us credit
And start having children, Bless the Lord!'

(*She laughs.*) Are you a poet, too?

MARCO (*abashed and furious*). I didn't write that.

PROSTITUTE. You're lying. You must have. Why deny it? Don't sell your soul for nothing. That's bad business. (*She laughs, waving the poem*

57

in her upraised hand, staring mockingly.) Going! Going! Gone! (*She lets it fall and grinds it under her feet into the earth – laughing.*) Your soul! Dead and buried! You strong man! (*She laughs.*)

MARCO (*threateningly*). Give me what was wrapped up in that, d'you hear!

PROSTITUTE (*scornfully. Takes the miniature from her bosom*). You mean this? I was bringing it back to you. D'you think I want her ugly face around? Here! (*She throws it at his feet. He leans down and picks it up, polishing it on his sleeve remorsefully. The Prostitute, walking away, calls back over her shoulder.*) I kissed it so you'd remember my kiss whenever you kiss her!

> (*She laughs. Marco starts as if to run after her angrily. Suddenly a shout rises from the lips of all the Tartars, the Minstrel and his drum become silent, and with one accord they raise their arms and eyes to the sky. Then the Minstrel chants.*)

MINSTREL. God of the Heaven, be in our souls! (*Then they all prostrate themselves on the ground as he chants.*) God of the Earth, be in our bodies!

> (*The Tartars sit up. The Minstrel begins again his drum-beat, crooning in a low monotone. The Polos rise and stretch sleepily.*)

58

MARCO (*inquisitively*). Two Gods? Are they in one Person like our Holy Trinity?

MAFFEO (*shocked*). Don't be impious! These are degraded pagans – or crazy, that's a more charitable way to –

> (*From behind the wall comes the sound of martial Chinese music. The gate opens. The blinding glare of the setting sun floods in from beyond. A file of soldiers, accompanying a richly-dressed Court Messenger, comes through. He walks directly up to the Polos and bows deeply.*)

MESSENGER. The Great Kaan, Lord of the World, sent me – (*He looks around.*) But where are the hundred wise men of the West?

NICOLO (*confusedly*). We had two monks to start with – but they left us and went back.

MAFFEO (*warningly*). Ssst!

MESSENGER (*indifferently*). You will explain to the Kaan. I was ordered to arrange a welcome for them.

MAFFEO (*claps him on the back*). Well, here we are – and hungry as hunters! So your welcome will be welcome, Brother. (*The Messenger bows, starts back, the Polos following him, Maffeo calling.*) Get on the job, Mark! (*They pass through the gate.*)

MARCO (*wearily picks up the cases – then goading himself on*). Giddap! Cathay or bust!

'MARCO MILLIONS'

(He struggles through the gate. For a second he is framed in it, outlined against the brilliant sky, tugging a sample case in each hand. Then the gate shuts, the light fades out. The drum-beat and the chanting recede into the distance.)

DARKNESS

ACT ONE

SCENE. *Music from full Chinese and Tartar bands crashes up to a tremendous blaring crescendo of drums, gongs, and the piercing shrilling of flutes. The light slowly comes to a pitch of blinding brightness. Then, as light and sound attain their highest point, there is a sudden dead silence. The scene is revealed as the Grand Throne Room in the palace of Kublai, the Great Kaan, in the city of Cambaluc, Cathay — an immense octagonal room, the lofty walls adorned in gold and silver. In the far rear wall, within a deep recess like the shrine of an idol, is the throne of the Great Kaan. It rises in three tiers, three steps to a tier. On golden cushions at the top Kublai sits dressed in his heavy gold robes of state. He is a man of sixty but still in the full prime of his powers, his face proud and noble, his expression tinged with an ironic humour and bitterness yet full of a sympathetic humanity. In his person are combined the conquering indomitable force of a descendant of Chinghiz with the humanizing culture of the conquered Chinese who have already begun to absorb their conquerors.*

On the level of the throne below Kublai are: on his right a Mongol warrior in full armour with shield and spear, his face grim, cruel and fierce. On his left Chu-Yin, the Cathayan sage

61

*and adviser to the Kaan, a venerable old man
with white hair, dressed in a simple black robe.*

*On the main floor, grouped close to the throne,
are: on the right, the sons of the Kaan. Farther
away, the nobles and warriors of all degrees with
their wives behind them. On the left, the wives
and concubines of the Kaan, then the courtiers,
officers, poets, scholars, etc. — all the non-military
officials and hangers-on of government, with
their women beside them.*

*Marco stands, a sample case in each hand, be-
wildered and dazzled, gawking about him on
every side. His father and uncle, bowing, walk
to the foot of the throne and kneel before the Kaan.
They make frantic signals to Marco to do likewise
but he is too dazed to notice. All the people in the
room are staring at him. The Kaan is looking at
the two brothers with a stern air. An usher of
the palace comes quietly to Marco and makes violent gestures to him to kneel down.*

MARCO (*misunderstanding him — gratefully*).
Thank you, Brother. (*He sits down on one of the
sample cases, to the gasping horror of all the Court.
The Kaan is still looking frowningly at the two Polos
as he listens to the report of their Messenger escort.
He does not notice. An outraged Chamberlain rushes
over to Marco and motions him to kneel down. Bewilderedly.*) What's the trouble now?

KUBLAI (*dismissing the Messenger, having heard*

his report — addresses the Polos coldly). I bid you welcome, Messrs. Polo. But where are the hundred wise men of the West who were to dispute with my wise men of the sacred teachings of Lao-Tseu and Confucius and the Buddha and Christ?

MAFFEO (*hurriedly*). There was no Pope elected until just before —

NICOLO. And he had no wise men, anyway.

> (*The Kaan now sees Marco and a puzzled expression of interest comes over his face.*)

KUBLAI. Is he with you?

NICOLO (*hesitantly*). My son, Marco, your Majesty — still young and graceless.

KUBLAI. Come here, Marco Polo.

> (*Marco comes forward, trying feebly to assume a bold, confident air.*)

MAFFEO (*in a loud, furious aside*). Kneel, you ass!

> (*Marco flounders to his knees.*)

KUBLAI (*with a smile*). I bid you welcome, Master Marco.

MARCO. Thank you, sir — I mean, your Lordship — your — (*Then suddenly.*) Before I forget — the Pope gave me a message for you, sir.

KUBLAI (*smiling*). Are you his hundred wise men?

MARCO (*confidently*). Well – almost. He sent me in their place. He said I'd be worth a million wise men to you.

NICOLO (*hastily*). His Holiness meant that Marco, by leading an upright life – not neglecting the practical side, of course – might set an example that would illustrate, better than wise words, the flesh and blood product of our Christian civilization.

KUBLAI (*with a quiet smile*). I shall study this apotheosis with unwearied interest, I foresee it.

MARCO (*suddenly – with a confidential air*). Wasn't that just a joke, your asking for the wise men? His Holiness thought you must have a sense of humour. Or that you must be an optimist.

KUBLAI (*with a smile of appreciation*). I am afraid your Holy Pope is a most unholy cynic. (*Trying to solve a riddle in his own mind – musingly.*) Could he believe this youth possesses that thing called soul which the West dreams lives after death – and might reveal it to me? (*Suddenly to Marco.*) Have you an immortal soul?

MARCO (*in surprise*). Of course! Any fool knows that.

KUBLAI (*humbly*). But I am not a fool. Can you prove it to me?

MARCO. Why, if you had no soul, what would happen when you die?

KUBLAI. What, indeed?

MARCO. Why, nothing. You'd be dead – just like an animal.

KUBLAI. Your logic is irrefutable.

MARCO. Well, I'm not an animal, am I? That's certainly plain enough. (*Then proudly.*) No, sir! I'm a man made by Almighty God in His Own Image for His greater glory!

KUBLAI (*staring at him for a long moment with appalled appreciation – ecstatically.*) So you are the Image of God! There is certainly something about you, something complete and unanswerable – but wait – a test!

> (*He claps his hands, pointing to Marco. Soldiers with drawn swords leap forward and seize him, trussing up his hands behind his back.*)

MAFFEO (*grovelling*). Mercy! He is only a boy!

NICOLO (*grovelling*). Mercy! He is only a fool!

KUBLAI (*sternly*). Silence! (*To Marco, with inhuman calm.*) Since you possess eternal life, it can do you no harm to cut off your head. (*He makes a sign to a soldier, who flourishes his sword.*)

MARCO (*trying to conceal his fear under a quavering, joking tone*). I might – catch – cold!

KUBLAI. You jest, but your voice trembles. What! Are you afraid to die, immortal youth? Well, then, if you will confess that your soul is a

stupid invention of your fear and that when you
die you will be dead as a dead dog is dead —

MARCO (*with sudden fury*). You're a heathen liar!
(*He glares defiantly. His father and uncle moan with
horror.*)

KUBLAI (*laughs and claps his hands. Marco is
freed. The Kaan studies his sullen but relieved face
with amusement*). Your pardon, Marco! I suspected a flaw, but you are perfect. You cannot
imagine your death. You are a born hero. I must
keep you near me. You shall tell me about your
soul and I will listen as to a hundred wise men
from the West! Is it agreed?

MARCO (*hesitatingly*). I know it's a great honour,
sir — but, forgetting the soul side of it, I've got to
eat.

KUBLAI (*astonished*). To eat?

MARCO. I mean, I'm ambitious. I've got to succeed, and — (*Suddenly blurts out.*) What can you
pay me?

KUBLAI. Ha! Well, you will find me a practical
man, too. I can start you upon any career you
wish. What is your choice?

MAFFEO (*interposing eagerly*). If I might speak to
the boy in private a minute — give him my humble
advice — he is so young — (*Maffeo and Nicolo
hurriedly lead Marco down to the foreground.*) You've
made a favourable impression — God knows why —
but strike while the iron is hot, you ninny! Ask to

be appointed a Second Class government commission-agent.

MARCO (*offended*). No! I'll be first-class or nothing!

MAFFEO. Don't be a fool! A First Class agent is all brass buttons and no opportunities. A Second Class travels around, is allowed his expenses, gets friendly with all the dealers, scares them into letting him in on everything – and gets what's rightfully coming to him! (*Then with a crafty look and a nudge in the ribs.*) And, being always in the secret, you'll be able to whisper to us in time to take advantage –

MARCO (*a bit flustered – with bluff assertion*). I don't know. The Kaan's been square with me. After all, honesty's the best policy, isn't it?

MAFFEO (*looking him over scathingly*). You'd think I was advising you to steal – I, Maffeo Polo, whose conservatism is unquestioned!

MARCO (*awed*). I didn't mean –

MAFFEO (*solemnly*). Do you imagine the Kaan is such a Nero as to expect you to live on your salary?

MARCO (*uncertainly*). No, I suppose not. (*He suddenly looks at Maffeo with a crafty wink.*) When I do give you a tip, what do I get from Polo Brothers?

MAFFEO (*between appreciation and dismay*). Ha! You learn quickly, don't you? (*Then hastily.*) Why, we – we've already thought of that – trust

us to look after your best interests — and decided
to — to make you a junior partner in the firm — eh,
Nick? — Polo Brothers and Son — doesn't that
sound solid, eh?

MARCO (*with a sly grin*). It's a great honour —
a very great honour. (*Then meaningly.*) But as
neither of you are Neros, naturally you'll also
offer me —

MAFFEO (*grinning in spite of himself*). Hmm!
Hmm! You Judas!

MARCO. A fair commission —

NICOLO (*blustering — but his eyes beaming with
paternal pride*). You young scamp!

MAFFEO (*laughing*). Ha-ha! Good boy, Mark!
Polos will be Polos!

> (*They all embrace laughingly. Kublai, who
> has been observing them intently, turns
> to Chu-Yin and they both smile.*)

KUBLAI. Did their Pope mean that a fool is a
wiser study for a ruler of fools than a hundred wise
men could be? This Marco touches me, as a child
might, but at the same time there is something
warped, deformed — Tell me, what shall I do with
him?

CHU-YIN. Let him develop according to his own
inclination and give him also every opportunity
for true growth if he so desires. And let us observe
him. At least, if he cannot learn, we shall.

KUBLAI (*smilingly*). Yes. And be amused. (*He calls commandingly.*) Marco Polo! (*Marco turns rather frightened and comes to the throne and kneels.*) Have you decided?

MARCO (*promptly*). I'd like to be appointed a commission-agent of the Second Class.

KUBLAI (*somewhat taken aback, puzzled*). You are modest enough!

MARCO (*manfully*). I want to start at the bottom!

KUBLAI (*with mocking grandeur*). Arise then, Second Class Marco! You will receive your agent's commission at once. (*Then with a twinkle in his eye.*) But each time you return from a journey you must relate to me all the observations and comments of your soul on the East. Be warned and never fail me in this!

MARCO (*confused but cocksurely*). I won't. I'll take copious notes. (*Then meaningly.*) And I can memorize any little humorous incidents –

MAFFEO (*apprehensively*). Blessed Saviour! (*He gives a violent fit of coughing.*)

MARCO (*looks around at him questioningly*). Hum? (*Misinterpreting his signal.*) And may I announce to your Majesty that a signal honour has just been conferred on me? My father and uncle have taken me into the firm. It will be Polo Brothers and Son from now on, and any way we can serve your Majesty –

KUBLAI (*a light coming over his face*). Aha! I

begin to smell all the rats in Cathay! (*The two elder Polos are bowed to the ground, trembling with apprehension. Kublai laughs quietly.*) Well, I am sure you wish to celebrate this family triumph together, so you may go. And accept my congratulations, Marco!

MARCO. Thank you, your Majesty. You will never regret it. I will always serve your best interests, so help me God!

> (*He goes grandly, preceded hurriedly by the trembling Nicolo and Maffeo. Kublai laughs and turns to Chu-Yin, who is smiling.*)

CURTAIN

ACT TWO

SCENE. *The Little Throne Room in the bamboo summer palace of the Kaan at Xanadu, the City of Peace — smaller, more intimate than the one at Cambaluc, but possessing an atmosphere of aloof dignity and simplicity fitting to the philosopher ruler who retreats here to contemplate in peace the vanity of his authority.*

> *About fifteen years have elapsed. It is a beautiful sunlit morning in late June. The Kaan reclines comfortably on his cushioned bamboo throne. His face has aged greatly. The expression has grown mask-like, full of philosophic calm. He has the detached air of an idol. Kukachin, a beautiful young girl of twenty, pale and delicate, is sitting at his feet. Her air is grief-stricken. A flute player in the garden is playing a melancholy air. Kukachin recites in a low tone:*

KUKACHIN. My thoughts in this autumn are lonely and sad,
A chill wind from the mountain blows in the garden.
The sky is grey, a snowflake falls, the last chrysanthemum
Withers beside the deserted summer-house.
I walk along the path in which weeds have grown.

71

My heart is bitter and tears blur my eyes.
I grieve for the days when we lingered together
In this same garden, along these paths between
flowers.
In the spring we sang of love and laughed with
youth
But now we are parted by many leagues and years
And I weep that never again shall I see your face.

> (*She finishes and relapses into her attitude
> of broken resignation. The flute player
> ceases his playing. Kublai looks down
> at her tenderly.*)

KUBLAI (*musingly*). Sing while you can. When
the voice fails, listen to song. When the heart
fails, be sung asleep. (*Chidingly.*) That is a sad
poem, Little Flower. Are you sad because you
must soon become Queen of Persia? But Arghun
is a great hero, a Khan of the blood of Chinghiz.
You will be blessed with strong sons able to dare
the proud destiny of our blood.

KUKACHIN (*dully*). Your will is my law.

KUBLAI. Not my will. The will of life to con-
tinue the strong. (*Forcing a consoling tone.*) Come,
Little Flower. You have been fading here. See
how pale you have grown! Your eyes are listless!
Your lips droop even in smiling! But life at the
Court of Persia is gay. There will be feasts, cele-
brations, diverting pleasures. You will be their
Queen of Beauty.

KUKACHIN (*with a sigh*). A Queen may be only a woman who is unhappy.

KUBLAI (*teasingly*). What despair! You talk like the ladies in poems who have lost their lovers! (*Kukachin gives a violent start which he does not notice and a spasm of pain comes over her face.*) But, never mind, Arghun of Persia is a hero no woman could fail to love.

KUKACHIN (*starting to her feet – desperately*). No! I can bear his children, but you cannot force me to – (*She breaks down, weeping.*)

KUBLAI (*astonished – gazing at her searchingly*). Have I ever forced you to anything? (*Then resuming his tone of tender teasing.*) I would say, rather, that ever since you were old enough to talk, the Ruler of Earth, as they innocently call your grandfather, has been little better than your slave.

KUKACHIN (*taking his hand and kissing it*). Forgive me. (*Then smiling at him.*) Have I been so bad as that? Has my love for you, who have been both father and mother to me, brought you no happiness?

KUBLAI (*with deep emotion*). You have been a golden bird singing beside a black river. You took your mother's place in my heart when she died. I was younger then. The river was not so black – the river of man's life so deep and silent – flowing with an insane obsession – whither? – and why? (*Then suddenly forcing a smile.*) Your poem

73

has made me melancholy. And I am too old, if not too wise, to afford anything but optimism! (*Then sadly.*) But now you in your turn must leave me, the river seems black indeed! (*Then after a pause – tenderly.*) If it will make you unhappy, you need not marry Arghun Khan.

KUKACHIN (*recovering herself – resolutely*). No. Your refusal would insult him. It might mean war. (*Resignedly.*) And Arghun is as acceptable as any other. Forgive my weakness. You once told me a Princess must never weep. (*She forces a smile.*) It makes no difference whether I stay or go, except that I shall be homesick for you. (*She kisses his hand again.*)

KUBLAI (*gratefully*). My little one. (*He strokes her hair. After a pause during which he looks at her thoughtfully – tenderly.*) We have never had secrets from each other, you and I. Tell me, can you have fallen in love?

KUKACHIN (*after a pause – tremblingly*). You must not ask that – if you respect my pride! (*With a pitiful smile.*) You see – he does not even know –

> (*She is blushing and hanging her head with confusion. Chu-Yin enters hurriedly from the right. He is very old but still upright. He is a bit breathless from haste, but his face is wreathed in smiles.*)

CHU-YIN (*making an obeisance*). Your Majesty, do you hear that martial music? His Honour,

Marco Polo, Mayor of Yang-Chau, seems about to visit you in state! (*The strains of a distant band can be heard.*)

KUBLAI (*still looking at Kukachin, who has started violently at the mention of Marco's name — worriedly*). Impossible! In love? . . . (*Then to Chu-Yin — preoccupiedly.*) Eh? Marco? I have given no order for him to return.

CHU-YIN (*ironically*). No doubt he comes to refresh your humour with new copious notes on his exploits. Our Marco has made an active mayor. Yang-Chau, according to the petition for mercy you have received from its inhabitants, is the most governed of all your cities. I talked recently with a poet who had fled from there in horror. Yang-Chau used to have a soul, he said. Now it has a brand new Court House. And another, a man of wide culture, told me, our Christian mayor is exterminating our pleasures and our rats as if they were twin breeds of vermin!

KUBLAI (*irritably*). He is beginning to weary me with his grotesque antics. A jester inspires mirth only so long as his deformity does not revolt one. Marco's spiritual hump begins to disgust me. He has not even a mortal soul, he has only an acquisitive instinct. We have given him every opportunity to learn. He has memorized everything and learned nothing. He has looked at everything and seen nothing. He has lusted for everything and loved nothing. He is only a shrewd and crafty greed. I shall send him home to his native wallow.

CHU-YIN (*in mock alarm*). What? Must we lose our clown?

KUKACHIN (*who has been listening with growing indignation*). How dare you call him a clown? Just because he is not a dull philosopher you think —

KUBLAI (*astounded — admonishingly*). Princess!

KUKACHIN (*turns to him — on the verge of tears — rebelliously*). Why are you both so unjust? Has he not done well everything he was ever appointed to do? Has he not always succeeded where others failed? Has he not by his will-power and determination risen to the highest rank in your service? (*Then, her anger dying — faltering.*) He is strange, perhaps, to people who do not understand him, but that is because he is so different from other men, so much stronger! And he has a soul! I know he has!

KUBLAI (*whose eyes have been searching her face — aghast*). Kukachin! (*She sees he has guessed her secret and at first she quails and shrinks away, then stiffens regally and returns his gaze unflinchingly. Chu-Yin looks from one to the other comprehendingly. Finally Kublai addresses her sternly.*) So, because I have allowed this fool a jester's latitude, because I permitted him to amuse you when you were a little girl, and since then, on his returns, to speak with you — a Princess! — (*Then brusquely.*) I shall inform the ambassadors you will be ready to sail for Persia within ten days. You may retire.

(*She bows with a proud humility and walks off* L. *Kublai sits in a sombre study, frowning and biting his lips. The blaring of Marco's band grows steadily nearer.*)

CHU-YIN (*gently*). Is intolerance wisdom? (*A pause. Then he goes on.*) I have suspected her love for him for a long time.

KUBLAI. Why didn't you warn me?

CHU-YIN. Love is to wisdom what wisdom seems to love — a folly. I reasoned, love comes like the breath of wind on water and is gone, leaving calm and reflection. I reasoned, but this is an enchanted moment for her and it will remain a poignant memory to recompense her when she is no longer a girl but merely a Queen. And I reasoned, who knows but some day this Marco may see into her eyes and his soul may be born, and that will make a very interesting study — for Kukachin, and her grandfather, the Son of Heaven and Ruler of the World! (*He bows mockingly.*) And for the old fool who is I!

KUBLAI (*bewilderedly*). I cannot believe it! Why, since she was a little girl, she has only talked to him once or twice every two years or so!

CHU-YIN. That was unwise, for thus he has remained a strange, mysterious dream-knight from the exotic West, an enigma with something

about him of a likable boy who brought her home
each time a humble, foolish, touching little gift!
And also remember that on each occasion he
returned in triumph, having accomplished a task —
a victor, more or less, acting the hero. (*The band
has crashed and dinned its way into the courtyard.*)
As now! Listen! (*He goes to the window and looks
down — with ironical but intense amusement.*) Ah!
He wears, over his Mayor's uniform, the regalia
of Cock of Paradise in his secret fraternal order
of the Mystic Knights of Confucius! The band of
the Xanadu lodge is with him as well as his own!
He is riding on a very fat white horse. He dis-
mounts, aided by the steps of your Imperial
Palace! He slaps a policeman on the back and
asks his name! He chucks a baby under the chin
and asks the mother its name. She lies and says
'Marco' although the baby is a girl. He smiles.
He is talking loudly so that everyone can overhear.
He gives the baby one yen to start a savings
account and encourage its thrift. The mother
looks savagely disappointed. The crowd cheers.
He keeps his smile frozen as he notices an artist
sketching him. He shakes hands with a one-
legged veteran of the Manzi campaign and asks
his name. The veteran is touched. Tears come
to his eyes. He tells him — but the Polo forgets
his name even as he turns to address the crowd.
He waves one hand for silence. The band stops.
It is the hand on which he wears five large jade
rings. The other hand rests upon — and pats —

78

the head of a bronze dragon, our ancient symbol of Yang, the celestial, male principle of the Cosmos. He clears his throat, the crowd stands petrified, he is about to draw a deep breath and open his mouth carefully in position one of the five phonetic exercises – (*Here Chu-Yin chuckles*). But I am an old man full of malice and venom and it embitters me to see others unreasonably happy, so – (*Here, just as Marco is heard starting to speak, he throws open the window and calls in a loud, commanding tone.*) Messer Polo, His Imperial Majesty commands that you stop talking, dismiss your followers, and repair to his presence at once!

MARCO'S VOICE (*very faint and crestfallen*). Oh – all right – I'll be right there.

KUBLAI (*cannot control a laugh in spite of himself – helplessly*). How can one deal seriously with such a child-actor?

CHU-YIN (*coming back from the window – ironically.*) Most women, including Kukachin, love children – and all women must take acting seriously in order to love at all.

> (*Just as he finishes speaking, Kukachin enters from* L. *She is terribly alarmed. She throws herself at Kublai's feet.*)

KUKACHIN. Why did you summon him? I told you he does not know. It is all my fault! Punish me, if you will! But promise me you will not harm him!

KUBLAI (*looking down at her—sadly*). Is it my custom to take vengeance? (*Then as people are heard approaching—quickly.*) Compose yourself! Remember again, Princesses may not weep! (*She springs to her feet, turns away for a moment, then turns back, her face rigidly calm and emotionless. Kublai nods with appreciation of her control.*) Good. You will make a Queen. (*She bows and retires backward to the left side of the throne. At the same moment, Nicolo and Maffeo Polo enter ceremoniously from* R. *They wear the regalia of officers in the Mystic Knights of Confucius over their rich merchants' robes. (This costume is a queer jumble of stunning effects that recall the parade uniforms of our modern Knights Templar, of Columbus, of Pythias, Mystic Shriners, the Klan, etc.) They are absurdly conscious and proud of this get-up—like two old men in a children's play. Kublai and Chu-Yin regard them with amused astonishment. Even Kukachin cannot restrain a smile. They prostrate themselves at the foot of the throne. Then just at the right moment, preceded by a conscious cough, Marco Polo makes his entrance. Over his gorgeous uniform of Mayor, he wears his childishly fantastic regalia as chief of the Mystic Knights of Confucius. As he steps on, he takes off his gilded, laced hat with its Bird of Paradise plumes and bows with a mechanical dignity on all sides. He has the manner and appearance of a successful movie star at a masquerade ball, disguised so that no one can fail to recognize him. His regular, good-looking, well-groomed face is carefully arranged into the grave responsible expression of a Senator from the South of the United States of America about to propose an amendment to the Constitution restricting the migration of non-Nordic birds into Texas, or prohibiting the practice of the laws of biology within the twelve-mile limit. He moves in stately fashion to the throne and prostrates himself before the Kaan. Kukachin stares at him with boundless admiration, hoping to catch his eye. The Kaan looks from her to him and his face grows stern. Chu-Yin is enjoying himself.)* Rise. *(Marco does so. Kublai continues dryly.)* To what do I owe the honour of this unexpected visit?

MARCO *(hastily, but with full confidence).* Well, I was sending in to your treasury the taxes of Yang-Chau for the fiscal year, and I knew you'd be so astonished at the unprecedented amount I had sweated out of them that you'd want to know how I did it — so here I am. *(An awkward pause. Marco is disconcerted at the Kaan's steady impersonal stare. He glances about — sees the Princess — welcomes this opportunity for diverting attention. Bowing with humble respect.)* Pardon me, Princess. I didn't recognize you before, you've so grown up. *(Flatteringly.)* You look like a Queen.

KUKACHIN *(falteringly).* I bid you welcome, Your Honour.

KUBLAI *(as a warning to Kukachin to control her emotion).* The Princess will soon be Queen of Persia.

81

MARCO (*flustered and awed, bowing to her again – flatteringly*). Then – Your Majesty – if I may be humbly permitted (*bowing to Kublai*) – to offer my congratulations – and before I settle down to discussing business – if Her Highness – Majesty – will accept a small token of my esteem – (*Here he stamps his foot. An African Slave, dressed in a pink livery with green hat and shoes and stockings and carrying a golden wicker basket, enters. He kneels, presents the basket to Marco, who lifts the cover and pulls out a small Chow puppy with a pink ribbon tied around its neck. He steps forward and offers this to the Princess, with a boyish grin.*) A contribution to your zoo – from your most humble servant!

KUKACHIN (*taking it – flushing with pleasure*). Oh, what a little darling! (*She cuddles the puppy in her arms.*)

MARCO (*boastfully*). He's a genuine, pedigreed pup. I procured him at great cost – I mean he's extra well-bred.

KUKACHIN. Oh, thank you so much, Marco Polo! (*Stammering.*) I mean, Your Honour.

KUBLAI (*warningly*). His Honour wishes to talk business, Princess.

KUKACHIN (*controlling herself*). I ask pardon. (*She bows and retires to L.R., where she stands fondling the puppy and watching Marco.*)

MARCO (*plunging in confidently on what he thinks is a sure point of attack*). My tax scheme, Your

Majesty, that got such wonderful results, is simplicity itself. I simply reversed the old system. For one thing, I found they had a high tax on excess profits. Imagine a profit being excess! Why, it isn't humanly possible! I repealed it. And I repealed the tax on luxuries. I found out that the great majority in Yang-Chau couldn't afford luxuries. The tax wasn't democratic enough to make it pay! I crossed it off and I wrote on the statute books a law that taxes every necessity in life, a law that hits every man's pocket equally, be he beggar or banker! And I got results!

CHU-YIN (*gravely*). In beggars?

KUBLAI (*with a chilling air*). I have received a petition from the inhabitants of Yang-Chau enumerating over three thousand cases of your gross abuse of power!

MARCO (*abashed only for a moment*). Oh, so they've sent that vile slander to you, have they? That's the work of a mere handful of radicals —

KUBLAI (*dryly*). Five hundred thousand names are signed to it. (*Still more dryly.*) Half a million citizens accuse you of endeavouring to stamp out their ancient culture!

MARCO. What! Why, I even had a law passed that anyone caught interfering with culture would be subject to a fine! It was Section One of a blanket statute that every citizen must be happy or go to jail. I found it was the unhappy ones who were always making trouble and getting discontented. You see, here's the way I figure it; if a man's good, he's happy – and if he isn't happy, it's a sure sign he's no good to himself or anyone else and he had better be put where he can't do harm.

KUBLAI (*a bit helplessly now*). They complain that you have entirely prohibited all free expression of opinion.

MARCO (*feelingly*). Well, when they go to the extreme of circulating such treasonable opinions against me, isn't it time to protect your sovereignty by strong measures? (*Kublai stares at this effrontery with amazement. Marco watches this impression and hurries on with an injured dignity.*) I can't believe, Your Majesty, that this minority of malcontents can have alienated your long-standing high regard for me!

KUBLAI (*conquered – suddenly overpowered by a great smile*). Not so! You are the marvel of mankind! And I would be lost without you!

MARCO (*flattered but at the same time nonplussed*). I thank you! (*Hesitatingly.*) But, to tell the truth, I want to resign, anyhow. I've done all I could. I've appointed five hundred committees to carry on my work and I retire confident that with the system I've instituted everything will go on automatically and brains are no longer needed. (*He adds as a bitter afterthought.*) And it's lucky they're not, or Yang-Chau would soon be a ruin!

KUBLAI (*with mock seriousness*). In behalf of the population of Yang-Chau I accept your resignation, with deep regret for the loss of your unique and extraordinary services. (*Then suddenly in a strange voice.*) Do you still possess your immortal soul, Marco Polo?

MARCO (*flustered*). Ha-ha! Yes, of course – at least I hope so. But I see the joke. You mean that Yang-Chau used to be a good place to lose one. Well, you wouldn't know the old town now. Sin is practically unseen. (*Hurrying on to another subject – boisterously.*) But however much I may have accomplished there, it's nothing to the big surprise I've got in reserve for you. May I demonstrate? (*Without waiting for permission, takes a piece of printed paper like a dollar bill from his pocket.*) What is it? Paper. Correct! What is it worth? Nothing. That's where you're mistaken. It's worth ten yen. No, I'm not a liar! See ten yen written on it, don't you? Well, I'll tell you the secret. This is money, legally valued at ten yens' worth of anything you wish to buy, by order of His Imperial Majesty, the Great Kaan! Do you see my point? Its advantages over gold and silver coin are obvious. It's light, easy to carry – (*Here he gives a prodigious wink*) wears out quickly, can be made at very slight expense, and yields enormous profit. Think of getting ten yen for this piece of paper. Yet it can be done. If you make the people believe it's worth it, it is! After all, when you stop to think, who was it first told them gold was money? I'll bet anything it was some quick-thinker who'd just discovered a gold mine!

(*Kublai and Chu-Yin stare at him in petrified incredulity. He mistakes it for admiration and is flattered. Bows and lays his paper money on the Kaan's knee.*) You're stunned, I can see that. It's so simple – and yet, who ever thought of it before me? I was amazed myself. Think it over, Your Majesty, and let the endless possibilities dawn on you! And now I want to show another little aid to government that I thought out. (*He makes a sign to his uncle and father. The former takes a mechanical contrivance out of a box and sets it up on the floor. It is a working model of a clumsy cannon. Nicolo, meanwhile, takes children's blocks out of his box and builds them into a fortress wall. Marco is talking. His manner and voice have become grave and portentous.*) It all came to me, like an inspiration, last Easter Sunday when Father and Uncle and I were holding a little service. Uncle read a prayer which spoke of Our Lord as the Prince of Peace. Somehow, that took hold of me. I thought to myself, well, it's funny, there always have been wars and there always will be, I suppose, because I've never read much in any history about heroes who waged peace. Still, that's wrong. War is a waste of money which eats into the profits of life like thunder! Then why war, I asked myself? But how are you going to end it? Then the flash came! There's only one workable way, and that's to conquer everybody else in the world so they'll never dare fight you again! An impossible task, you object? Not any more! This invention you see before you

makes conquering easy. Let me demonstrate
with these models. On our right, you see the
fortress wall of a hostile capital. Under your
present system with battering rams, to make an
effective breach in this wall would cost you the
lives of ten thousand men. Valuing each life con-
servatively at ten yen, this amounts to one hundred
thousand yen! This makes the cost of breaching
prohibitive. But all of this waste can be saved.
How? Just keep your eyes on your right and
permit my exclusive invention to solve this prob-
lem. (*He addresses the fortress in a matter-of-fact
tone.*) So you won't surrender, eh? (*Then in a
mock-heroic falsetto, answering himself like a ventrilo-
quist.*) We die but we never surrender! (*Then
matter-of-factly.*) Well, Brother, those heroic senti-
ments do you a lot of credit, but this is war and
not a tragedy. You're up against new methods
this time, and you'd better give in and avoid waste-
ful bloodshed. (*Answering himself.*) No! Victory
or Death! (*Then again.*) All right, Brother, don't
blame me. Fire! (*His uncle fires the gun. There is a
bang, and a leaden ball is shot out which knocks a big
breach in the wall of blocks. Marco beams. Kukachin
gives a scream of fright, then a gasp of delight, and
claps her hands. Marco bows to her the more gratefully as Kublai and Chu-Yin are staring at him with
a queer appalled wonder that puzzles him although
he cannot imagine it is not admiration.*) I see you are
stunned again. What made it do that, you're
wondering? This! (*He takes a little package out*

87

of his pocket and pours some black powder out of it on his palm.) It's the same powder they've been using here in children's fireworks. They've had it under their noses for years without a single soul ever having creative imagination enough to visualize the enormous possibilities. But you can bet I did! It was a lad crying with a finger half blown off where he held a fire-cracker too long that first opened my eyes. I learned the formula, improved on it, experimented in secret, and here's the gratifying result! (*He takes the cannon ball from his father who has retrieved it.*) You see? Now just picture this little ball magnified into one weighing twenty pounds or so and then you'll really grasp my idea. The destruction of property and loss of life would be tremendous! No one could resist you!

KUBLAI (*after a pause – musingly*). I am interested in the hero of that city who preferred death to defeat. Did you conquer his immortal soul?

MARCO (*with frankness*). Well, you can't consider souls when you're dealing with soldiers, can you? (*He takes his model and places it on the Kaan's knee with the paper money.*) When you have time, I wish you'd look this over. In fact – and this is the big idea I've been saving for the last – consider these two inventions of mine in combination. You conquer the world with this – (*He pats the cannon-model*) and you pay for it with this. (*He pats the paper money – rhetorically.*) You become the

88

bringer of peace on earth and good-will to men, and it doesn't cost you a yen hardly. Your initial expense – my price – is as low as I can possibly make it out of my deep affection for your Majesty – only a million yen.

KUBLAI (*quickly*). In paper?

MARCO (*with a grin and a wink*). No. I'd prefer gold, if you don't mind. (*Silence. Marco goes on meaningly.*) Of course, I don't want to force them on you. I'm confident there's a ready market for them elsewhere.

KUBLAI (*grimly smiling*). Oh, I quite realize that in self-protection I've got to buy them – or kill you!

MARCO (*briskly*). Then it's a bargain? But I've still got one proviso – that you give us permission to go home. (*Kukachin gives a little gasp. Marco goes on feelingly.*) We're homesick, Your Majesty. We've served you faithfully, and frankly now that we've made our fortune we want to go home and enjoy it. There's no place like home, Your Majesty! I'm sure even a King in his palace appreciates that.

KUBLAI (*with smiling mockery*). But – who can play your part? And your mission – your example! What will your Pope say when you tell him I'm still unconverted?

MARCO (*confidently*). Oh, you will be – on your

death-bed, if not before – a man of your common sense.

KUBLAI (*ironically*). Courtier! (*Then solemnly.*) But my last objection is insurmountable. You haven't yet proved you have an immortal soul!

MARCO. It doesn't need proving.

KUBLAI. If you could only bring forward one reliable witness.

MARCO. My Father and Uncle can swear –

KUBLAI. They think it is a family trait. Their evidence is prejudiced.

MARCO (*worried now – looks at Chu-Yin hopefully*). Mr. Chu-Yin ought to be wise enough to acknowledge –

CHU-YIN (*smiling*). But I believe that what can be proven cannot be true.

> (*Marco stands puzzled, irritated, looking stubborn, frightened and foolish. His eyes wander about the room, finally resting appealingly on Kukachin.*)

KUKACHIN (*suddenly steps forward – flushed but proudly*). I will bear witness he has a soul.

> (*Kublai looks at her with a sad wonderment, Chu-Yin smilingly, Marco with gratitude, Nicolo and Maffeo exchange a glance of congratulation.*)

KUBLAI. How can you know, Princess?

KUKACHIN. Because I have seen it – once, when he bound up my dog's leg, once when he played with a slave's baby, once when he listened to music over water and I heard him sigh, once when he looked at sunrise, another time at sunset, another at the stars, another at the moon, and each time he said that Nature was wonderful. And all the while, whenever he has been with me I have always felt – something strange and different – and that something must be His Honour's soul, must it not?

KUBLAI (*with wondering bitterness*). The eye sees only its own sight.

CHU-YIN. But a woman may feel life in the unborn.

KUBLAI (*mockingly but sadly*). I cannot contest the profound intuitions of virgins and mystics. Go home, Your Honour, Immortal Marco, and live for ever! (*With forced gaiety.*) And tell your Pope your example has done much to convert me to wisdom – if I could find the true one!

KUKACHIN (*boldly now*). And may I humbly request, since His Honour, and his father and uncle, are experienced masters of navigation, that they be appointed, for my greater safety, to attend me and command the fleet on my voyage to Persia?

KUBLAI (*astonished at her boldness – rebukingly*). Princess!

KUKACHIN (*returning his look – simply*). It is the

last favour I shall ever ask. I wish to be converted to wisdom, too — one or another — before I become a name.

KUBLAI (*bitterly*). I cannot deny your last request, even though you wish your own unhappiness. (*To the Polos.*) You will accompany the Princess.

MARCO (*jubilantly*). I'll be only too glad! (*Turning to the Princess.*) It'll be a great pleasure! (*Then briskly.*) And have we your permission to trade in the ports along the way?

KUKACHIN (*to Marco — embarrassed*). As you please, Your Honour.

MARCO (*bowing low*). I'll promise it won't disturb you. It's really a scheme to while away the hours, for I warn you in advance this is liable to be a mighty long trip.

KUKACHIN (*impulsively*). I do not care how long — (*She stops in confusion.*)

MARCO. Now if I had the kind of ships we build in Venice to work with I could promise you a record passage, but with your tubby junks it's just as well to expect the worst and you'll never be disappointed. (*Familiarly.*) And the trouble with any ship, for a man of action, is that there's so little you can do. I hate idleness where there's nothing to occupy your mind but thinking. I've been so used to being out, overcoming obstacles, getting things done, creating results where there weren't any before, going after the impossible – well – (*Here he gives a little deprecating laugh*) all play and no work makes Jack a dull boy. I'm sure I'd make a pretty dull person to have around if there wasn't plenty to do. You might not believe it, but when I'm idle I actually get gloomy sometimes!

KUKACHIN (*eagerly*). But we shall have dancers on the ship and actors who will entertain us with plays –

MARCO (*heartily*). That'll be grand. There's nothing better than to sit down in a good seat at a good play after a good day's work in which you know you've accomplished something, and after you've had a good dinner, and just take it easy and enjoy a good wholesome thrill or a good laugh and get your mind off serious things until it's time to go to bed.

KUKACHIN (*vaguely*). Yes. (*Then, eager to have him pleased.*) And there will be poets to recite their poems –

MARCO (*not exactly overjoyed*). That'll be nice. (*Then very confidentially – in a humorous whisper.*) I'll tell you a good joke on me, Your Highness. I once wrote a poem myself; would you ever believe it, to look at me?

KUKACHIN (*smiling at him as at a boy – teasingly*), No?

MARCO (*smiling back like a boy*). Yes, I did too, when I was young and foolish. It wasn't bad stuff either, considering I'd had no practice. (*Frowning with concentration.*) Wait! Let me see if I can remember any — oh, yes — 'You are lovely as the gold in the sun.' (*He hesitates.*)

KUKACHIN (*thrilled*). That is beautiful!

MARCO. That's only the first line. (*Then jokingly.*) You can consider yourself lucky. I don't remember the rest.

KUKACHIN (*dropping her eyes — softly*). Perhaps on the voyage you may be inspired to write another.

KUBLAI (*who has been staring at them with weary amazement*). Life is so stupid, it is mysterious!

DARKNESS

94

ACT TWO

SCENE TWO

SCENE: *The wharves of the Imperial Fleet at the sea-port of Zayton — several weeks later. At the left, stern to, is an enormous junk, the flagship. The wharf extends out, rear, to the right of her. At the right is a warehouse, from a door in which a line of half-naked slaves, their necks, waists, and right ankles linked up by chains, form an endless chain which revolves mechanically, as it were, on sprocket wheels in the interiors of the shed and the junk. As each individual link passes out of the shed it carries a bale on its head, moved with mechanical precision across the wharf, disappears into the junk, and reappears a moment later, having dumped its load, and moves back into the shed. The whole process is a man-power original of the modern devices with bucket scoops that dredge, load coal, sand, etc. By the side of the shed, a foreman sits with a drum and gong with which he marks a perfect time for the slaves, a four-beat rhythm, three beats of the drum, the fourth a bang on the gong as one slave at each end loads and unloads. The effect is like the noise of a machine.*

A bamboo stair leads up to the high poop of the junk from front, left. It is just getting dawn. A forest of masts, spars, sails of woven bamboo laths, shuts out all view of the harbour at the end of the wharf. At the foot of the stairs, Chu-Yin

95

stands like a sentinel. Above on top of the poop, the figures of Kublai and Kukachin are outlined against the lightening sky.

KUBLAI (*brokenly*). I must go. (*He takes her in his arms.*) We have said all we can say. Little Daughter, all rare things are secrets which cannot be revealed to anyone. That is why life must be so lonely. But I love you more dearly than anything on earth. And I know you love me. So perhaps we do not need to understand. (*Rebelliously.*) Yet I wish some Power could give me assurance that in granting your desire I am acting for your happiness, and for your eventual deliverance from sorrow to acceptance and peace. (*He notices she is weeping — in self-reproach.*) Old fool! I have made you weep again! I am death advising life how to live! Be deaf to me! Strive after what your heart desires! Who can ever know which are the mistakes we make? One should be either sad or joyful. Contentment is a warm sty for the eaters and sleepers! (*Impulsively.*) Do not weep! Even now I can refuse your hand to Arghun. Let it mean war!

KUKACHIN (*looking up and controlling herself — with a sad finality*). You do not understand. I wish to take this voyage.

KUBLAI (*desperately*). But I could keep Polo here. (*With impotent anger.*) He shall pray for his soul on his knees before you!

KUKACHIN (*with calm sadness*). Do I want a

slave? (*Dreamily.*) I desire a captain of my ship on a long voyage in dangerous, enchanted seas.

KUBLAI (*with a fierce defiance of fate*). I am the Great Kaan! I shall have him killed! (*A pause.*)

CHU-YIN (*from below, recites in a calm, soothing tone*). The noble man ignores self. The wise man ignores action. His truth acts without deeds. His knowledge venerates the unknowable. To him birth is not the beginning nor is death the end. (*Kublai's head bends in submission. Chu-Yin continues tenderly.*) I feel there are tears in your eyes. The Great Kaan, Ruler of the World, may not weep.

KUBLAI (*brokenly*). Ruler? I am my slave! (*Then controlling himself — forcing an amused teasing tone.*) Marco will soon be here, wearing the self-assurance of an immortal soul and his new admiral's uniform! I must fly in retreat from what I can neither laugh away nor kill. Write when you reach Persia. Tell me — all you can tell — particularly what his immortal soul is like! (*Then tenderly.*) Farewell, Little Flower! Live. There is no other advice possible from one human being to another.

KUKACHIN. Live — and love!

KUBLAI (*trying to renew his joking tone*). One's ancestors, particularly one's grandfather. Do not forget me!

KUKACHIN. Never! (*They embrace.*)

o

KUBLAI (*chokingly*). Farewell. (*He hurries down the ladder — to Chu-Yin.*) You remain — see him — bring me word — (*He turns his head up to Kukachin.*) For the last time, farewell, Little Flower of my life! May you know happiness! (*He turns quickly and goes.*)

KUKACHIN. Farewell! (*She bows her head on the rail and weeps.*)

CHU-YIN (*after a pause*). You are tired, Princess. Your eyes are red from weeping and your nose is red. You look old — a little homely, even. The Admiral Polo will not recognize you. (*Kukachin dries her eyes hastily.*)

KUKACHIN (*half-smiling and half-weeping at his teasing*). I think you are a very horrid old man!

CHU-YIN. A little sleep, Princess, and you will be beautiful. The old dream passes. Sleep and awake in the new. Life is perhaps most wisely regarded as a bad dream between two awakenings, and every day is a life in miniature.

KUKACHIN (*wearily and drowsily*). Your wisdom makes me sleep. (*Her head sinks back on her arms and she is soon asleep.*)

CHU-YIN (*after a pause — softly*). Kukachin! (*He sees she is asleep — chuckles.*) I have won a convert. (*Then speculatively.*) Youth needs so much sleep and old age so little. Is that not a proof that from birth to death one grows steadily closer to complete life? Hum.

(He ponders on this. From the distance comes the sound of Polo's band playing the same martial air as in the previous scene. Chu-Yin starts — then smiles. The music quickly grows louder. The Princess awakes with a start.)

KUKACHIN *(startled)*. Chu-Yin! Is that the Admiral coming?

CHU-YIN *(dryly)*. I suspect so. It is like him not to neglect a person in the city when saying good-bye.

KUKACHIN *(flurriedly)*. I must go to my cabin for a moment. *(She hurries back.)*

CHU-YIN *(listens with a pleased, ironical smile as the band gets rapidly nearer. Finally it seems to turn a corner near by, and a moment later, to a deafening clangour, Marco enters, dressed in a gorgeous Admiral's uniform. Two paces behind, side by side, walk Maffeo and Nicolo, dressed only a trifle less gorgeously as Commodores. Behind them comes the band. Marco halts as he sees Chu-Yin, salutes condescendingly, and signals the band to be silent. Chu-Yin bows gravely and remarks as if answering an argument in his own mind).* Still, even though they cannot be house-broken, I prefer monkeys because they are so much less noisy.

MARCO *(with a condescending grin)*. What's that — more philosophy? *(Clapping him on the back.)* Well, I like your determination. *(He wipes his*

99

brow with a handkerchief.) Phew! I'll certainly be glad to get back home where I can hear some music that I can keep step to. My feet just won't give in to your tunes. (*With a grin.*) And look at the Old Man and Uncle. They're knock-kneed for life. (*Confidentially.*) Still, I thought the band was a good idea — to sort of cheer up the Princess, and let people know she's leaving at the same time. (*As people begin to come in and stare at the poop of the ship.*) See the crowd gather? I got them out of bed, too!

CHU-YIN (*ironically*). You also woke up the Princess. You sail at sunrise?

MARCO (*briskly — taking operations in hand*). Thank you for reminding me. I've got to hurry. (*To his Father and Uncle.*) You two better get aboard your ships and be ready to cast off when I signal. (*They go off. He suddenly bawls to some one in the ship.*) Much more cargo to load?

A VOICE. Less than a hundred bales, sir.

MARCO. Good. Call all hands on deck and stand by to put sail on her.

A VOICE. Aye-aye, sir.

MARCO. And look lively, damn your lazy souls! (*To Chu-Yin — complacently.*) You've got to impose rigid discipline on shipboard.

CHU-YIN (*inquisitively*). I suppose you feel your heavy responsibility as escort to the future Queen of Persia?

MARCO (*soberly*). Yes, I do. I'll confess I do. If she were a million yens' worth of silk or spices I wouldn't worry an instant, but a Queen, that's a different matter. However, when you give my last word to His Majesty, you can tell him that I've always done my duty by him and I won't fail him this time. As long as I've a breath in me, I'll take care of her!

CHU-YIN (*with genuine appreciation*). That is bravely spoken.

MARCO. I don't know anything about brave speaking. I'm by nature a silent man, and I let my actions do the talking. But, as I've proved to you people in Cathay time and again, when I say I'll do a thing, I do it!

CHU-YIN (*suddenly with a sly smile to himself*). I was forgetting. His Majesty gave me some secret last instructions for you. You are, at some time every day of the voyage, to look carefully and deeply into the Princess's eyes and note what you see there.

MARCO. What for? (*Then brightly.*) Oh, he's afraid she'll get fever in the tropics. Well, you tell him I'll see to it she keeps in good condition. I'll do what's right by her without considering fear or favour. (*Then practically.*) Then, of course, if her husband thinks at the end of the voyage that my work deserves a bonus — why, that's up to him. (*Inquisitively.*) She's never seen him, has she?

CHU-YIN. No.

MARCO (*with an air of an independent thinker*). Well, I believe in love matches myself, even for Kings and Queens. (*With a grin.*) Come to think of it, I'll be getting married to Donata myself when I get home.

CHU-YIN. Donata?

MARCO (*proudly*). The best little girl in the world! She's there waiting for me.

CHU-YIN. You have heard from her?

MARCO. I don't need to hear. I can trust her. And I've been true to her, too. I haven't ever thought of loving anyone else. Of course, I don't mean I've been any he-virgin. I've played with concubines at odd moments when my mind needed relaxation — but that's only human nature. (*His eyes glistening reminiscently.*) Some of them were beauties, too! (*With a sigh.*) Well, I've had my fun and I suppose it's about time I settled down.

CHU-YIN. Poor Princess!

MARCO. What's that? Oh, I see, yes, I sympathize with her, too — going into a harem. If there's one thing more than another that proves you in the East aren't responsible, it's that harem notion. (*With a grin.*) Now in the West we've learned by experience that one at a time is trouble enough.

CHU-YIN (*dryly*). Be sure and converse on love

and marriage often with the Princess. I am certain you will cure her.

MARCO (*mystified*). Cure her?

CHU-YIN. Cure her mind of any unreasonable imaginings.

MARCO (*easily*). Oh, I'll guarantee she'll be contented, if that's what you mean. (*The human chain in back finishes its labours and disappears into the shed. The crowd of people has been steadily augmented by new arrivals, until a small multitude is gathered standing in silence staring up at the poop. Marco says with satisfaction.*) Well, cargo's all aboard, before schedule, too. We killed six slaves but, by God, we did it! And look at the crowd we've drawn, thanks to my band!

CHU-YIN (*disgustedly*). They would have come without noise. They love their Princess.

MARCO (*cynically*). Maybe, but they love their sleep, too. I know 'em!

> (*A cry of adoration goes up from the crowd. With one movement they prostrate themselves as the Princess comes from the cabin dressed in a robe of silver and stands at the rail looking down.*)

THE CROWD (*in a long, ululating whisper*). Farewell – farewell – farewell – farewell!

KUKACHIN (*silences them with a motion of her hand*). I shall know the long sorrow of an exile

As I sail over the green water and the blue water
Alone under a strange sky amid alien flowers and
  faces.
My eyes shall be ever red with weeping, my heart
  bleeding,
While I long for the land of my birth and my child-
  hood
Remembering with love the love of my people.
(*A sound of low weeping comes from the crowd.*) Fare-
well!

THE CROWD. Farewell – farewell – farewell –
farewell!

MARCO (*feeling foolish because he is moved*). Damn
it! Reciting always makes me want to cry about
something. Poetry acts worse on me than wine
that way. (*He calls up – very respectfully.*) Princess! We'll be sailing at once. Would you mind
retiring to your cabin? I'm afraid you're going to
catch cold standing bareheaded in the night air.

KUKACHIN (*tremulously – grateful for his solici-
tude*). I am in your charge, Admiral. I am grateful
that you should think of my health, and I obey.

> (*She turns and goes back into her cabin. The
> crowd silently filters away, leaving only
> the band.*)

MARCO (*proudly and fussily*). You can't have
women around when you're trying to get something done. I can see where I'll have to be telling
her what to do every second. Well, I hope she'll

take it in good part and not forget I'm acting in her husband's interests, not my own. (*Very confidentially.*) You know, apart from her being a Princess, I've always respected her a lot. She's not haughty and she's — well, human, that's what I mean. I'd do anything I could for her, Princess or not! Yes, sir!

CHU-YIN (*wonderingly*). There may be hope — after all.

MARCO. What's that?

CHU-YIN. Nothing. Enigma!

MARCO. There's always hope! Don't be a damned pessimist! (*Clapping him on the back.*) Enigma, eh? Well, if that isn't like a philosopher — to start in on riddles just at the last moment! (*He ascends half-way up the ladder to the poop, then turns back to Chu-Yin with a chuckle.*) Take a fool's advice and don't think so much or you'll get old before your time! (*More oratorically.*) If you look before you leap, you'll decide to sit down. Keep on going ahead and you can't help being right! You're bound to get somewhere! (*He suddenly breaks into a grin again.*) There! Don't ever say I never gave you good advice! (*He springs swiftly to the top deck and bellows.*) Cast off there amidships! Where the hell are you — asleep? Set that foresail! Hop, you kidney-footed gang of thumb-fingered infidels! (*He turns with a sudden fierceness on the band, who are standing stolidly, awaiting orders.*) Hey you! Didn't I tell you to strike up when I set foot on the deck? What do you think I paid you in advance for — to wave me good-bye? (*The band plunges madly into it. A frenzied cataract of sound results. Chu-Yin covers his ears and moves away, shaking his head, as Marco leans over the rail and bawls after him.*) And tell the Kaan — anything he wants — write me — just Venice — they all know me there — and if they don't, by God, they're going to!

DARKNESS

ACT TWO

SCENE THREE

SCENE: *Poop deck of the royal junk of the Princess Kukachin at anchor in the harbour of Hormuz, Persia — a moonlight night some two years later. On a silver throne at C. Kukachin is sitting dressed in a gorgeous golden robe of ceremony. Her beauty has grown more intense, her face has undergone a change, it is the face of a woman who has known real sorrow and suffering. In the shadow of the highest deck in rear her women-in-waiting are in a group, sitting on cushions. On the highest deck in rear Sailors lower and furl the sail of the mizzenmast, every movement being carried out in unison with a machine-like rhythm. The bulwarks of the junk are battered and splintered, the sail is frayed and full of jagged holes and patches. In the foreground (the port side of deck) the two elder Polos are squatting. Each has a bag of money before him from which they are carefully counting gold coins and packing stacks of these into a chest that stands between them.*

MARCO (*his voice, hoarse and domineering, comes from the left just before the curtain rises*). Let go that anchor!

> (*A meek 'Aye-aye, sir,' is heard replying and then a great splash and a long rattling of chains. The curtain then rises, dis-*

107

covering the scene as above. Marco's voice is again heard, 'Lower that miz-zensail! Look lively now!')

BOATSWAIN (*with the sailors*). Aye-aye, sir! (*They lower the sail, and begin to tie it up trimly.*)

MAFFEO (*looking up and straightening his cramped back – with a relieved sigh*). Here's Persia! I'll be glad to get on dry land again. Two years on this foreign tub are too much.

NICOLO (*with a grunt, intent on the money*). Keep counting if you want to finish before we go ashore. It's nine hundred thousand now in our money, isn't it?

MAFFEO (*nods – counting again*). This lot will bring it to a million. (*He begins stacking and packing again.*)

BOATSWAIN (*chanting as his men work*).
    Great were the waves,
    Volcanoes of foam
    Ridge after ridge
    To the rim of the world!
    Great were the waves!

CHORUS OF SAILORS. Great were the waves!

BOATSWAIN. Fierce were the winds!
    Demons screamed!
    Their claws rended
    Sails into rags,
    Fierce were the winds!

CHORUS. Fierce were the winds!

BOATSWAIN. Fire was the sun!
Boiled the blood black,
Our veins hummed
Like bronze kettles.
Fire was the sun!

CHORUS. Fire was the sun!

BOATSWAIN. Long was the voyage!
Life drifted becalmed,
A dead whale awash
In the toil of tides.
Long was the voyage!

CHORUS. Long was the voyage!

BOATSWAIN. Many have died!
Sleep in green water.
Wan faces at home
Pray to the sea.
Many have died!

CHORUS. Many have died!

KUKACHIN (*chants the last line after them – sadly*).
Many have died!

(*After a brooding pause she rises and chants in a low voice.*)

If I were asleep in green water,
No pang could be added to my sorrow,
Old grief would be forgotten,
I would know peace.

SAILORS. There is peace deep in the sea
But the surface is sorrow.

WOMEN. Kukachin will be a Queen!
    A Queen may not sorrow
    Save for her King!

KUKACHIN. When love is not loved it loves death.
When I sank drowning, I loved Death.
When the pirate's knife gleamed, I loved Death.
When fever burned me, I loved Death.
But the man I love saved me.

SAILORS. Death lives in a silent sea,
    Grey and cold under cold grey sky,
    Where there is neither sun nor wind
    Nor joy nor sorrow!

WOMEN. Kukachin will be a wife.
    A wife must not sorrow
    Save for her man.

KUKACHIN. A hero is merciful to women.
Why could not this man see or feel or know?
Then he would have let me die.

SAILORS. There are harbours at every voyage-end
Where we rest from the sorrows of the sea.

WOMEN. Kukachin will be a mother.
    A mother may not sorrow
    Save for her son.

*(Kukachin bows her head in resignation. A
    pause of silence. Marco Polo enters
    briskly from below on L. He is dressed
    in full uniform, looking spick and span*

and self-conscious. His face wears an
expression of humorous scorn. He bows
ceremoniously to the Princess, his atti-
tude a queer mixture of familiarity and
an uncertain awe.)

MARCO. Your Highness – (*Then ingratiatingly*)
– or I suppose I'd better say Majesty now that
we've reached Persia – I've got queer news for
you. A boat just came from the shore with an
official notification that your intended husband,
Arghun Khan, is dead and I'm to hand you over
to his son, Ghazan, to marry. (*He hands her a*
sealed paper.) See!

KUKACHIN (*letting the paper slip from her hand*
without a glance – dully). What does it matter?

MARCO (*admiringly – as he picks it up*). I must
say you take it coolly. Of course, come to think
of it, never having seen either, one's as good as
another. (*He winds up philosophically.*) And you'll
be Queen just the same, that's the main thing.

KUKACHIN (*with bitter irony*). So you think that
is happiness? (*Then, as Marco stares at her uncer-*
tainly, she turns away and looks out over the sea with
a sigh – after a pause.) There, where I see the
lights, is that Hormuz?

MARCO. Yes. And I was forgetting, the messenger said Ghazan Khan would come to take you
ashore to-night.

KUKACHIN (*with sudden fear*). So soon? To-

III

night? (*Then rebelliously.*) Is the granddaughter of the Great Kublai no better than a slave? I will not go until it pleases me!

MARCO. Good for you! That's the spirit! (*Then alarmed at his own temerity – hastily.*) But don't be rash! The Khan probably meant whenever you were willing. And don't mind what I just said.

KUKACHIN (*looks at him with a sudden dawning of hope – gently*). Why should you be afraid of what you said?

MARCO (*offended*). I'm not afraid of anything – when it comes to the point!

KUKACHIN. What point?

MARCO (*nonplussed*). Why – well – when I feel some one's trying to steal what's rightfully mine, for instance.

KUKACHIN. And now – here – you do not feel that?

MARCO (*with a forced laugh, thinking she is joking*). Ha! Well – (*Uncertainly.*) That is – I don't catch your meaning – (*Then changing the subject abruptly.*) But here's something I want to ask you. Your grandfather entrusted you to my care. He relied on me to prove equal to the task of bringing you safe and sound to your husband. Now I want to ask you frankly if you yourself won't be the first to acknowledge that in spite of typhoons, shipwrecks, pirates and every other known form of bad luck, I've brought you through in good shape?

KUKACHIN (*with an irony almost hysterical*). More than anyone in the world, I can appreciate your devotion to duty! You have been a prodigy of heroic accomplishment! In the typhoon when a wave swept me from the deck, was it not you who swam to me as I was drowning?

MARCO (*modestly*). It was easy. Venetians make the best swimmers in the world.

KUKACHIN (*even more ironically*). When the pirates attacked us, was it not your brave sword that warded off their curved knives from my breast and struck them dead at my feet?

MARCO. I was out of practice, too. I used to be one of the crack swordsmen of Venice – and they're the world's foremost, as everyone knows.

KUKACHIN (*with a sudden change – softly*). And when the frightful fever wasted me, was it not you who tended me night and day, watching by my bedside like a gentle nurse, even brewing yourself the medicines that brought me back to life?

MARCO (*with sentimental solemnity*). My mother's recipes. Simple home remedies – from the best friend I ever had!

KUKACHIN (*a trifle wildly*). Oh, yes, you have been a model guardian, Admiral Polo!

MARCO (*quickly*). Thank you, Princess. If I have satisfied you – then if I might ask you a favour, that you put in writing all you've just said in your first letter to the Great Kaan, and also tell your husband?

KUKACHIN (*suddenly wildly bitter*). I will assuredly! I will tell them both of your heroic cruelty in saving me from death! (*Intensely.*) Why could you not let me die?

MARCO (*confusedly*). You're joking. You certainly didn't want to die, did you?

KUKACHIN (*slowly and intensely*). Yes!

MARCO (*puzzled and severe*). Hum! You shouldn't talk that way.

KUKACHIN (*longingly*). I would be asleep in green water!

MARCO (*worried — suddenly reaches out and takes her hand*). Here now, young lady! Don't start getting morbid!

KUKACHIN (*with a thrill of love*). Marco!

MARCO. I believe you're feverish. Let me feel your pulse!

KUKACHIN (*violently*). No! (*She draws her hand from his as if she had been stung.*)

MARCO (*worried*). Please don't be unreasonable. There'd be the devil to pay if you should suffer a relapse of that fever after I sweated blood to pull you through once already! Do you feel hot?

KUKACHIN (*wildly*). No! Yes! On fire!

MARCO. Are your feet cold?

KUKACHIN. No! Yes! I don't know!

(*Gravely Marco kneels, removes a slipper, and feels the sole of her foot — then pats her foot playfully.*)

MARCO. No. They're all right. (*He gets up — professionally.*) Any cramps?

KUKACHIN. You fool! No! Yes! My heart feels as if it were bursting!

MARCO. It burns?

KUKACHIN. Like a red ember flaring up for the last time before it chills into grey ash for ever!

MARCO. Then something must have disagreed with you. Will you let me see your tongue?

KUKACHIN (*in a queer hysterical state where she delights in self-humiliation*). Yes! Yes! Anything! I am a Princess of the Imperial blood of Chinghiz and you are a dog! Anything! (*She sticks out her tongue, the tears streaming down her face as he looks at it.*)

MARCO (*shakes his head*). No sign of biliousness. There's nothing seriously wrong. If you would only try to sleep a while —

KUKACHIN. O Celestial God of the Heavens! What have I done that Thou shouldst torture me? (*Then wildly to Marco.*) I wished to sleep in the depths of the sea. Why did you awaken me?

MARCO (*worried again*). Perhaps it's brain fever. Does your head ache?

KUKACHIN. No! Does your immortal soul?

MARCO. Don't blaspheme! You're talking as if you were delirious! (*Then pleadingly.*) For Heaven's sake, try and be calm, Princess! What if your husband, Ghazan Khan, should find you in such a state?

KUKACHIN (*calming herself with difficulty – after a pause, bitterly*). I suppose you are relieved to get me here alive and deliver me – like a cow!

MARCO (*injuredly*). I've only carried out your own grandfather's orders!

KUKACHIN (*forcing a smile*). Won't you miss being my guardian? (*Striving pitifully to arouse his jealousy.*) When you think of Ghazan protecting me and nursing me when I am sick – and – and loving me? Yes! I will compel him to love me, even though I never love him! He shall look into my eyes and see that I am a woman and beautiful!

MARCO. That's a husband's privilege.

KUKACHIN. Or a man's – a man who has a soul! (*Mockingly but intensely.*) And that reminds me, Admiral Polo! You are taking advantage of this being the last day to shirk your duty!

MARCO. Shirk! No one can ever say –!

KUKACHIN. It was my grandfather's special command, given to you by Chu-Yin, you told me, that every day you should look into my eyes.

MARCO (*resignedly*). Well, it isn't too late yet, is it?

116

(He moves toward her with a sigh of half-impatience with her whims.)

KUKACHIN. Wait. This is the one part of your duty in which I shall have to report you incompetent.

MARCO (*hurt*). I've done my best. I never could discover anything out of the way.

KUKACHIN. There must be something he wished you to find. I myself feel there is something, something I cannot understand, something you must interpret for me! And remember this is your last chance! There is nothing in life I would not give — nothing I would not do — even now it is not too late! See my eyes as those of a woman and not a Princess! Look deeply! I will die if you do not see what is there! (*She finishes hysterically and beseechingly.*)

MARCO (*worried — soothingly*). There! There! Certainly, Princess! Of course, I'll look. And will you promise me that afterwards you'll lie down?

KUKACHIN. Look! See! (*She throws her head back, her arms outstretched. He bends over and looks into her eyes. She raises her hands slowly above his head as if she were going to pull it down to hers. Her lips part, her whole being strains out to him. He looks for a moment critically, then he grows tense, his face moves hypnotically toward hers, their lips seem about to meet in a kiss. She murmurs.*) Marco!

MARCO (*his voice thrilling for this second with oblivious passion.*) Kukachin!

MAFFEO (*suddenly slapping a stack of coins into the chest with a resounding clank*). One million!

MARCO (*with a start, comes to himself and backs away from the Princess in terror*). What, Uncle? Did you call?

MAFFEO. One million in God's money! (*He and Nicolo lock and fasten the box jubilantly.*)

KUKACHIN (*in despair*). Marco!

MARCO (*flustered*). Yes, Princess. I saw something queer! It made me feel feverish too! (*Recovering a bit – with a sickly smile.*) Oh, there's trouble there, all right! You must be delirious! I advise you to go to sleep.

KUKACHIN (*with wild despair pulls out a small dagger from the bosom of her dress*). I obey! I shall sleep for ever!

> (*But Marco, the man of action, springs forward and wresting the dagger from her hand, flings it over the side. She confronts him defiantly, her eyes wild with grief and rage. He stares at her, dumbfounded and bewildered.*)

MARCO (*bewildered*). I never believed people – sane people – ever seriously tried –

KUKACHIN (*intensely*). I implored an ox to see

my soul! I no longer can endure the shame of living!

MARCO (*sheepishly*). You mean it was a terrible insult when I called you – by your name?

KUKACHIN (*bursting into hysterical laughter*). Yes! How dared you!

MARCO (*hastily*). I ask pardon, Princess! Please forgive me! My only excuse is, I forgot myself. I'll have to stop overworking or I'll suffer a nervous breakdown. I felt like one of those figures in a puppet show with some one jerking the wires. It wasn't me, you understand. My lips spoke without me saying a word. And here's the funniest part of it all, and what'll explain matters in full, if you can believe it. It wasn't you I was seeing and talking to, not a Princess at all, you'd changed into some one else, some one I've got a good right to – just a girl –

KUKACHIN (*again clutching at hope*). A girl – a woman – you saw in me?

MARCO (*enthusiastically, groping in his shirt front*). Yes. Here she is! (*He jerks the locket out of an under pocket and presents it to her proudly.*) The future Mrs. Marco Polo! (*The Princess takes it mechanically and stares at it in a stupor as Marco rambles on.*) You may believe it or not, but like a flash she was standing there in your place and I was talking to her, not you at all!

119

KUKACHIN (*dully*). But it was my name you spoke.

MARCO (*confused*). I meant to say Donata. That's her name. We're going to be married as soon as I get home. (*Then as she stares at the miniature – proudly.*) Pretty, isn't she?

KUKACHIN (*dully*). She may have married another.

MARCO (*confidently*). No. Her family needs an alliance with our house.

KUKACHIN. She may have had lovers.

MARCO (*simply*). Oh, no. She's not that kind.

KUKACHIN (*staring at the picture*). She will be middle-aged – fat – and stupid!

MARCO (*with a grin*). Well, I don't mind a wife being a bit plump – and who wants a great thinker around the house? Sound common sense and a home where everything runs smooth, that's what I'm after.

KUKACHIN (*looks from him to the miniature*). There is no soul even in your love, which is no better than a mating of swine! And I –! (*A spasm of pain covers her face – then with hatred and disdain.*) Pig of a Christian! Will you return to this sow and boast that a Princess and a Queen –? (*With rage.*) Shall I ask as my first wedding present from Ghazan Khan that he have you flayed and thrown into the street to be devoured by dogs?

MAFFEO AND NICOLO (*who have pricked up their ears at this last, rush to the Princess, dragging their box between them, and prostrate themselves at her feet*). Mercy! Mercy!

> (*She seems not to hear or to see them but stares ahead stonily. Marco beckons Maffeo to one side.*)

MARCO (*in a whisper*). Don't be afraid. She doesn't mean a word of it. She's hysterical. Listen, I just noticed the royal barge coming. I'll go and meet the Khan. You keep her from doing anything rash until he gets here.

MAFFEO. Yes.

> (*He goes back and crouches again before the Princess, keeping a wary eye on her, but she seems turned to stone. Marco comes down and goes off L. There is the blare of a trumpet, the reflections of lanterns and torches, the sound of running about on deck and Marco's voice giving commands. The Women come out to attend the Princess. She remains rigid, giving no sign.*)

WOMEN (*in chorus*).
The lover comes,
Who becomes a husband,
Who becomes a son,
Who becomes a father —
In this contemplation lives the woman

KUKACHIN (*her face now a fatalistic mask of acceptance*).

> I am not.
> Life is.
> A cloud hides the sun.
> A life is lived.
> The sun shines again.
> Nothing has changed.
> Centuries wither into tired dust.
> A new dew freshens the grass.
> Somewhere this dream is being dreamed.

(*From* L. *Marco comes escorting Ghazan Khan, attended by a train of nobles and slaves with lights. He can be heard saying: 'She is a little feverish — the excitement —' All are magnificently dressed, glittering with jewels. Ghazan is a young man, not handsome but noble and manly looking. He comes forward and bows low before her, his attendants likewise. Then he looks into her face and stands fascinated by her beauty. She looks back at him with a calm indifference.*)

GHAZAN (*after a pause — his voice thrilling with admiration*). If it were possible for a son who loved a noble father to rejoice at that father's death, then I should be that guilty son! (*As she makes no reply.*) You have heard? Arghun Khan is dead. You must bear the humiliation of accepting his son for husband, a crow to replace an eagle! Forgive me. But with your eyes to watch I may become at least a shadow of his greatness.

KUKACHIN (*calmly*). What am I? I shall obey the eternal will which governs your destiny and mine.

GHAZAN (*impetuously*). You are more beautiful than I had dared to dream! It shall not be I who rules, but you! I shall be your slave! Persia shall be your conquest and everywhere where songs are sung they shall be in praise of your beauty! You shall be Queen of Love —!

KUKACHIN (*sharply, with pain*). No!

(*She drops the locket on the floor and grinds it into pieces under her foot.*)

MARCO (*excitedly*). Princess! Look out! You're stepping on —

(*She kicks it away from her. Marco stoops on his knees and begins picking up the wreckage in his handkerchief. Kukachin turns to Ghazan and points to Marco.*)

KUKACHIN. My first request of you, my Lord, is that you reward this Christian who has brought me here in safety. I ask, as a fitting tribute to his character, that you give an immense feast in his honour. Let there be food in tremendous amounts! He is an exquisite judge of quantity. Let him be urged to eat and drink until he can hold no more, until he becomes his own ideal figure, an idol of stuffed self-satisfaction! Will you do this? (*She is a trifle hectic now and her manner has grown wilder.*)

GHAZAN. Your wish is my will!

KUKACHIN (*pointing to a magnificent lion in diamonds on his breast*). What is that wonderful glittering beast?

GHAZAN. It is the emblem of the Order of the Lion, which only great heroes and kings of men may wear.

KUKACHIN (*gives a laugh of wild irony*). Great heroes – kings of men? (*Then eagerly.*) Will you give it to me? I implore you! (*Ghazan, fascinated, yet with a wondering glance, unpins it and hands it to her without a word. She prods Marco, who is still collecting the pieces of the locket, with her foot.*) Arise! Let me give you the noble Order of the Lion! (*She pins the blazing diamond figure on the breast of the stunned Marco, laughing with bitter mockery.*) How well it is set off on the bosom of a sheep! (*She laughs more wildly.*) Kneel again! Bring me a chest of gold! (*Ghazan makes a sign. Two slaves bring a chest of gold coins to her. She takes handfuls and throws them over the kneeling forms of the Polos, laughing.*) Here! Guzzle! Grunt! Wallow for our amusement!

> (*The two elder are surreptitiously snatching at the coins, but Marco jumps to his feet, his face flushing.*)

MARCO (*in a hurt tone*). I don't see why you're trying to insult me —just at the last moment. What have I done? (*Then suddenly forcing a smile.*) But I realize you're not yourself.

GHAZAN (*sensing something*). Has this man offended you? Shall he be killed?

KUKACHIN (*wearily*). No. He has amused me. Let him be fed. Stuff him with food and gold and send him home. And you, My Lord, may I ask that this first night I be allowed to remain on board alone with my women? I am weary!

GHAZAN. Again your wish is my will, even though I will not live until I see you again!

KUKACHIN (*exhaustedly*). I am humbly grateful. Good night, My Lord.

> (*She bows. Ghazan and the Court bow before her. They retire toward* L., *Marco talking earnestly to the oblivious Ghazan, whose eyes are riveted on the Princess, who has turned away from them. The two elder Polos, carrying their chest, their pockets stuffed, trudge along last.*)

MARCO. The close confinement of a long voyage. I think probably her spleen is out of order.

> (*They are gone from sight. Kukachin's shoulders quiver as, her head bowed in her hands, she sobs quietly. The ship can be heard making off.*)

WOMEN. Weep, Princess of the Wounded
Heart,
Weeping heals the wounds of sorrow
Till only the scars remain
And the heart forgets.

KUKACHIN (*suddenly runs up to the upper deck and
stands outlined against the sky, her arms outstretched
– in a voice which is a final, complete renunciation,
calls*). Farewell, Marco Polo!

MARCO (*his voice comes from over the water, cheery
and relieved*). Good-bye, Your Majesty – and all
best wishes for long life and happiness!

(*The Princess sinks to her knees, her face
hidden in her arms on the bulwark.*)

CURTAIN

ACT THREE

SCENE ONE

SCENE: *One year later.*

The Grand Throne Room in the Imperial palace at Cambaluc. Kublai squats on his throne, aged and sad, listening with an impassive face to General Bayan who, dressed in the full military uniform and armour of the Commander-in-Chief, is explaining earnestly with several maps in his hand. On Kublai's left stands Chu-Yin, who is reading. Behind Bayan are grouped at attention all the generals of his army with a multitude of young staff officers, all gorgeously uniformed and armoured. From the room on the right, the ballroom, a sound of dance music and laughter comes through the closed doors.

BAYAN (*impressively – pointing to the map*). Here, Your Majesty, is the line of the river Danube which marks the Western boundary of your Empire. Beyond it, lies the West. Our spies report their many petty states are always quarrelling. So great is their envy of each other that we could crush each singly and the rest would rejoice. We can mobilize one million horsemen on the Danube within a month. (*Proudly.*) We would ride their armies down into the sea! Your Empire would extend from ocean to ocean!

KUBLAI (*wearily*). It is much too large already. Why do you want to conquer the West? It must

127

be a pitiful land, poor in spirit and material wealth. We have everything to lose by contact with its greedy hypocrisy. The conqueror acquires first of all the vices of the conquered. Let the West devour itself.

BAYAN (*helplessly*). But – everywhere in the East there is peace!

KUBLAI (*with hopeless irony*). Ah! And you are becoming restless?

BAYAN (*proudly*). I am a Mongol – a man of action!

KUBLAI (*looking at him with musing irony*). Hum! You have already conquered the West, I think.

BAYAN (*puzzled*). What, Your Majesty? (*Then persuasively.*) The West may not be strong, but it is crafty. Remember how that Christian, Polo, invented the engine to batter down walls? It would be better to wipe out their cunning now before they make too many engines to weaken the power of men. (*Then with a sudden inspiration.*) And it would be a righteous war! We would tear down their Christian Idols and set up the image of the Buddha!

KUBLAI. Buddha, the Prince of Peace?

BAYAN (*bowing his head, as do all his retinue*). The Gentle One, The Good, The Kind, The Pitiful, The Merciful, The Wise, The Eternal Contemplative One!

KUBLAI. In His Name?

BAYAN (*fiercely*). Death to those who deny Him!

ALL (*with a great fierce shout and a clanking of swords*). Death!

KUBLAI (*looks up at the ceiling quizzically*). A thunderbolt? (*Waits.*) No? Then there is no God! (*Then to Bayan with a cynical, bitter smile.*) August Commander, if you must have war, let it be one without fine phrases — a practical war of few words, as that Polo you admire would say. Leave the West alone. Our interests do not conflict — yet. But there is a group of islands whose silk industry is beginning to threaten the supremacy of our own. Lead your gallant million there — and see to it your war leaves me in peace!

BAYAN. I hear and I obey! (*He turns to his staff exultantly.*) His Majesty has declared war!

ALL (*with a fierce cheer*). Down with the West!

BAYAN (*hastily*). No. Not yet. Down with Japan! (*They cheer with equal enthusiasm — then he harangues them with the air of a patriotic exhorter.*) His Majesty's benevolence and patience have been exhausted by the continued outrages against our silk nationals perpetrated by unscrupulous Japanese trade-pirates who, in spite of his protests, are breeding and maintaining silkworms for purposes of aggression! We fight in the cause of moral justice, that our silk-makers may preserve their share of the eternal sunlight! (*A long cheer.*)

KUBLAI (*smiling — distractedly*). War without

P 129

rhetoric, please! Polo has infected you with cant! The West already invades us! Throw open the doors! Music! (*The doors are thrown open. The dance music sounds loudly.*) Go in and dance, everyone! You, too, General! I revoke my declaration of war – unless you learn to dance and be silent! (*They all go into the ballroom, Bayan stalking majestically with an injured mien.*) But dancing makes me remember Kukachin whose little dancing feet –! Shut the doors! Music brings back her voice singing! (*Turning to Chu-Yin – harshly.*) Wisdom! No, do not read! What good are wise writings to fight stupidity? One must have stupid writings that men can understand. In order to live even wisdom must be stupid!

A CHAMBERLAIN (*enters hurriedly and prostrates himself*). A courier from Persia!

KUBLAI (*excitedly*). From Kukachin! Bring him here! (*The Chamberlain dashes to the door and a moment later the Courier enters, travel-stained and weary. He sinks into a heap before the throne. Kublai shouts at him impatiently.*) Have you a letter?

COURIER (*with a great effort holds out a letter*). Here!

> (*He collapses. Chu-Yin hands the letter up to Kublai, who takes it eagerly from him. He begins to read at once. The Chamberlain comes back with a cup of wine. The Courier is revived and gets to his knees, waiting humbly.*)

CHU-YIN (*goes back to Kublai, who has finished reading the short note and is staring sombrely before him*). And did the Little Flower save his Immortal Soul? (*Kublai does not look at him, but mutely hands him the letter. Chu-Yin becomes grave. He reads aloud.*) 'Arghun had died. I am the wife of his son, Ghazan. It does not matter. He is kind, but I miss my home and you. I doubt if I shall be blessed with a son. I do not care. I have lost my love of life. My heart beats more and more wearily. Death woos me. You must not grieve. You wish me to be happy, do you not? And my body may resist Death for a long time yet. Too long. My soul he has already possessed. I wish to commend the unremitting attention to his duty of Admiral Polo. He saved my life three times at the risk of his own. He delivered me to Ghazan. Send him another million. You were right about his soul. What I had mistaken for one I discovered to be a fat woman with a patient virtue. By the time you receive this they will be married in Venice. I do not blame him. But I cannot forgive myself — nor forget — nor believe again in any beauty in the world. I love you the best in life. And tell Chu-Yin I love him too.'

> (*He lets the letter in his hand drop to his side, his eyes filling, his voice grown husky. Kublai stares bleakly ahead of him.*)

KUBLAI (*at last rouses himself — harshly to the Courier*). Did the Queen give you this in person?

COURIER. Yes, Your Majesty – with a generous gift.

KUBLAI. I can be generous too. Did she appear – ill?

COURIER. Yes. I could scarcely hear her voice.

KUBLAI. You brought no other word?

COURIER. Not from the Queen. I came privately from her. But Admiral Polo suspected my departure and gave me a verbal message which he caused me to memorize.

KUBLAI (*harshly – his eyes beginning to gleam with anger*). Ha! Go on! Repeat!

COURIER (*stopping for a moment to freshen his memory*). He said, tell the Great Kaan that 'in spite of perils too numerous to relate, I have delivered my charge safely to Ghazan Khan. In general, she gave but little trouble on the voyage, for although flighty in temper and of a passionate disposition, she never refused to heed my advice for her welfare, and as I informed His Majesty, King Ghazan, the responsibilities of marriage and the duties of motherhood will sober her spirit and she will settle down as a sensible wife should. This much I further add, that in humble obedience to your final instructions given me by Mr. Chu-Yin, I looked daily into her eyes.'

KUBLAI (*bewilderedly to Chu-Yin*). What? Did you –?

CHU-YIN (*miserably*). Forgive an old fool! I

132

meant it partly in jest as a last chance – to cure her – or to awaken him.

COURIER (*continuing*). 'But I have never noted any unnatural change in them except toward the termination of our trip, particularly on the last day, when I noticed a rather strained expression, but this I took to be fever due to her Highness's spleen being sluggish after the long confinement on shipboard.'

KUBLAI (*choking with wrath*). O God of the Sombre Heavens!

COURIER. And he gave me no money for delivering the message, but he promised that you would reward me nobly.

KUBLAI (*with wild laughter*). Ha-ha-ha! Stop! Do you dare to madden me? (*Then suddenly raging.*) Out of my sight, dog, before I have you impaled! (*The terror-stricken Courier scrambles out like a flash. Kublai stands up with flashing eyes – revengefully.*) I have reconsidered! I shall conquer the West! I shall lead my armies in person! I shall not leave one temple standing nor one Christian alive who is not enslaved! Their cities shall vanish in flame, their fields shall be wasted! Famine shall finish what I leave undone! And of the city of Venice not one vestige shall remain! And of the body of Marco Polo there shall not be a fragment of bone nor an atom of flesh which will not have shrieked through ten days' torture before it died!

133

CHU-YIN. Master! (*He throws himself on his face at Kublai's feet.*) Do not torture yourself! Is this Wisdom? Is this the peace of the soul?

KUBLAI (*distractedly*). To revenge oneself – that brings a kind of peace!

CHU-YIN. To revenge equally the wrong of an equal perhaps, but this –? Can you confess yourself weaker than his stupidity?

KUBLAI. He has murdered her!

CHU-YIN. She does not accuse him. What would be her wish?

KUBLAI (*his anger passing – wearily and bitterly, after a pause*). Rise, my old friend, it is I who should be at your feet, not you at mine! (*He sinks dejectedly on his throne again. After a pause, sadly.*) She will die. Why is this? What purpose can it serve? My hideous suspicion is that God is only an infinite, insane energy which creates and destroys without other purpose than to pass eternity in avoiding thought. Then the stupid man becomes the Perfect Incarnation of Omnipotence and the Polos are the true children of God! (*He laughs bitterly.*) Ha! How long before we shall be permitted to die, my friend? I begin to resent life as the insult of an ignoble inferior with whom it is a degradation to fight! (*Broodingly – after a pause.*) I have had a foreboding she would die. Lately, to while away time, I experimented with the crystal. I do not believe the magic nonsense about it, but

I do consider that, given a focus, the will can perhaps overcome the limits of the senses. Whatever the explanation be, I looked into the crystal and willed to see Kukachin in Persia and she appeared, sitting alone in a garden, beautiful and sad, apart from life, waiting – (*Brokenly.*) My eyes filled with tears. I cried out to her – and she was gone! (*Then suddenly – to the Chamberlain.*) Bring me the crystal! (*To Chu-Yin as the Chamberlain goes.*) Marco, the true ruler of the world, will have come to Venice by this time. My loathing grows so intense I feel he must jump into the crystal at my bidding. And – in the cause of wisdom, say – we must see what he is doing now. (*The Chamberlain returns with the crystal. Kublai takes it eagerly from his hand and stares fixedly into it.*)

CHU-YIN (*protestingly*). Why do you wish to hurt yourself further?

KUBLAI (*staring fixedly*). I shall observe dispassionately. It is a test of myself I want to make as a penalty for my weakness a moment ago. (*He sees something.*) Ah – it begins. (*A pause. The light grows dimmer and dimmer on the stage proper as it begins to come up on the extreme foreground.*) I see – a city whose streets are canals – it is evening – a house. I begin to see through the walls – Ah!

> (*The lights come up again on the back stage as the forestage is fully revealed. The Kaan on his throne and Chu-Yin are seen dimly, behind and above, like be-*

ings on another plane. At the centre of the forestage is a great banquet table garishly set with an ornate gold service. A tall major-domo in a gorgeous uniform enters and stands at attention as the procession begins. First come the Guests, male and female, a crowd of good substantial bourgeois, who stare about with awe and envy and are greatly impressed by the gold plate.)

A MAN. They've laid out a pile of money here!

A WOMAN. Is that gold service really gold?

ANOTHER. Absolutely. I can tell without biting it.

A MAN. They must have cash, whoever they are.

A WOMAN. Do you think they're really the Polos?

ANOTHER. They looked like greasy Tartars to me.

ANOTHER. That was their queer clothes.

A MAN. And remember they've been gone twenty-odd years.

ANOTHER. In spite of that, I thought I could recognize Maffeo.

A WOMAN. Will Donata know Marco, I wonder?

'MARCO MILLIONS'

A MAN. What's more to her point, will he recognize her?

A WOMAN. Imagine her waiting all this time!

ANOTHER. How romantic! He must be terribly rich – if it's really him.

A MAN. We'll soon know. That's why we were invited.

A WOMAN. Ssshh! Here comes Donata now. How old she's getting to look!

ANOTHER. And how fat in the hips!

A MAN (*jokingly*). That's the way I like 'em, and perhaps Marco –

> (*Donata enters on the arm of her father, a crafty, wizened old man. She has grown into a stout middle-age, but her face is unlined and still pretty in a bovine, good-natured way. All bow and they return this salutation.*)

ALL. Congratulations, Donata!

> (*She blushes and turns aside in an incongruous girlish confusion.*)

FATHER (*proud but pretending querulousness*). Don't tease her now! The girl's nervous enough already. And it may not be Marco after all, but only a joke some one's put up on us.

A WOMAN. No one could be so cruel!

ALL (*suddenly with a great gasp*). Oh, listen! (*An*

137

orchestra vigorously begins a flowery, sentimental Italian tune. This grows into quite a blare as the musicians enter from the right, six in number, in brilliant uniforms.) Oh, look! (*The musicians form a line, three on each side by the stairs on right.*) Oh, see! (*A procession of servants begins to file one by one through the ranks of musicians, each carrying on his head or upraised hand an enormous platter on which are whole pigs, fowl of all varieties, roasts, vegetables, salads, fruits, nuts, dozens of bottles of wine. The servants arrange these on the table, in symmetrical groups, with the trained eye for display of window-dressers, until the table, with the bright light flooding down on it, closely resembles the front of a pretentious delicatessen store. Meanwhile*) See! What a turkey! Such a goose! The fattest pig I ever saw! What ducks! What vegetables! Look at the wine! A feast for the gods! And all those servants! An army! And the orchestra! What expense! Lavish! They must be worth millions! (*The three Polos make their grand entrance from the stairs on right, walking with bursting self-importance between the files of musicians who now blare out a triumphant march. The two elder precede Marco. All three are dressed in long robes of embroidered crimson satin reaching almost to the ground. The guests give a new united gasp of astonishment.*) Is it they? Is that old Nicolo? That's Maffeo's nose! No! It isn't them at all! Well, if it's a joke, I don't see the point. But such robes! Such hand embroidery! Such material! They must be worth millions!

138

DONATA (*falteringly*). Is that him, father? I can't tell. (*She calls faintly.*) Marco!

> (*But he pretends not to hear. He gives a sign at which the three take off their robes and hand them to the servants. They have even more gorgeous blue ones underneath. Marco addresses the servants in a false voice.*)

MARCO. My good men, you may sell these rich robes and divide the proceeds among yourselves! And here is a little something extra.

> (*He tosses a handful of gold to the servants and another to the musicians. A mad scramble results. The guests gasp. They seem inclined to join in the scramble.*)

GUESTS. How generous! What prodigality! What indifference to money! They throw it away like dirt. They must be worth millions!

MARCO (*in the same false voice*). Our guests look thirsty. Pass around the wine. (*The servants do so. The guests gaze, smell, taste.*)

ALL. What a vintage! What flavour! What bouquet! How aged! It must have cost twenty lire a bottle! (*At another signal the three Polos take off their blue robes.*)

MARCO (*regally*). Give those to the musicians! (*They are revealed now in their old dirty, loose Tartar*

*travelling dress, and look quite shabby. The guests
gape uncertainly. Then Marco declares grandly.*) You
look astonished, good people, but this is a moral
lesson to teach you not to put too much faith in
appearances, for behold!

> (*He slits up the wide sleeves of his own robe,
> as do his father and uncle, and now the
> three, standing beside a big empty space
> which has been purposely left at the very
> centre of the table at the front, lower
> their opened sleeves, and, as the musi-
> cians, obeying this signal, start up a
> great blare, let pour from them a perfect
> stream of precious stones which forms a
> glittering multi-coloured heap. This is
> the final blow. The guests stare pop-
> eyed, open-mouthed, speechless for a
> second. Then their pent-up admiration
> breaks forth.*)

ALL. Extraordinary! Jewels! Gems! Rubies!
Emeralds! Diamonds! Pearls! A king's ransom!
Millions!

MARCO (*suddenly with his hail-fellow-well-met
joviality*). Well, folks, are you all tongue-tied?
Isn't one of you going to say welcome home? And
Miss Donata, don't I get a kiss? I'm still a
bachelor!

> (*Immediately with mad shouts of 'Bravo!'
> 'Welcome home!' 'Hurrah for the Po-*

los!' etc., etc., the guests bear down on them in a flood. There is a confused whirl of embraces, kisses, back-slaps, handshakes and loud greetings of all sorts. Marco manages to get separated and pulls Donata down front to the foreground.)

DONATA (*half swooning*). Marco!

MARCO (*moved*). My old girl! (*They kiss, then he pushes her away.*) Here! Let me get a good look at you! Why, you're still as pretty as a picture and you don't look a day older!

DONATA (*exaltedly*). My beloved prince!

MARCO (*jokingly*). No, if I was a prince I'd never have remained single all these years in the East! I'm a hero, that's what! And all the twenty-odd years I kept thinking of you, and I was always intending to write — (*He pulls the pieces of the miniature wrapped in the handkerchief out of his pocket.*) Here's proof for you! Look at yourself! You're a bit smashed, but that was done in a hand-to-hand fight with pirates. Now don't I deserve another kiss?

DONATA (*giving it*). My hero! (*Then jealously.*) But I know all the heathen women must have fallen in love with you.

MARCO. Oh, maybe one or two or so — but I didn't have time to waste on females. I kept my

nose to the grindstone every minute. (*Proudly.*)
And I got results. I don't mind telling you, Donata, I'm worth over two millions! How's that for
keeping my promise? Worth while your waiting,
eh? (*He slaps her on the back.*)

DONATA. Yes, my wonder boy! (*Then worriedly.*) You said there were one or two women?
But you were true in spite of them, weren't
you?

MARCO. I tell you I wouldn't have married the
prettiest girl in Cathay! (*This with emphasis. Then
abruptly.*) But never mind any other girl. (*He
chucks her under the chin.*) What I want to know is
when this girl is going to marry me?

DONATA (*softly*). Any time!

(*They hug. The guests group about them
kittenishly, pointing and murmuring,
'What a romance! What a romance!'*)

DONATA'S FATHER (*seizing the opportunity*).
Friends, I take this opportunity to announce pub-
licly the betrothal of my daughter, Donata, to
Marco Polo of this City! (*Another wild round of
congratulations, kisses, etc.*)

MARCO (*his voice sounding above the hubbub*).
Let's eat, friends! (*They swirl to their places behind
the long table. When they stand their faces can be seen
above the piles of food, but when they sit they are out of
sight.*) No ceremony among friends. Just pick

your chair. All ready? Let's sit down then! (*With one motion they disappear.*)

VOICE OF DONATA'S FATHER. But, first, before we regale ourselves with your cheer, won't you address a few words to your old friends and neighbours who have gathered here on this happy occasion?

(*Applause. Marco is heard expostulating, but finally he gives in.*)

MARCO. All right, if you'll promise to go ahead and eat and not wait for me. (*His head appears, his expression full of importance. Servants flit about noisily. He coughs and begins with dramatic feeling.*) My friend and neighbours of old, your generous and wholehearted welcome touches me profoundly. I would I had the gift of oratory to thank you fittingly, but I am a simple man, an ordinary man, I might almost say, – a man of affairs used to dealing in the hard facts of life, a silent man given to deeds not words – (*Here he falters fittingly.*) And so now – forgive my emotion – words fail me – (*Here he clears his throat with an important cough and bursts forth into a memorized speech in the grand Chamber of Commerce style.*) But I'll be glad to let you have a few instructive facts about the silk industry as we observed it in the Far East, laying especial emphasis upon the keystone of the whole silk business – I refer to the breeding of worms! (*A few hungry guests start to eat. Knives and forks and spoons rattle against plates. Soup is heard. Marco strikes a good listening attitude so that he will be sure not to miss a word his voice utters, and warms to his work.*) Now, to begin with, there are millions upon millions of capital invested in this industry, millions of contented slaves labour unremittingly millions of hours per annum to obtain the best results in the weaving and dyeing of the finished product, but I don't hesitate to state that all this activity is relatively unimportant beside the astounding fact that in the production of the raw material there are constantly employed millions upon millions upon millions of millions of worms!

ONE VOICE (*rather muffled by roast pig*). Hear!

> (*But the rest are all absorbed in eating and a perfect clamour of knives and forks resounds. Marco begins again, but this time the clamour is too great, his words are lost, only the one he lays such emphasis upon can be distinguished.*)

MARCO. Millions! . . . millions! . . . millions! . . . millions!

KUBLAI (*who from the height of his golden throne, crystal in hand, has watched all this with fascinated disgust while Chu-Yin has sat down to read again, now turns away with a shudder of loathing — and in spite of himself, a shadow of a smile — and lets the crystal fall from his hand and shatter into bits with a loud report. Instantly there is darkness and from high*

144

up in the darkness Kublai's voice speaking with a pitying scorn). The Word became their flesh, they say. Now all is flesh! And can their flesh become the Word again?

DARKNESS

ACT THREE

SCENE TWO

SCENE. *Grand Throne Room in the Imperial Palace at Cambaluc, about two years later. The walls tower majestically in shadow, their elaborate detail blurred into a background of half-darkness.*

Kublai sits at the top of his throne, cross-legged in the posture of an idol, motionless, wrapped in contemplation. He wears a simple white robe without adornment of any sort. A brilliant light floods down upon him in one concentrated ray. His eyes are fixed on a catafalque, draped in heavy white silk, which stands in the centre of the room, emphasized by another downpouring shaft of light.

Chu-Yin stands on the level below, on Kublai's left. On the main floor are the nobles and people of the Court, grouped as in Act One, Scene Six.

There is a long pause clamorous with the pealing of the thousands of bells in the city, big and little, near and far. Every figure in the room is as motionless as the Kaan himself. Their eyes are kept on him with the ardent humility and respect of worship. Behind their impassive faces, one senses a tense expectancy of some sign from the throne. At last, Kublai makes a slight but imperious motion of command with his right hand.

Immediately the women all turn with arms out-stretched toward the catafalque. Their voices rise together in a long, rhythmic wail of mourning; their arms with one motion move slowly up; their voices attain a prolonged note of unbearable poignancy; their heads are thrown back, their arms appeal to Heaven in one agonized gesture of despair. Here the Kaan makes the same barely perceptible sign of command again. The voices are instantly silenced. With one motion, the women throw themselves prostrate on the floor. The bells, except for one slow deep-toned one in the palace itself, are almost instantly hushed. At the same instant, from outside, at first faint, but growing momentarily in volume, comes the sound of funeral music. A moment later the funeral procession enters. The men sink to the cross-legged position of prayer, their heads bowed.

First come the musicians, nine in number, men in robes of bright red. They are followed by the chorus of nine singers, five men and four women, all of them aged, with bent bodies, their thin, cracked voices accompanying the music in queer, breaking waves of lamentation. These are masked, the men with a male mask of grief, the women with a female. All are dressed in deep black with white edging to their robes. After them comes a troupe of young girls and boys, dressed in white with black edging, moving

147

slowly backward in a gliding, interweaving dance pattern. Their faces are not masked but are fixed in a disciplined, traditional expression of bewildered, uncomprehending grief that is like a mask. They carry silver censers which they swing in unison toward the corpse of the Princess Kukachin, carried on a bier directly behind them on the shoulders of eight princes of the blood in black armour.

Accompanying the bier, one at each corner, are four priests – the foremost two, a Confucian and a Taoist, the latter two, a Buddhist and a Moslem. Each walks with bent head, reading aloud to himself from his Holy Book.

The princes lift the bier of Kukachin to the top of the catafalque. Her body is wrapped in a winding sheet of deep blue, a jewelled golden head-dress is on her black hair, her face is white and clear as a statue's. The young boys and girls place their smoking censers about the catafalque, the incense ascending in clouds about the Princess as if it were bearing her soul with it. The music and the singing cease as the dancers, singers, and musicians form on each side, and to the rear, of the catafalque and sink into attitudes of prayer.

Kublai speaks to the priests in a voice of command in which is weariness and disbelief.

KUBLAI. Peace! She does not need your prayers. She was a prayer! (*With one motion they shut their*

*books, raise their heads and stare before them in silence
Kublai continues – sadly.*) Can words recall life to
her beauty? (*To the Priest of Tao.*) Priest of Tao,
will you conquer death by your mystic Way?

PRIEST OF TAO (*bowing his head in submission –
fatalistically*). Which is the greater evil, to possess
or to be without? Death is.

CHORUS (*in an echo of vast sadness*). Death is.

KUBLAI (*to the Confucian*). Follower of Confucius, the Wise, have you this wisdom?

PRIEST OF CONFUCIUS (*slowly*). Before we know
life, how can we know death? (*Then as the Taoist,
submissively.*) Death is.

CHORUS (*as before*). Death is.

KUBLAI (*to the Buddhist Priest*). Worshipper of
Buddha, can your self-overcoming overcome that
greatest overcomer of self?

BUDDHIST PRIEST. This is a thing which no god
can bring about: that what is subject to death
should not die. (*Then as the others, submissively.*)
Death is.

CHORUS (*as before*). Death is.

KUBLAI (*wearily*). And your answer, priest of
Islam?

PRIEST OF ISLAM. It is the will of Allah! (*Submissively.*) Death is.

CHORUS. Death is. Death is. Death is. (*Their
voices die away.*)

KUBLAI (*after a pause*). What is death? (*A long pause. His eyes rest in loving contemplation on the body of Kukachin. Finally he speaks tenderly to her with a sad smile.*) Girl whom we call dead, whose beauty is even in death more living than we, smile with infinite silence upon our speech, smile with infinite forbearance upon our wisdom, smile with infinite remoteness upon our sorrow, smile as a star smiles! (*His voice appears about to break. A muffled sound of sobbing comes from the prostrate women. Kublai regains control over his weakness and rises to his feet — with angry self-contempt.*) No more! That is for poets! (*With overstressed arrogance — assertively.*) I am the Great Kaan!

(*Everyone in the room rises with one motion of assertion.*)

CHORUS (*accompanied by a clangour of brass from the musicians — recite with discordant vigour*).

> Greatest of the Great!
> Son of Heaven!
> Lord of Earth!
> Sovereign of the World!
> Ruler over Life and Death!

KUBLAI (*silences them by an imperious gesture — and now even the great palace bell is stilled — half-mockingly but assertively*). The Son of Heaven? Then I should know a prayer. Sovereign of the World? Then I command the World to pray!

(*With one motion all sink to the position of prayer.*) In silence! Prayer is beyond words! Contemplate the eternal life of Life! Pray thus! (*He himself sinks to the position of prayer – a pause – then slowly.*) In silence – for one concentrated moment – be proud of life! Know in your heart that the living of life can be noble! Know that the dying of death can be noble! Be exalted by life! Be inspired by death! Be humbly proud! Be proudly grateful! Be immortal because life is immortal. Contain the harmony of womb and grave within you! Possess life as a lover – then sleep requited in the arms of death! If you awake, love again! If you sleep on, rest in peace! Who knows which? What does it matter? It is nobler not to know!

> (*A pause of silence. He rises to his feet. With one motion all do likewise. Kublai sits back on his cushions again, withdrawing into contemplation. The Mongol Chronicler comes forward to fulfil his function of chanting the official lament for the dead. He declaims in a high, wailing voice accompanied by the musicians and by the Chorus who sway rhythmically and hum a rising and falling mourning accompaniment.*)

CHRONICLER. We lament the shortness of life. Life at its longest is brief enough.
Too brief for the wisdom of joy, too long for the knowledge of sorrow.

Sorrow becomes despair when death comes to the young, untimely.

Oh that her beauty could live again, that her youth could be born anew.

Our Princess was young as Spring, she was beautiful as a bird or flower.

Cruel when Spring is smitten by Winter, when birds are struck dead in full song, when the budding blossom is blighted!

Alas that our Princess is dead, she was the song of songs, the perfume of perfumes, the perfect one!

Our sobs stifle us, our tears wet the ground, our lamentations sadden the wind from the West. (*Bows submissively – speaks.*)

Yet we must bow humbly before the Omnipotent.

CHORUS. We must be humble.

CHRONICLER. Against Death all Gods are powerless.

CHORUS. All Gods are powerless. (*Their voices die into silence.*)

KUBLAI (*after a pause – wearily*). Leave her in peace. Go. (*The Court leaves silently at his command in a formal, expressionless order. The four priests go first, beginning to pray silently again. They are followed by the nobles and officials with their women coming after. Finally the young boys and girls take up their censers and dance their pattern out backward, preceded by the musicians. Only the Chorus remain, grouped in a semi-circle behind the catafalque,*

152

motionless, and Chu-Yin who stays at the left hand of Kublai. The music fades away. Kublai takes his eyes from the dead girl with a sigh of bitter irony.) Oh, Chu-Yin, my Wise Friend, was the prayer I taught them wisdom?

CHU-YIN. It was the wisdom of pride. It was thy wisdom.

CHORUS (*echoing sadly*). Thy wisdom.

KUBLAI. Was it not truth?

CHU-YIN. It was the truth of power. It was thy truth.

CHORUS (*as before*). Thy truth.

KUBLAI. My pride, my power? My wisdom, my truth? For me there remains only – her truth! (*Then after staring at Kukachin for a second, bitterly.*) Her truth! She died for love of a fool!

CHU-YIN. No. She loved love. She died for beauty.

KUBLAI. Your words are hollow echoes of the brain. Do not wound me with wisdom. Speak to my heart! (*Sadly – his eyes again on Kukachin.*) Her little feet danced away the stamp of armies. Her smile made me forget the servile grin on the face of the World. In her eyes' mirror I watched myself live protected from life by her affection – a simple old man dying contentedly a little, day after pleasant day.

CHU-YIN (*bowing – compassionately*). Then weep, old man. Be humble and weep for your child. The old should cherish sorrow. (*He bows again and goes out silently.*)

KUBLAI (*after a pause, gets up and descending from his throne, slowly approaches the catafalque, speaking to the dead girl softly as he does so – with a trembling smile.*) I think you are hiding your eyes, Kuka-chin. You are a little girl again. You are playing hide-and-seek. You are pretending. Did we not once play such games together, you and I? You have made your face still, you have made your face cold, you have set your lips in a smile so remote – you are pretending even that you are dead! (*He is very near her now. His voice breaks – more and more intensely.*) Let us stop playing! It is late. It is time you were asleep. Open your eyes and laugh! Laugh now that the game is over. Take the blindfold from my dim eyes. Whisper your secret in my ear. I – I am dead and you are living! Weep for me, Kukachin! Weep for the dead! (*He stretches his arms out to her beseechingly – pauses, standing beside the body, staring down at her; then, after a moment, he passes his hand over her face – tremblingly – with a beautiful tenderness of grief.*) So, little Kukachin – so, Little Flower – you have come back – they could not keep you – you were too homesick – you wanted to return – to gladden my last days – (*He no longer tries to control his grief. He sobs like a simple old man, bending and kissing his*

154

granddaughter on the forehead – with heart-breaking playfulness.) I bid you welcome home, Little Flower! I bid you welcome home! (*He weeps, his tears falling on her calm white face.*)

CURTAIN

EPILOGUE

The play is over. The lights come up brilliantly in the theatre. In an aisle seat in the first row a Man rises, conceals a yawn in his palm, stretches his legs as if they had become cramped by too long an evening, takes his hat from under the seat and starts to go out slowly with the others in the audience. But although there is nothing out of the ordinary in his actions, his appearance excites general comment and surprise, for he is dressed as a Venetian merchant of the later Thirteenth Century. In fact, it is none other than Marco Polo himself, looking a bit sleepy, a trifle puzzled, and not a little irritated as his thoughts, in spite of himself, cling for a passing moment to the play just ended. He appears quite unaware of being unusual and walks in the crowd without self-consciousness, very much as one of them. Arrived in the lobby his face begins to clear of all disturbing memories of what had happened on the stage. The noise, the lights of the streets, recall him at once to himself. Impatiently he waits for his car, casting a glance here and there at faces in the groups around him, his eyes impersonally speculative, his bearing stolid with the dignity of one who is sure of his place in the world. His car, a luxurious limousine, draws up at the curb. He

*gets in briskly, the door is slammed, the car edges
away into the traffic and Marco Polo, with a
satisfied sigh at the sheer comfort of it all, resumes
his life.*

THE END